pg. 148

*X marks Mr. Hoover Dining with Australian friends,
Under the Union Jack.*

THE STRANGE CAREER OF
MR. HOOVER
UNDER TWO FLAGS

BY

JOHN HAMILL

ILLUSTRATED
AND
DOCUMENTED

NEW YORK : WILLIAM FARO, INC. : 1931

PUBLISHER'S NOTE

To say that the manuscript out of which grew this book, was the most amazing ever brought to us, would be to put the case very mildly.

Our chief care, once we had decided to publish this chronicle of the career of Mr. Hoover, was to make certain of the facts. To that end it was necessary to hunt up verifications in some of the farthest reaches of the globe. The accomplishment of this was not always easy, and in some cases it was almost impossible. The difficulties were not always of time and space. At many sources we came only to find that someone had already been there before us, going over the hard-beaten track of Mr. Hoover's past, and taking, buying up, and otherwise obliterating important records. Even in *The New York Public Library,* books and records would suddenly disappear from the shelves, not to be found again after numerous exhaustive searches by the authorities.

But we have finally accomplished our task. We have documentary proof for every syllable of this extraordinary work.

According to the laws of our state (and of most civilized states), it is the duty of a citizen, once such matters have been brought to his attention, to help to bring them to light. It is probably possible (in theory) to even punish one for failing to do so. Yet some of the biggest American publishers turned this book down. And as for encouragement in the bringing out of the book—. "Do you realize," we were warned on all sides, "that you are in danger of antagonizing the most powerful man in the living world?"

Maybe so. But we are still old-fashioned enough to believe that nothing is more powerful than truth: nothing so potent as fact. And so we submit the facts, amazing as they are.

August 29, 1931

CONTENTS

PREFACE

WHEN Herbert Hoover returned to the United States in April, 1917, he was virtually a stranger in his own country. He had been practically an absentee for exactly twenty years, during fifteen of which he had resided in London, where he was taken for granted to be an Englishman, so much so that his name appeared regularly on the voting lists. Prior to September 1912, he had never spent more than a few weeks at a time in this country, which he occasionally passed through on his way to Australia. However, he spent a few months here during the winters of 1912 and 1913 in connection with some very peculiar financial business which I shall refer to later.

He was, indeed, so much unknown to Americans that, with the exception of an interview to a reporter friend of the *New York Sun* on his arrival in September, 1912, we find no mention of him whatever in the Eastern newspapers until the end of 1914, nor in the press of California, of which he claimed to be a resident, other than a few references in 1913 and 1914 to Herbert C. Hoover, a London financier, of the notorious Western Ocean Syndicate, which was making desperate and unscrupulous efforts to gain control of the independent oil lands of California for England. Even the year book "Who's Who on the Pacific Coast" for 1913, and which contains over 3,000 names, does not mention him. Indeed, outside of his immediate associates, he was an "unknown" to the American public, even of California.

Subsequent to the end of October 1914, when he was "wangled" into the position of Chairman of the Belgian Relief Commission by the Belgian Francqui, his co-director of and collaborator in the "taking" of the Chinese Kaiping Coal Mines, as it was described by Chancellor Joyce in the English Chancery Court,

Hoover obtained considerable publicity, mostly in the form of remarkably inaccurate statements issued by himself regarding the food situation in Belgium, with the object of obtaining subscriptions for his Commission, which had the monopoly of buying, begging, shipping and selling relief to the Belgium National Relief Committee, of which Francqui was in charge. You will notice that I have used the word "selling." That is the correct word. The relief was sold, not given away. Prior to the Food Administration racket it was the greatest individual "business" in the World, and, as we shall see, quite a profitable one for many of those concerned.

When Hoover turned up in Washington in April 1917, and it was announced a few weeks later that he had been appointed Food Administrator, there was a gulp of amazement. Not one member of the Senate or the House knew his record. And, as Mr. McElmore of Texas said in the House: "this man, a mining engineer, who has not been a citizen of the United States for all of twenty years and whose home and interests are all in a foreign land, who knows absolutely nothing of farming and cattle raising, yet has been brought over here to assume a dictatorship over our producers and invested with such autocratic powers that to disobey his mandates may mean prison walls for all who may dare offend. With a population of more than 100,000,-000 to choose from, why was it necessary to go out of the United States to get a man to preside as dictator over our American producers and invest him with autocratic powers greater than those ever exercised by kaiser, emperor or czar? Have we become so fallen that there is not one of our own citizens to be trusted with these autocratic powers, one whose interests are in the United States and whose ideals are for and of America? But, Mr. Speaker, this is not all. Not only

SILVER FALLS CITY.

ONLY TWENTY-FIVE DOLLARS BUYS A LOT IN THIS BEAUTIFUL CITY.

The town site is 22 miles a little south of east of Salem, and only four and one half miles north of the line of the Oregon Pacific Rail Road. Here, at an altitude of about 500 feet above the sea level surrounded by fragrant Pine, Hemlock and Cedar forests, in full view of a beautiful cataract which makes a sheer plunge of nearly two hundred feet, into an emerald pool below. The tired denizens of city, town or farm, can pitch their tents or swing their hammocks, or, if they prefer, build their cottages there and take the world easy, while the dog star rages, feasting themselves meanwhile, on fruits, chickens milk and eggs from neighboring farm houses, or replenish their larders from the adjacent trout streams, or natural preserves of game.

The pure mountain air is wonderfully exhilerating. The water is clear and cold and puts new life and vigor into the invalids frame. The town site lies in a true thermal belt, being exempt from late and early frosts as has been demonstrated by the fruit growers along the same line of elevation.

The proprietors announce that the income from the sale of lots for the first year will be largely expended in improving and beautifying the place, thus enhancing the value of all the property alike and giving all purchasers an equal benefit of the money expended. The title to the land is perfect, (U. S. Patent,) and every purchaser will receive a warranty deed for the property sold to him. For fuller particulars, apply to

OREGON LAND CO.

Even the U. S. Survey has been unable to locate this city so pursuasively advertised by Mr. Hoover's first office.

do we propose to make this 'food dictator' by far the most powerful autocrat this country has ever seen, but the bill also carries with it an appropriation of $150,-000,000 of the people's money, which will be placed at his disposal to do with as he pleases. In addition to this, we are asked to appropriate $2,500,000 for office forces, and so forth; and he also asks for the sum of $150,000 with which to erect an office building. * * * Mr. Speaker, perhaps the most remarkable and most extraordinary thing that ever happened in the United States is found in the statement that Mr. Hoover has been made 'food dictator' and clothed with great autocratic powers weeks before a bill has even been passed by Congress creating the office. He already has an army of assistants and clerks doing his bidding and has leased an entire hotel building, with its furnishings, etc., where he maintains his offices and where he and numerous assistants also maintain their homes. No eastern potentate ever exercised greater autocratic powers than those now being exercised by Mr. Herbert C. Hoover, of Red House, Hornton Street, London, England, and who, it seems, did not have to wait for Congress to act before assuming the role of food dictator and taking charge of the produce of 45,000,000 American farmers of the United States."

When Mr. McElmore made these remarks he had no animus against Herbert Hoover. All he knew of him was from a report he had received from the Merchants Association of New York. Other Congressmen and Senators knew still less. Even Senator Phelan of California, which Hoover claimed as his home state, showed his entire ignorance of Hoover's record by reading in the Senate a newspaper man's "inspired" account of him, which was entirely without foundation. What amazed Mr. McElmore was that Hoover had actually taken up the job and started the racketeering that went with it, weeks before the office had ever been created by Congress.

To put through the bill creating Hoover's appointment as food dictator, and present him in a favorable light to the American public, a great campaign of Hoover propaganda was started in the twenty-five newspapers which had been selected by big banking and munition manufacturing interests to control public opinion in the United States. This was supplemented by descriptive articles in magazines of great circulation, such as *The Saturday Evening Post* and by literature distributed by Hoover's own *Food Administration Office*.

To give an idea of the extent to which they went with this propaganda, I shall again quote the Congressional Record of August 3rd, 1917 (Mr. McElmore speaking):

"Mr. Hoover may be the most honest and most honorable man that ever trod this mundane sphere, but as an American citizen, Mr. Speaker, I am not in favor of clothing any man, whether or not he be sent to us by England, with unlimited autocratic powers and placing in his hands $150,000,000 of the people's money—to use as he pleases—and the destiny of the 45,000,000 producers in this country. That Mr. Hoover is a most wise man I am ready to admit, for he tells us so himself, and I take it that he speaks knowingly. In fact, he is a little ahead of Solomon, for Solomon, though a man of exceeding human wisdom, did not, as I understand it, perform miracles, while Mr. Hoover does. At least, that is the conclusion I draw from some of the literature sent to the newspapers by the publicity department of his administration, a sample of which I will here give:

> Publicity Department, Food Administration,
> Food Conservation Section,
> Washington, D. C., July 14, 1917.

To the EDITOR:

Herewith I am enclosing to you some material that has been sent out from the Food Conservation Section of the Food Administration to the news associations and by them sent over their wires. I feel that there are stories in this material that you have not seen and that these may be of use to you.

Your name is on the mailing list of the Food Conservation Section, and after this news stories will be mailed to you Mondays, Wednesdays and Fridays.

I hope you will find something useful to your paper and to the great cause of food saving.

> Faithfully yours,
> KATHERINE LECKIE.

Among the many items of this 'material' sent to the different papers throughout the country, we have this item which is of special interest, as it refers to Mr. Hoover himself and shows the exalted opinion the gentleman has of Mr. Herbert Hoover. The item bears date of July 13, 1917, and reads as follows:

> (*For release July* 13, 1917)
> Food Administration,
> Food Conservation Section,

Post office clerks rubbed their eyes today when they found in an incoming mail sack a letter bearing no other address than 'Mr. Miracle-Man Hoover, Washington.' On a guess as for whom it was intended the letter was carried to

Herbert Hoover, United States Food Administrator. The guess proved correct. The writer
tells of the pressing need of food conservation,
and adds 'God bless you in your service to our
country.'

A distinguished Member of the United States
Senate, in discussing this highly interesting news
item on the floor of the Senate a few days ago,
expressed himself as follows:

'This statement is being sent out by Mr.
Hoover about himself, in order that he may thereby glorify himself by having it printed in all
the papers of the country. It is, I assume, sent
out at Government expense.' "

We have all read the captions: "the hero of Tientsin" "the great engineer," "the doctor of sick mining
companies," "the great administrator," "the great humanitarian," "the relief expert," "the saviour of Europe,"
"the dear old Quaker." These and others were all
greedily swallowed by the public. A little truth makes
the grossest fictions palatable, and fiction grows by what
it feeds on. A real miracle came to pass. A glamor
was cast about a man who was a stranger in his own
country. He became a legendary hero in his lifetime,
a prophet of prosperity—until overtaken by a fact.

I have compiled Hoover's record during those twenty
years of his foreign residence. It has not been an easy
matter, for Hoover is not only very secretive but seems
to enjoy a singular genius for treading without leaving
tracks. Works of reference, when I inquired for them,
were strangely missing in many of our libraries. Publications had disappeared from the market in Europe,
where others had covered the ground before me. But
not all tracks were invisible. I offer here what I know
about Mr. Hoover. Everything can be verified by official
records, reliable works of reference, and publications of
repute.

THE BOOK

CHAPTER THE FIRST

EARLY DAYS

HERBERT HOOVER was born on August 10, 1874, in the village of West Branch, Iowa. He was of German descent, an ancestor, Andreas Huber, having settled in North Carolina about 1740. The descendants of this Huber later migrated West with other members of the Quaker sect to which they belonged, and eventually settled in Iowa. In one of the "inspired" biographies of Hoover, which was published in 1920, it was claimed stoutly that he was of French Huguenot origin. This was probably meant to explain his devotion to the Allies' cause and why he had no consideration for the naughty German babies who were to be condemned to starve in November, 1918. However, the genealogists, those curious exploiters of one of our human weaknesses, have traced him back to the German Fatherland.

Hoover's parents were poor folk, his father Jesse being a country blacksmith, who died when Herbert was six years old. According to all accounts, Hoover's mother, Huldah, was a religious woman, who preached at the Friends' meeting houses. But unfortunately she died when he was only nine years of age, before she could have exercised any permanent influence on the boy's character. After his mother's death, Herbert was separated from his sister and his brother Theodore, and sent to live with his uncle Allan on a farm in Cedar County, a few miles away. He did not remain there long and went to stay with his uncle John Minthorn at Newberg, Oregon, where he lived in the Highland Friends Colony on the outskits of the town. Dr.

John, as he called himself, was then opening a new school at Newberg, for Dr. John was in the land business and, as every real estate agent knows, a school is a prime requisite to attract new settlers. Here Herbert Hoover did chores about the school. In 1887, Dr. John moved to Salem, Oregon, where with B. S. Cook he took over the management of the Oregon Land Company, and, according to the various biographies of his early life, Hoover worked there as office boy for his uncle.

When Uncle John Minthorn moved to Salem, Hoover was thirteen years old. His life so far had been a hard one; he was an orphan and had to work for the relatives who supported him, so that his education was much neglected. He seems to have had no comrades or playmates and developed that extreme secretiveness that is so impressively commented on by his biographer Rose Wilder Lane, and which still remains one of the most dominant traits of his character. He appears to have missed all those "thrills that come once in a lifetime" to the normal American boy, and evidently suffered from a grave psychological reflex that probably had a physiological background. Although his enthusiastic campaigners renovated the old swimming hole in 1928, Hoover has never been seen in it or in any other. He has never taken part in any sports or outdoor games. He seems to have missed all the fun we have come to associate with the very thought of boyhood. This was certainly not due to any timidity on Hoover's part. Timidity has never been one of Hoover's weaknesses. He appeared, rather, to be conscious of some physical defect or other which he was anxious to conceal, and which, taken in conjunction with his lifelong addictedness to double-breasted coats and very high collars, has led to various pathological surmises.

Hoover lived in Salem with his uncle John from the age of thirteen to seventeen, living with him and actively helping him in his business, the Oregon Land Company. As this was the formative period of the lad's character and undoubtedly must have had a tremendous influence on his later life, it behooves us to see what kind of a gentleman was his Quaker uncle, Dr. John Minthorn.

The best that can be said about this uncle John Minthorn is that he was a pious humbug. He had been an Indian agent. He claimed to be a doctor. He preached and taught on Sundays. And he was engaged in the business of selling undeveloped land. With Cook, he managed the Oregon Land Company, carrying on, according to Miss Lane, an extensive advertising campaign in a thousand newspapers, telling the people of other States how much better off they would be by coming to Oregon and investing their savings in some of his land. Or rather, he told them they did not have to come, they could send their money by mail. And how could they refuse to do this after reading Dr. John's 50 page "compendium," first published in April, 1888, which started right off on the inside front cover in large type as follows!

WE HAVE

NO CYCLONES — NO BLIZZARDS — NO TORNADOES — NO EARTHQUAKES — NO THUNDER — NO LIGHTNING — NO HAILSTONES — NO COLD WINTERS — NO HOT SUMMERS — NO SUNSTROKE — NO HYDROPHOBIA — NO FAILURE OF CROPS — NO SCARCITY OF FUEL — NO FLOODS — NO DROUGHT — NO IRRIGATION NEEDED — NO GRASSHOPPERS — NO CHINTZ BUGS — NO POTATO BUGS — NO HESSIAN FLY

— NO CENTIPEDES — NO TARANTULAS — NO MOSQUITOES — NO RATTLESNAKES — NO ALKALI LAND — NO SANDY LAND — THE LARGEST STRAWBERRIES AND CHERRIES — THE BEST PRUNES, PEARS AND PLUMS — THE FINEST APPLES — BEST SPRINGS — THE HEALTHIEST COUNTRY IN THE UNITED STATES.

Now, Uncle John did not belong to any "Truth in Advertising" Association, but we must admit that he was qualifying. There are many other claims he might have made for the Williamette Valley in Oregon and, indeed, in the next issue of his "Compendium" published in 1889, he added: NO HOT NIGHTS IN SUMMER — GRASS GROWS ALL WINTER. He failed to state, however, what made the grass grow all Winter. According to his advertisements, he had for sale 500,000 acres of land at prices ranging from $3 to $80 per acre, the price depending to some extent on the "gullability" of the "idiot" who bought it. And how could anyone fail to buy land in such a Paradise where there was not even hydrophobia? Then too, there were the attractions of the City of Salem, which, according to Uncle John's "Compendium," included the State House, Insane Asylum, State Penitentiary, Deaf and Dumb School, Blind School and Orphan Asylum. How could any "moron" refuse to come and live in a community so well equipped to look after him? They came and bought lots of undeveloped land, and some, who could not make the journey, even sent their money by mail.

For those who did not want to be farmers, but wished to have a stake in a city, Uncle John was equally well prepared. Page 45 of the original "Compendium" is entirely given up to the advertising of lots in Silver Falls City under the caption: ONLY $25 BUYS A

LOT IN THIS BEAUTIFUL CITY. This beautiful
city must have been like the heavenly city Uncle John
preached about on Sundays, for nobody ever succeeded
in discovering it. Even the United States Survey never
seems to have located it. And yet there must have
been many "idiots" who put up their good money for
sites for their future homesteads in this beautiful city
of dreams with the wonderful name, for Uncle John's
business prospered for a time and in 1889 we find the
Oregon Land Company occupying half the ground floor
of the three story brick and iron building of the State
Insurance Co., in what was known as the Bank Block
in Salem, three doors south of the First National Bank.

There were, however, rival land sharks in Salem, and
according to his biographer Rose Wilder Lane, young
Hoover hit on the idea of getting the jump on competi-
tors by meeting all newcomers at the station with his
uncle's buggy and taking them out at once to Dr. John's
office, something in the nature of "bunco steering," as
it is vulgarly called. Prospective buyers were brought
to the imposing office in the Bank Block and were there
met by the severe looking black coated Quaker manager
and duly impressed. This environment undoubtedly
made a strong impression on young Hoover.

However, some of the buyers became dissatisfied.
Things had not been as represented. A few of those
who sent their money by mail, occasionally turned up
to see the beautiful Silver Fall City where they had
bought their lots. Trouble began to brew in the Bank
Block building. Miss Lane, on page 89 of her story of
Hoover describes a scene: "Do you mean to insinuate
that I am not an honest man?" "Well, didn't you say
that—" and then she goes on to tell how young Hoover
turned out the light, the old style bar-room trick before
guns were drawn.

In 1891 the Oregon Land Company went out of business and young Hoover decided to turn to something more promising. Professor Kellogg and Will Irwin tell the story of the visiting mining man who had impressed young Hoover with the mysteries of geology. There was a demand for geologists who could tell the formations of the soil and the probable locations of important minerals. Who would dare dispute with a man who could talk glibly of "metamorphic" rocks or who could describe a new formation as "neozoic" and an old one as "paleozoic." It was much as if one called a Swiss cheese an "eroded lactiferous postprandial conglomerate." This appealed to Hoover's peculiar mentality; he would become a geologist.

Just then the new *Leland Stanford Junior University* was opening up at Palo Alto, some thirty miles from San Francisco. It was not the least bit like the institution that it is today. It had plenty of land, a few buildings not yet complete, and no students. People who had any means could, of course, send their sons to the established University of California, so that the new college was obliged to send out agents to recruit students from the neighboring States, mostly from among the small farmers' sons who wished to obtain a college education at nominal fees. One of these, a Dr. Swain, came to Portland advertising the new college, and to him Hoover presented himself. He had received so meagre an education that he could not even pass the entrance tests in English, let alone other subjects. But the new school was not particular. It had to obtain students somehow and was willing to stretch a point for the young "rubes" who formed the great majority of the new entrants. Dr. Swain, too, was a Quaker and took some interest in the lad, suggesting that he go at once to Palo Alto, where he would receive some private tuition before the commencement of classes.

Hoover accordingly packed up in June 1891 and set out for Palo Alto, and entered the new university in the following Fall, being actually the first student to take up residence in Encina Hall. It was not expensive there. Tuition was free. Circular No. 4 of the University published in 1891 tells us that "Board in Encina and Robe Halls is furnished at cost, the price at present being fixed at $20 per month. This includes board, furnished rooms, light, heat and attendance. * * * The expenses of the student, exclusive of clothing and railway fares, need not exceed $200 per year." This circular goes on to state that there were opportunities for a student earning all or part of his expenses, and Hoover took advantage of this to help pay his expenses by collecting the other boys' laundry.

One may guess that at that time *Leland Stanford Junior University* was not exactly a "nobby" institution and the educational standards were correspondingly low. The requirements for a Bachelor of Arts degree were only the equivalent of four years' work, of fifteen hours of lecture or recitation weekly. Hoover, as we have said, took geology, the course of instruction which consisted of Elementary Geology, Topographic Geology (which has to do with map work) and Palaeontology (which deals with fossils). The text book was "Geikie's Textbook of Geology" and the whole program was up to about our present high school standard. The geology class had not been organized in 1891 and for the first semester Hoover was obliged to attend the Mechanical Engineering class, where he learned the use of carpenter's tools and a little drawing, arithmetic and algebra.

This semester absorbed at the tender age of seventeen, is the only engineering education Hoover ever had. But it must have possessed a miraculous quality, for in 1929 he was awarded the John Fritz medal, the greatest honor in the engineering profession.

English was a compulsory subject at the examinations, and in this subject, notwithstanding the low standard of the requirements, Hoover failed regularly every semester. He could not write English, or spell English correctly. As William Hard, the author of *Who's Hoover*, which contains the worst of the propagandist pre-election hero-worship blather, admits:

"He was deficient in words as objects of study, deficient also in words as vehicles of expression."

Even at his final examination, Hoover again flunked in English, and V. P. Kellogg, another of his hero worshipping spellbinders, who was a professor at Stanford at the time, admits in his book *Hoover, the Man* that his examination papers in English had to be rewritten for him by Professor J. P. Smith, for the college had to grind out degrees to attract new students, and all the students in the class had to be graduated, no matter what their attainments. We therefore find that all seven students who took up geology in 1892 were graduated in 1895, irrespective of their attainments, and they included Hoover.

So, with a college diploma in geology more or less forced on him, we find Herbert Hoover, at twenty-one. There had been nothing remarkable about his three and a half years at Stanford. Unlike other lads, he kept very much to himself. He took no part in sports or games, nor even in the student activities, except in his last year when, as a senior, he was elected honorary treasurer of the student body, a position that must have appealed to him, although it cannot have placed a great strain on his financial ability, since most of the boys there were just as unembarrassed with money as he was. His only other activity there was the rather significantly feminine one of collecting laundry, which added a little to his meagre resources. His vacations, too, were not spent with friends or other boys. The first Summer he accompanied his teacher Dr. Branner, who was State Geologist of Arkansas, and the following two summer vacations he went with Waldemar Lindgren, State Geologist of California, who was making a survey of the Nevada City mining region, as his helper, carrying his geologist's pick, for which Hoover just received his board and pocket money, for there was no salary attached to the job.

But let us have a somewhat closer look at this very ordinary young man who was to develop into such an extraordinary and important international personality. We have a description from Will Irwin, who was also at Stanford in 1895. He describes Hoover as tall, slender, with a slight stoop, mouse colored hair, hazel eyes, and the round face, double-breasted coat and high collar we are all familiar with. As regards his character, we have the evidence of his secretiveness. He could not play as other lads play. He could not laugh. William Hard, his apologist, tells us in *Who's Hoover* that "he had a laugh which was only a chuckle. He choked the chuckle before the sound of it could become an obvious noise." His religious opinions are not known, for, although brought up as Quaker in his childhood, he does not appear, in his subsequent twenty years of residence abroad, to have professed any religion or attended any church.

When Hoover left Stanford in April, 1895, he again accompanied Lindgren as helper on the geological survey in the Nevada City district. The survey was completed in October of the same year and Hoover had to begin looking for a job. The construction of the new electric power works on the Yuba River had caused a revival of mining in the vicinity of Nevada City, and some of the old gold mines were again opening up. But there was no opening there for geologists, for they had been mining gold there for close on fifty years and there was not a miner in the camp who did not know more about the geology of the district than any raw young college alumnus. Hoover hung around the camp for a while, but necessity is a hard stepmother and he was eventually glad to get a job as trammer in the old Mayflower mine, which had just been taken over by Lane, Hobart and Hayward. This job consisted in hauling the underground trolleys containing the ore and paid the current wage of $2.50 a day. It was tiresome, monotonous, trying work down there, over a thousand feet from the light of day, and Hoover had no liking for physical labor. He was laid off after a few months by Boss Davis and we find him back in San Francisco in the Spring of 1896 once more out of work and looking for a job.

Professor V. P. Kellogg and William Hard, in their panegyrics of Hoover, tell with gusto the story of how he made his first connection with Louis Janin, the Belgian mining engineer of San Francisco. Janin's business was not what it used to be, and his brothers and his own son Louis, Jr., had gone abroad. However, at the time Hoover presented himself looking for a job, Janin happened to be engaged as expert in the very important mining case of the *Carson City Gold and Silver Mining Company* versus *The North Star Mining Company* regarding apex and lateral rights, and told the young man that what he needed was a typist. It was not a big job, it paid thirty dollars a month, but it was better than starvation. Professor Kellogg tells how Hoover not only did not know how to use a typewriter, but was woefully deficient in spelling. However, Hoover got the job. The story goes that the few months Hoover had spent working underground in the Mayflower gave him knowledge regarding the course of the gold vein in dispute that was valuable to Janin, and helped Janin to win the case for his clients. Janin just then was negotiating for the purchase of the Steeple Rock Mining Company in Carlisle, N. M., on behalf of an English syndicate, and started using Hoover as outside man, sending him on tours of inspection to Carlisle and other places. He also had him for some months in Ruett County in Colorado, superintending the digging of a water ditch. This covers Hoover's activities for the year 1896, half office boy and half handy man.

CHAPTER THE SECOND

OFF TO AUSTRALIA

WE have seen how Louis Janin, the mining engineer of San Francisco, had taken on Hoover as a kind of office boy in the Spring of 1896, and how he had subsequently found use for his services in connection with the water ditch in Colorado and the reopening of the little bankrupt gold mine of Carlisle, N. M., which Janin had bought for the English "Exploration Company." This mine was refitted with ten stamps (machines for breaking the ore) and started milling in November of 1896 with a mining engineer in charge. Hoover was kept on for a while in the smeltery, but he was not equipped for the job. He had had no training as a mining engineer which, of all professions, is the one that requires the most varied and extensive knowledge. As Henry Louis said in the Inaugural Address at the Durham College of Science on October 17th, 1895, a mining engineer must know chemistry, physics, mechanics, electricity, assaying, and metallurgy. and the present day curriculum of Columbia University not only includes these subjects, but also accounting, mine ventilation, sanitation and a host of others, of all of which Hoover was blissfully ignorant. Hoover was not a mining engineer then, or at any subsequent time, but he overcame that difficulty, as we shall see, by the very simple process of converting himself into an expert. The public does not trouble to enquire into the qualifications of the expert.

The discovery of gold, especially the rich finds at Coolgardie in 1892 and Kalgoorlie in 1893, had attracted considerable attention to the British colony of Western Australia. Financial syndicates were formed by the unscrupulous financiers Whitaker Wright and Horatio Bottomley, who succeeded in getting hold of some rich properties, which enabled them to pay dividends and drive the British public gambling-mad. A Mr. Charles Algernon Moreing, of the London firm of mining engineers Bewick, Moreing & Co., took advantage of the gambling fever to promote his own financial syndicate, which almost immediately managed to secure the little twelve acre Hannan's Brownhill gold mine in Kalgoorlie. This little mine proved to be a veritable Bonanza, for it secured for Moreing a following among the British investing public. He followed up his success by promoting several other financial companies, which, in turn, floated other mining companies, all under the management of Bewick, Moreing & Co. The gold mining district in Western Australia was, however, a howling desert, and Moreing had great difficulty in finding British mining engineers to go there or stay there. Few of them cared to stand the climate and the separation from civilization. Besides, Californian mining engineers were just then giving a good account of themselves in South Africa, and were in great demand. They had the traditions of fifty years of gold mining behind them. They were capable, adaptable and could stand the hot climate. Accordingly, Moreing, who was familiar with our West, having mining interests in Montana, asked Louis Janin to send him out a good man. This was in December of 1896. Janin selected L. P. Goldstone, manager of the Kentuck mine in Nevada City, California, and sent him on to London. Goldstone was a very capable man, who had formerly been with the California State Mining Bureau, and he went to London and made such a good impression on Moreing that he was engaged to take charge of one of Moreing's Western Australian mines (the Consolidated Murchison) at a salary of $7,500 a year and expenses.

Almost immediately afterwards, Moreing got word of the resignation of his field agent in Coolgardie, Mr. Harry P. Woodward, and he again applied to Janin for a Californian, or rather told Janin to send him another experienced man about thirty-five years old. There were plenty of experienced Californian mining engineers at the time who would be glad to get this job, which paid four thousand dollars a year, but Janin sent Hoover, who was not yet twenty-three. Why he did so we can only surmise, but it was probably because he had no further work for him, or else because he considered him well adapted for the peculiar work he would have to do. So, on Wednesday, March 27th, 1897, Hoover left San Francisco for London on his way to Western Australia.

All of Hoover's sycophant pre-election biographers tell how Janin impressed on Hoover that he was supposed to be thirty-five years of age, and they further narrate how he grew a mustache and beard for the occasion, although we rather doubt this part of the story, for nobody appears to have ever seen Hoover with either a mustache or a beard. It was no trouble at all, however, to Hoover to say that he was thirty-five.

He arrived in Liverpool, took the train to London, reported to Moreing in his offices at Broad St. House, and there gave Moreing his record, which was later published in the Australian mining press. To those of us who are familiar with Hoover's record it appears rather modest, but here it is, as he gave it:

"Graduate in Mining, Stanford University, U. S. A.

1 year Geologist, Geological Survey, Arkansas (lead and zinc investigation),

2 1/2 years Geologist, U. S. Geological Survey (gold and silver).

1 year Surveyor, Assayer, Foreman and Superintendent at Grass Valley, Nevada City, Angelo Camp, California; Clifton, Arizona, etc.

3 years mostly Chief Assistant to Louis Janin, during which time he made the usual examinations all over the Western U. S. A. In charge at New Mexico and Four Mile, Colorado."

But Mr. Moreing, head of Bewick Moreing, was not in a position to judge, for he himself was not a qualified mining engineer, although his firm had charge of so many mining properties. The firm of Bewick Moreing & Co. was very pleased to acquire the services of such a self-styled notable mining expert at such a relatively low salary and, after receiving his instructions, perhaps we should say secret instructions, judging from this firm's methods of working, Hoover sailed for Western Australia at once by the S/S *Victoria*. He was off to the new found land of gold.

What a thrill this voyage would have afforded to the ordinary college graduate of the barnyard type such as Hoover was! Down the English Channel, past the glorious Isle of Wight, along the Spanish and Portuguese coasts, into Gibralter where there was time to go ashore and visit the famous Rock, then on again to Malta, where there were another few hours on shore, hen off to sleepy Brindisi, down to the Greek coast and across the blue Mediterranean to busy Port Said, the home of the riff raff and the donkey boy. The voy-

age through the Suez Canal was truly wonderful and
weird by the moonlight night in the deadly stillness
of the desert. After passing Ismailia the steamer proceeded to Suez, and then through the Red Sea to Aden,
where the passengers had a few hours on shore with
time to have a look at the picturesque native village,
and then on across the Indian Ocean. It was now
mid-April and it was very hot. The sun stood in the
sky like a blazing ball of gold, the sea was a million
dimples of living liquid gold, everything suggested gold
in an inferno of heat. What could Hoover have thought
of on that eventful trip if not of gold! He was going
down to the new West Australian goldfields as field
agent, and it was his job to find gold.

      "Cursed craze for gold," as Vergil wrote in
      Latin 2,000 years ago, "how thou dost affect the
      minds of man!"

In Colombo, Ceylon, the steamer docked for a whole
day, giving the passengers an opportunity of admiring
the tropical scenery, and then she headed south to the
Southern Cross. The next ten days were dull and
monotonous, the temperature much cooler and the as-
pect of sea and sky cold and grey, for the Australian
Winter was approaching. The first glimpse of Western Australia was depressing after the brilliant tropical scenery of Colombo. Once past Cape Lewin, as
King George Sound was reached, the rugged expanse
of precipitous bush-covered headland suggested England
but only momentarily, for as far as the eye could see
there was no sign of human handiwork, nothing to
break the everlasting solitude. At the entrance to King
George Sound stood Cape Vancouver. Here the coast
line receded rapidly to form a natural harbor-opening,
and beyond it rose the beautiful landlocked bay,

Princess Royal Harbor, on the northern shore of which rests the little town of Albany, a sleepy place of rather scattered appearance with slate roofed houses. As the S/S *Victoria* approached the town, a yellow flag was run up on shore, the dreaded quarantine flag, which meant that the passengers would be for some time the guests of the Western Australian Government. On May 13th, 1897, Herbert Hoover landed at Albany.

While Hoover is making this eventful voyage, let us look over his new employers, Bewick Moreing & Co. In 1885, Thomas J. Bewick, a brother of the Bishop of Newcastle, and an engineer who had had some experience in lead mining in the North of England, formed a partnership with his son Thomas Burrell Bewick and with a pupil named Charles Algernon Moreing. Bewick was then a man of sixty-four and his son was rather delicate, so that the whole management of the new company devolved on the junior partner Moreing, who was most active and enterprising. The new firm engaged in furnishing reports on, and taking over the management of, mining properties, and gradually acquired an interest in mining and exploration companies in the United States, South Africa and Western Australia. In 1897 it had, in addition to its main office in London, branch offices at Perth and Coolgardie in Western Australia and at Umtali and Salisbury (Mashonaland) in South Africa.

Moreing, too, was something of a financier. Taking advantage of the West Australian gold mining "boom" originated by Wright and Bottomley, he decided to also enter the promoting game. He would have the advantage over these other promoters, who made their profits simply by market gambling, by being the manager of any companies he promoted, and could thus

appoint employees in the mines who would consider
his interests first. In other words he would have the
inside information, and have it first. Accordingly, in
the Summer of 1894 he promoted the *London & Western
Australian Exploration Company Limited* with a flow-
ery prospectus showing as a member of the Board of
Directors no less a personage than the late Lord Roberts.
It was the usual "come-on" English promoters used
to attract investors, this of embellishing the prospectus
with the name of some member of the nobility or prominent personage, the so-called "guinea pigs." Sixty-
seven thousand, five hundred shares at a pound (or five
dollars) a share were sold to the public. The promoter
retained free of charge fifteen hundred "deferred"
shares of no par value, for his services. The directors
were, of course, nominees of Moreing and they agreed
to finance the expenses of a field agent in the employ
of Bewick Moreing & Co., to prospect for gold in Western Australia. This agent, W. A. Mercer, was immediately successful. At Kalgoorlie he is said to have come
across a couple of immigrant Italians, who held two
six acre claims, which showed very little gold on the
surface. However, Mercer was a competent and clever
man and he came to the conclusion that he had made
a "find." He promptly offered the Italians five thousand
pounds ($25,000) and a one-tenth interest in a new
company to be formed. The story goes that the Italians
demurred, thinking that the offer was not enough,
whereupon Mercer offered them one-twentieth, and the
poor Italians, thinking this a better offer, accepted.
The *Hannan's Brownhill Gold Mining Co.* was at once
floated on the London market by Moreing's *London &
Western Exploration Co.* which financed the deal, and
received considerably more than a third of the shares

in the new *Hannan's Brownhill Gold Mining Company.*
These shares were worth an enormous premium, for
the mine proved itself to be a veritable Aladdin's cave.
Moreing promptly proceeded to take effective control
of the *London & Western Australian Exploration Company.* At its very first annual meeting he gave back the
shareholders the money they had put up by declaring
a 100% dividend out of the enormous profits made from
the flotation of the *Hannan's Brownhill* mine, and then
forced through a scheme of reconstruction by increas-
ing the capital to three hundred thousand pounds
($1,500,000) and giving the shareholders in the old
company one hundred and thirty-five thousand shares
in the new company (two for one) and giving himself
also a hundred and thirty-five thousand shares in the
new company in exchange for the fifteen hundred
shares in the old company that he had taken free of
charge. This was ninety for one. Then, by allotting
himself and his friends a few of the unissued shares,
he had acquired effective control of the company at no
cost whatever. This most shrewd and unusual method
of finance was not new. It is not known who taught
it to Mr. Moreing. But there is no doubt of how well
Mr. Moreing taught it to his American employee, Herbert
Hoover.

The success of the flotation of the rich little *Hannan's
Brownhill* mine proved the turning point in the fortunes
of Bewick Moreing & Co., or rather Moreing. In this
enterprise he had associated with him Edmund Davis
and Walton Fitzjames Turner, names that, for over
a quarter of a century have been of sinister import to
the British investor. As long as the public was willing to put up the money for them to gamble with,
Moreing and his friends were going to put no obstacles

in the way, so that we find them promoting a whole series of financial companies: the *London & Western Australian Investment Co. Ltd.*, the *Continental & Western Australian Trust Ltd.*, the *London & New Zealand Exploration Co. Ltd.* and the *Anglo-Continental Gold Syndicate Ltd.*, of which we shall hear a good deal later. The method of operation of all these financial companies, including the original *London & Western Australian Company* was very simple. The public bought their shares and provided the funds. The directors, Moreing and his gang, had their field agents running around in the gold fields looking for claims they could "jump" or buy for a trifle. Then the programme was to put a few men working on the "property" and then have it visited by a mining "expert," who was generally the same field agent who acquired it, and who would cable to London glowing accounts of his "discovery." The next step was to float a company in London based on these fine reports with a capital of twenty to a hundred times what the property had cost. Most of these properties might have been payable but for the fact of being overcapitalized. But this was of little purport to Bewick Moreing & Co., who made their profits as "insiders" and earned their handsome fees for managing the properties or, in other words, keeping them alive as long as possible. There was no killing the *Hannan's Brownhill*. It was far too rich. It gorged with gold. It was used as the advertisement, the "come-on."

We accordingly find that on Hoover's arrival in Western Australia in May 1897, his employers, Bewick Moreing & Co., had the management of numerous mining properties in that region which they had helped to promote, among them being the *East Murchison United*,

the *Bellevue Proprietary,* the *Hampton Plains Estate,*
Menzie's Gold Estates, Mertzy's Reward, Menzie's Gold
Development, Menzie's Consolidated Gold Mines, Lynd-
hurst Goldfields, and others, none of which with the
exception of the first named ever paid a single dividend.
On the contrary, they resulted in the loss of millions
of dollars to the unfortunate investors. Or perhaps we
should not say "loss?" Did not Mr. Hoover fifteen years
later, on the occasion of the Nigerian tin deals, in
which he and his friend Edmund Davis took such a
prominent part, explain that such money is not lost
but simply transferred into the pockets of the "insiders"
from those of the "idiots" who buy the shares?

When Hoover landed in Albany on May 13th, 1897,
he was herded with the other passengers into the quarantine shed, a bare, chilly room, where he had to remain
five days until the danger of infection was over. However, he had his luck with him, for among the passengers was Professor Modest Maryanski, the Polish mining expert, who had first discovered "telluride" gold
in Western Australia. Hoover learned more about gold
in those few days than he had ever done before in his life.
Telluride gold, to give a non-technical explanation, is
gold in such a fine state of subdivision in the ore that
it is almost impossible to distinguish it from ordinary
country rock. On leaving the quarantine shed, Hoover
was met by his new boss in Western Australia, Mr.
Edward Hooper, who was the local partner and general
manager for Bewick Moreing & Co. Hooper took
Hoover to Perth, a distance of three hundred and thirty
miles, which it took sixteen hours to cover, changing
trains at Beverly, two hundred and forty-two miles
from Perth, to connect with the Government Railway
from Fremantle to Perth. The country traversed was

overwhelmingly monotonous with dense flat wastes of
forest and endless brush on either side. But what was
chiefly striking was the utter absence of human or
animal life everywhere, not even so much as a bird
being visible to break the eternal monotony. It was
a dreadful change from California. And there was
worse beyond, enough to discourage any young man
except one bent on the search for gold.

On arrival in Perth, Mr. Hooper took Hoover over
the rounds, which in Perth generally meant a visit to
the Weld Club and the Shamrock Hotel bar and various
rounds of drinks. Hoover must have appeared young
to him for a man of thirty-five, but Hooper had been
in the West of the U. S. A. and knew how difficult it
was to judge a man's age from his appearance. You
may be surprised that he fell for Hoover's record, as
he gave it, but there is, as the *Mining News* of London
said on January 23, 1913, "no science which more easily
lends itself to deception of this kind than does geology,
and when the hurriedly assimilated knowledge gained
from textbooks is aided by a small amount of practical
experience in the field, the average sort of person already referred to is sufficiently equipped to prove himself a disadvantage and a danger to any community."

Mr. Harry P. Woodward, whom Hoover was to re-
place at Coolgardie, had already left on April 10th for
Perth to take a position at a smaller salary from Mr.
Critchley Parker of the Australian Mining Standard
in Perth. With Mr. Woodward, this was a question
of principle. He had a reputation to maintain. He
was the son of one of the most famous geologists in
England. He had been through the School of Mines.
He had been Assistant Government Geologist of South
Australia for five years and Government Geologist to

Western Australia for eight years. He had a record of accomplishment as an explorer and geologist, and when he resigned in 1895 to enter the employment of Bewick Moreing & Co. the Government, as a mark of appreciation, conferred upon him the title of Honorary Consulting Geologist and Mining Engineer to the colony of Western Australia. He was a Justice of the Peace, a member of many engineering and geological societies, and a Freeman of the City of London. He had such a fine record that when he retired from Bewick Moreing & Co.'s service the great mining newspaper, the *Mining Journal* of London, at the other end of the world, issued a special supplement in his honor. Woodward had left the job with Bewick Moreing & Co. just because he could not make it jibe with his principles. He found that what was wanted of him he could not do. The work of field agent with Bewick Moreing & Co. did not call for a geologist but for a smart aleck, a claim jumper, a snooper and a spy, and this hardly fitted into the way of thinking of a man who, as the *Mining Journal* of June 26th, 1897, put it, "always, in his official capacity as Government Geologist, did his best to protect the British investor from the numerous spurious and worthless undertakings put forward by the unscrupulous to ensnare the public, and for which he received the usual thanks." This was the man whom Hoover was to succeed.

Hoover was not allowed to dally in Perth, but was sent right on to Coolgardie. This was a distance of four hundred and fifty miles, which it took the train twenty-four hours to cover. If the journey from Albany to Perth had been dreary, this was absolute desolation, nothing but interminable bush and scrub and the red sand everywhere. Along the road could be

seen camel caravans in charge of Afghans, and unfortunate individuals "humping their swag" trying to
tramp back to civilization hundreds of miles away, and
with small chances of ever getting there. For here
there was hardly a drop of water, and what there was,
was salty. The "soaks" or shallow wells along the
roads, which had collected a little rain water, were
scenes of bitter quarrels, every man fighting selfishly
to help himself first and cursing himself for wasting
his life and strength in such a country. Even the horses
and camels were mad with thirst.

On arrival in Coolgardie, Hoover proceeded to his
new residence, *The Homestead,* an attractive one story
frame house with veranda, at the entrance of the *Hampton Plains Estate* property, one of the "dud" companies
of his employers, which was located a mile or so out
of Coolgardie. Coolgardie has been described at this
period as a place of "sin, sand and sorrow." "Of all
the God forsaken places in the world this is the worst,"
wrote Charles Taylor, a Montana miner in 1896. And
yet, it was a thriving community. The railroad had
just been finished to Coolgardie and pushed on to Kalgoorlie, some twenty miles further east, the location
of the famous Golden Mile. Its population was some
five thousand mostly miners without their families,
for it was cruel to bring women and children into this
wilderness. And yet, ladies of leisure, lured by the
craze of gold, found their way there by the hundreds,
even from far away Japan. The town presented a
weird appearance, for timber and building materials
were so extremely dear that almost all the "houses"
consisted of hessian stretched on poles and covered
with corrugated iron roofs. Coolgardie was sometimes
visited by little local whirlwinds, called "willie willies,"

which frequently carried off quite a few of these resi-
dences in a cloud of dust. The main street, Bayley
Street, called after the discoverer of gold in Coolgardie, was a very wide thoroughfare lined with a
heterogeneous collection of corrugated iron shops, which
sold almost everything under the sun except fresh milk,
meat and fish. The staple food in Coolgardie was "tinned dog," as it was called, and the regular drink was
whisky, for beer cost just as much and was unpalatable,
there being no way of keeping it cool. Water was the
great luxury. The locally obtained water was seven
times as salty as sea water and had to be condensed.
A horse consumed sixty cents worth and a camel five
dollars worth, at a draft. It was dangerous for human
consumption on account of the prevalence of typhoid
fever, so that the only "drys" in Coolgardie at this
period were those who could not afford whisky. This
did not mean that the population was lawless. Quite
the contrary. There was no gun toting or shooting as
in Western United States mining camps, and practically
no crime of any description. Offenders, as a rule, received summary justice from the miners themselves
by being ordered to leave the settlement. Coolgardie,
then, this desert settlement four hundred and fifty
miles from the coast, away from all the amenities of
civilization, with its hessian huts, torrid heat, perpetual sand, plagues of flies, typhoid fever and absence of
washing water, was not the most desirable place in the
world to live in and certainly in no way comparable
to the beautiful Silver Falls City of Uncle John Minthorn.

However, men did not come here for comfort. They
came here for gold. Just as in that Summer of 1897
men were trekking north to the Klondyke to brave the

horrors of the Arctic cold, so they had to come out
here to face the heat and the drought. They were
gold hungry, had the gold fever. All they thought of
was gold. All they talked of was gold. Most of them
had come out as prospectors, and when they had no
luck and lost their little capital were compelled to
work in the mines where they breathed the gold dust
they had been so anxious to win and eventually fell
victims to the deadly poison. The miners were white
Australians, in great part of the prospector type we
have mentioned, and to a great extent of Irish origin,
descendants of patriots who had been transported to
Australia in bygone days for political offenses. There
was an admixture of English and Welsh miners who
had been attracted by the high rates of wages. These
high wages were, however, fictitious. For, although
a miner could earn from three pounds ten shillings to
four pounds ($17.50 to $20) a week, his board and
lodging set him back over fifteen dollars a week, and
with whisky at twenty-five cents a glass and beer at
a dollar a quart bottle, there was very little surplus.
Few of the miners who came out to this wilderness
ever could save enough to get back to the Coast. After
a few years labor they frequently succumbed to the
dreaded miner's complaint contracted in the badly
ventilated mines. To be laid off was practically a
death sentence. If no other work was available it
meant tramping back to the coast, and a few ever suc-
cessfully made the journey. Some disappeared completely, having probably wandered into the bush in
search of water. And any white man who went into
the bush alone was never seen again. The bodies of
others were sometimes found by the tracks with bleed-
ing feet and swollen tongues cleaving to the roofs of

their mouths, into which they had sometimes forced a jacknife in a last desperate effort to escape suffocation. The mining worker element was accordingly fairly stable, and there was always a fresh influx which made up for the loss from accident, disease or migration to other adjoining camps.

Such was the Coolgardie in which Herbert Hoover made his appearance in June, 1897, a miserable place to live in, dusty, oppressively hot, but more than prosperous. It was, indeed, thriving. Millions in gold were being produced from the mines. There was a constant influx of visitors, capitalists and experts. And the hotels did a roaring business. Coolgardie had its race track, a couple of clubs, and a Stock Exchange where large sums were won and lost in speculation. Traveling theatrical companies called occasionally. But with it all there was little distraction. The main resorts for all and sundry were the bars of the hotels where whisky was drunk and all discussed the latest finds, the latest prospects, and where all conversations were limited to gold. Of these hotels the most prominent was the *Victoria,* which was a modern up-to-date two story brick and stone building, the bar of which was frequented evenings by the "elite" in formal dress— the moose-ised white shirts and white duck or flannel pants. The wearing of such an outfit indicated opulence, just as did the appearance of having had a bath, for with the dust of Coolgardie a white suit could not be worn more than once. There were only a few of these "skyscraper" two-story stone and brick edifices in Coolgardie, the handsomest being that which contained the office of Bewick Moreing & Co. and which was to be Hoover's headquarters. This building had been erected by the *London & Western Australian Com-*

pany, which, as we have seen, had been more or less absorbed by Moreing. The most notable feature of this building was the large hall, which was used evenings as a "bootleg" stock exchange, where mining shares were bought and sold on open call, thus often making the market price, for any new development that had occurred during the day was at once reflected in the prices. Here rough, unkempt miners, most of whom did not look as if they were worth a quarter, bought and sold shares for tens of thousands of dollars.

Hoover's new job gave him the management of this office. He was the field agent for Bewick Moreing & Co., and his duties were to discover new mining properties for his firm. If he could not discover any he was to try and get hold of some in any other possible way. They were not overscrupulous. For Hoover's employers were not only mine managers, but mine promoters and speculators acting on inside information acquired from their activities as mine managers. Hoover's new duties also called for his superintending the more or less defunct mines in the Menzies district and the East Murchison mine at Lawlers, which was still a going concern.

He certainly gave himself a good send-off. Here is an "inspired" article which appeared in the Western Australian Goldfields *Courier* of June 19th, 1897, under the modest heading "An American Mining Expert":

"Among the most recent arrivals of American mining men in Western Australia is that of Mr. Herbert C. Hoover, who has recently taken up the management of Messrs. Bewick Moreing's business at Coolgardie when Mr. H. P. Woodward resigned. At a time such as this, when the "telluride" problem is attracting the attention of experienced metallurgists, Mr. Hoover's wide knowledge obtained in the treatment of such ores in Colorado should render him of great service to the mining industry generally, while his two years active connection with the United States official survey of the gold producing regions of California, Arizona and Colorado is, in itself, a guarantee of his geological qualifications. Mr. Hoover comes to this colony direct from California, leaving a highly responsible position on the staff of Louis Janin & Co., who are deservedly placed in the front rank of mining men of the United States, being engineers of worldwide reputation, doing business for the Rothschilds and other leading British and Continental capitalists. Apart from his connection with his late firm, however, Mr. Hoover has Mein, R. A. F. Penrose and Henry Bratsober, men of known repute in America, while among other mining undertakings in California, Nevada and New Mexico, which he has conducted with highly satisfactory results may be mentioned the development of the 'London Exploration' Company's mines at Steeple Rock in the last named State."

In July of 1897 Mr. Edward Hooper, the general manager came up to Coolgardie to make a tour of inspection of the Northern fields, and Hoover accompanied him. On August 27th, of that year the elder Mr. Bewick died and Edward Hooper was taken into the firm as partner. This necessitated Mr. Hooper's going to London and it was not until the following February that Ernest Williams arrived from South Africa to replace him and take charge of the Bewick Moreing business. Hoover meanwhile had a brief spell of authority. One of the first things he did was to try to break the wages of the miners on the East Murchison mine. There was a strike on the railroad at the time and this caused a slackening of mining, throwing some men out of work, and Hoover thought to take advantage of it. But he little knew the spirit of the miners, who rather than accept a cut in pay, went on strike. Hoover returned to Coolgardie, leaving the mine manager, Mr. Mitchell, to settle the strike. His kindest biographer, Rose Wilder Lane, tells us: "He had a sense of the vast egotism and cruelty of youth." This, in explanation of his discharging employees at a time when, as the *Mining World* tells us, men were dying of hunger in the goldfields. There was no sentiment of humanity or pity in him. Indeed, as Miss Lane writes: "When he heard that he was known in West Australia as a hard and ruthless man, he did not deny the indictment." And again she refers to him on page 225 of her book, as "Herbert Hoover, whose ruthlessness was known from Perth to the farthest reaches of the back country."

Hoover's hatred of the white worker is explained to some extent by the report to the *Australian Mail* of its correspondent who accompanied Hoover on one of his tours in February 1898. This report states:

"Upon the labour question Mr. Hoover is particularly bitter and is by no means yet accustomed to the saucy independence of the Australian miner."

Indeed, Hoover had such a dislike for the white miner, that he is said to have written an article to a mining publication in 1898 in which he advocated "removal of the restrictions on Asiatic labor." And this in a white country, where he, an alien, was earning his living.

You have read what Hoover's duties were, as field agent; mainly to find, buy or otherwise acquire mining property suitable for promoting a company in London. This called for keeping watch on the bidders in the evening at the "bootleg" Stock Exchange that was held in his offices, hanging round the hotel bars at night, to overhear a stray word let fall by a drinker, and then up at daybreak and out with his team of "brumbies," as the local ponies were called, to follow up the clews. One day in Cue, the same week at Lawlers, on to Menzies, and back to Coolgardie, thence to Norseman. In an interview with a reporter of the *Australian Mail* in January 1899, he himself claimed to have travelled over five thousand miles by team within twelve months, and yet this "expert" discovered no gold where ignorant immigrants were stumbling across it. What were his thoughts as he sped along behind his brumbies in a cloud of dust, plagued by swarms of flies, tortured by the blistering heat, which went as high as a hundred and twenty degrees in the shade, with desolation all around! He probably cursed the heat, the flies, and his bad luck, just as anyone else might do! He halts his team for a moment. Like shadows a couple of starving native black children speed out from the bush. *Gib it damper* (give us food), *gib it gabbi* (give us water)! A flick of his whip and a curse, and Hoover is on his way. If you think that Herbert Hoover could not curse, just read in the next chapter how Hoover called the Mandarin Chang, an expression so filthy that it would not even bear repetition in a Court of Law.

It has always been claimed for Hoover that he dis-

covered the *Sons of Gwalia* gold mine. But he no more
discovered it than Dr. Cook discovered the South Pole.
It was however the mine which made for him a reputation of the kind Mr. Moreing liked, and that led to his
future advancement. So we must tell our readers
something about it. The *Sons of Gwalia* mine was at
Leonora about two hundred miles north from Coolgardie and sixty miles by road from the rail head at
Menzies. It was disovered by a party of Welsh miners,
who pegged out their claim in July 1896, and gave it
the Welsh name *Sons of Gwalia*. Mr. G. W. Hall, a
Welsh mining engineer, who was prospecting in Western Australia, heard of it. He went out to look it
over and bought it on August 13th, 1896, for a price
of five thousand pounds ($25,000). He immediately
started to make it a marketable proposition by developing it, working it, and proving it. And in May
1897, when Hoover arrived in Australia, Hall had already the mine equipped with a ten stamp battery,
two Berdan and two Wheeler pans and a working
force of a hundred and ten men, and was producing
a thousand ounces ($20,000 worth) of gold a month.
Now that he had proved the mine, Hall set about
marketing it. Hall's partner in London, Pritchard
Morgan, dickered for a while with the Whitaker Wright
and Bottomley people, but the newspapers had begun
rapping these "crowds," and the prospects of floating
a company through them were not brilliant. They accordingly decided to try and promote the new company
through Moreing, who had a following as a result of
the success of the *Hannan's Brownhill* mine. Hall,
therefore, in the Fall of 1897, got in touch with Hoover,
who was temporarily in charge pending the arrival of
Ernest Williams, and interested him in the mine. He

held out to him the prospects of his becoming manager of the mine. Now, Hoover's great ambition had been to become a mine manager, for the managers in Western Australia generally managed to acquire enough wealth in a couple of years to retire on, and Hoover could never hope for such a job except from such a combination. The *Mine Managers Institute* in Coolgardie refused to recognize as a mine manager any man who could not produce credentials to prove that he had served for three years as a practical mine manager, and had even petitioned the Government in September 1897 not to issue a Government certificate to anyone who did not meet with these requirements. Hoover, accordingly, strongly recommended the deal to Moreing, and on November 17th, 1897, an agreement was signed between Moreing and Hall's people in London to float a new company to be called the *Sons of Gwalia Limited*. The capital was to be three hundred thousand pounds ($1,500,000) in three hundred thousand one pound ($5) shares, of which Hall and his partners were to get 100,000 shares, and fifty thousand pounds ($150,000) was to be put up as working capital by Moreing's promoting company, the *London & Western Australian Company*. The Moreing company's share was to be 200,000 shares for putting up the cash and floating the company. Now this mine was not a rich mine like many in the West Australian field that were producing several ounces of gold to the ton of ore. It had up to this time been yielding only about seven hundred tons of ore a month of a gold content of less than one ounce ($20 worth) of gold per ton, and then it was located over sixty miles from a railroad which would make transportation of supplies and machinery extremely expensive. It would take a great deal of

"ballyhoo" to "put it over" with the investing public,
and this Moreing and his friends proceeded to supply.
The company was registered and a prospectus published
"for information only," no shares being offered to the
public, as if the promoters were keeping a good thing
for themselves. Meanwhile production was stepped up
at the mine until it exceeded a thousand tons of
ore a month.

But there was a slight impediment: Mr. A. W.
Castle, Hall's mine manager would not make his
mine reports encouraging enough to start the ball
rolling. This was soon overcome. Hoover, having
taken an option for Moreing on an adjoining fifteen
acre property called *Gwalia No. 1 South,* news flashed
to London of the discovery of two large reef formations. A "formation" does not of course mean a "lode,"
or indicate anything in particular, but it was sufficient
for the promoters to get busy and introduce the shares
to the stock market in the first days of March at two
pounds and a quarter for the one pound share. The
process of "introducing" shares consisted in getting a
friendly broker to make a few "wash" sales with con-
federates, which would lead the public to believe that
the price quoted was the actual market value of the
shares. This price was ridiculous in comparison with
those of mines already paying large dividends and, to
maintain it, more "ballyhoo" than ever had to be in-
dulged in. The most essential thing was to get good
reports from the mine, Mr. Castle's being too sober
altogether. Moreing knew how to get these good reports.

On March 17th, 1898, Herbert Hoover took over
the *Sons of Gwalia* mine on behalf of the new company.
His friend Professor V. P. Kellogg tells us on page 75
of his book on Hoover how "he went out and took

personal charge of the opening up." Mr. Castle's last report had been cabled on March 12th. It was the best one so far and read:

> "200 foot level crosscut just intersected vein, width 4 feet equal parts quartz formation, assay value 3 ounces per ton."

Of course, the assay value may sometimes be double the value of the gold actually recovered from the ore, so there is no doubt but that this report was correct. But Castle could not see as much gold as Hoover, and here is the first cable after taking over:

> "March 21—Gwalia level No. 2—assays average per ton of 2240 lbs. 5 ounces. I have no doubt we can improve upon this. Level No. 1— cut No. 8—rich chute of ore—mine promises exceedingly well for the future."

It was no trouble at all for Hoover to improve on this. Here is his next cable:

> "March 24—Drive South in No. 2 level—lode is improving. Assays average 7 ounces 6 pennyweight per ton."

This cable coincided happily with a great "ballyhoo" dinner given at the Hotel Cecil in London and attended by several members of Parliament including Lloyd George, who in those days was not averse to being let in on a "good thing." Mr. Hall, in the course of his speech, reached the climax when he told of the cable just received which stated that the average of seven ounces was being maintained. Well, what did the average dumb investor think when he picked up his morning paper on March 29th, 1898, and read the account of this dinner and the wonderful mine that was "averaging" over seven ounces ($140) to the ton? Did he not think that there was another *Brownhill,* and rush to buy?

We must remember the class of people who mostly invested in mining shares in England in those days. They were the small tradesman, the artisan, the teacher, the widow, in general people who could never hope to save very much money and who were willing to take a little gamble in hopes of making enough to educate their children or put by a little competance for their old age. Now, there was nothing wrong with the *Sons of Gwalia* mine, only with the people who were exploiting it, and who, when they had shares to unload, did not hesitate to feed the public with stories of over a hundred and forty dollars of gold to the ton when the mine was actually producing twenty dollars. However, settling day in the shares had been fixed by the Stock Exchange for June 28th, 1898, and the campaign had to be kept up till then. On May 14th, 1898, the *Mining Journal* printed the mine report received by mail for the two weeks ending March 26th. It confirmed the cable read at the "booster" dinner at the Hotel Cecil, reading, in part:

> "The average of assays for the fortnight is 7 oz. 4 dwt. gold per ton. The last assay made today (quartz only) gave 55 oz. 10 dwts. 7 grains gold."

This campaign of encouraging reports continued. The report for the fortnight ending April 9th reads:

> "No. 9 shaft south drive No. 2 level 6 feet lode formation taken out given by washing an average of 4 ounces free gold. No. 1 winze average of samples gives 4 ounces free gold Samples taken across full width of winze about 5 feet, etc."

This was even better than the assay value report of 7 ounces. Just imagine four ounces of free gold obtained by washing! It must be a veritable Bonanza!

The result of these reports was that Moreing and his friends cleaned up a profit of some two million dollars on the flotation of the *Sons of Gwalia* mine.

With the success of the flotation of the *Sons of Gwalia* mine, Hoover became the "white haired boy" with Moreing. He unhesitatingly appointed Hoover manager of the mine in replacement of the Capable Mr. Castle, and in defiance of the local *Mine Managers Institute*. This was not a new occurrence.

Thus we find that Hoover in June, 1898, had at last realized his ambition of becoming a mine manager.

Now let us go back a little. Edward Hooper had left for England to become a partner of Moreing, and Ernest Williams, the new general manager, did not arrive from Johannesburg until February of 1898. In the meantime, enjoying a brief spell of authority, Hoover at once took advantage of it to send for his Stanford "crony" G. B. Wilson, who had taken his degree of Bachelor in Preliminary Law in 1896. That is how Mr. George Benton Wilson, who is now a corporation counsel in Los Angeles, came over to Australia in January 1898 as assistant to Hoover, and was described in the press as a mining engineer "of extensive Californian and Mexican experience."

Thus, in June 1898, we find Herbert Hoover installed as manager of the *Sons of Gwalia* mine. And yet no wonders took place. Production did not increase. The Government reports show us that in the six months he held that job the average monthly output was a little over a thousand tons a month with a gold yield of exactly one ounce to the ton. What became of the seven ounces six pennyweight that he had already reported? It does look as if there were something wrong somewhere. And yet, as manager, he had competent assistance. His boss, Ernest Williams, was a mining engineer with a fine record in South Africa, and his underground mine manager, John Alexander Agnew, was a young New Zealander, a graduate of the Thame School of Mines, and a very capable man, who, as we shall see, was later to play an important part in Hoover's activities.

Hoover was now definitely in the mining game. He was a mining expert. We know, of course, that many of the undesirable elements who have associated themselves with mining have given it a bad name, to such an extent that Mark Twain described a mine as "a hole in the ground with a liar on top." And yet there is really no cleaner or more profitable pursuit in life than mining, when in the hands of men of responsibility and integrity. Every dollar raised from the mine and added to the wealth of the nation comes without injury to fellowmen resulting from competitive trade and industry which so often thrives on the misfortunes of others.

Hoover had been a mine manager just six months, when in December 1898, he received a hurry call from London. There was hard work to be done in China. It called for a man tough, tenacious and relentless. But the salary was in proportion, twelve thousand, five hundred dollars a year. Moreing knew his man, he offered Hoover the job, and in December 1898, Hoover sailed for London to receive his instructions.

During his eighteen months residence in Western Australia, Hoover earned a reputation, as Rose Wilder Lane tells us, for ruthlessness. The truth about him is that he was absolutely unsocial. In all that time he does not seem to have taken part in any church or social activities, concert or entertainment, sport or game, not even fishing. So that on his departure there was no "send-off" as is usual in these frontier colonies. In a way, it was sad. He was only twenty-four. But the mask he wore and which he no longer could lay aside was that of a mining expert thirty-six years old.

He arrived in London during the first week of January 1899, and, having been touted as an important personage, gave an interview on arrival to the representative of the *Australian Mail*. He was very cautious about mentioning the *Sons of Gwalia*, which we know was nothing like what he had cracked it up to be. But, this interview alleges, he told the world that Moreing's *East Murchison* mine had forty thousand to fifty thousand tons of ore ready to stope above the hundred and seventy foot level of an average milling value of twenty-eight dwt. as well as twenty thousand tons of tailings, and that the profits of this mine for 1899 should reach ninety thousand pounds ($450,000). This statement might, of course, have meant to boost the shares of that mine, which had declared a 5% dividend a few days before. He also predicted that the four great gold mines of West Australia would prove to be the *East Murchison,* the *Bellevue,* the *Sons of Gwalia* and *Westralia Mount Morgans.*

After Hoover's arrival, the firm went into a "huddle" for a couple of weeks. There were Moreing and Davis and Turner. There was a great "coup" to be pulled off. No, dear reader, it is not a bank robbery they were planning. These gentlemen were not thieves. They were "financiers." What they were planning was the "absorption" of one of the greatest coal mines in the world, a property worth hundreds of millions of dollars.

Hoover was coached, received his instructions, and

left for New York, where he arrived at the end of January 1899, proceeding direct to San Francisco. From there he ran down to Monterey, where on February 10th, 1899, he was married by Father Ramon Mestress, a Roman Catholic priest, to Miss Lou Henry, who had been a fellow student of his in the geology class at Stanford, held the same diploma, and was just as much entitled to be called a mining engineer as he was. The following day they sailed from San Francisco for Shanghai.

CHAPTER THE THIRD

MANDARINS AND MOUNTEBANKS

IN connection with the flotation of the *Sons of Gwalia* mine, Moreing had been brought in touch with William Pritchard Morgan, a mining engineer, and partner of G. W. Hall, the man who had developed that mine. Pritchard Morgan had visited China in the beginning of 1897 and had been much impressed by the possibilities there. He, too, had made a considerable profit from the flotation of the new *Sons of Gwalia* company, but had been manoeuvered by Moreing out of a directorship in that company. So he again turned his attention to China and left for that country. Moreing was not to be outdone and followed suit. But whereas Morgan went to the province of Szechuan, Moreing went to the Northern province of Chi-li, and in June of 1898 we find him visiting the Kaiping coal mines. He came, saw and coveted. Here was an enormous coal deposit, with reserves of hundreds of millions of tons of coal, some of it equal to the best Welsh or Pennsylvania steam coal, within ninety miles of the great city of Tientsin and sixty miles of a deep water seaport, being operated and managed by the Chinese themselves. Something would have to be done about it.

This Chinese enterprise, the *Chinese Engineering & Mining Company*, was a private company with a capital of 1,500,000 Taels (roughly $1,000,000). The Chinese Government, which had an interest in the concern, had put in charge of it the Mandarin Chang-Yen-Mao, who relied largely on the advice of Gustav Detring, a German resident of Tientsin of great ability and foresight, who had devoted his life to the interests of China and who had the greatest influence with the Chinese Government. At the time of Moreing's visit, the mines were on a basis of great efficiency. Moreing himself tells us, in September 1898:

> "The number of persons employed underground is about 3,000, and the output from the Tongshan pit alone was 446,000 tons in 1896 and 425,000 in 1897. None can be spared for export; and were the output twenty times as great as it is, it would find ready market, for its quality is better than that of Japanese coal. The colliery has its own foundry, machine shop, brickmaking and other works, and altogether is a very significant instance of what Chinese enterprise is capable of. A new shaft—as good a piece of work as I have ever seen—has just been sunk, and the aggregate output will be largely increased in a few months."

This company had also executed important public works. It had built a canal fourteen miles long from the mines to Lutai, and fifty miles of railroad from Tong-ku to Ku-yeh. It had a fleet of six steamers. It had also erected large buildings with a compound and wharves along the river Pei-ho in the American concession, a parcel of land that had been ceded by China to the United States in 1861, and at the time Moreing arrived they were busy constructing a harbor in the ice-free port of Ching-Wan-Tao, having bought all the property for 10 miles around. To finance this great undertaking, which would give it an outlet for its coal to the open sea for shipment by steamers of large tonnage, it had issued bonds bearing 12% interest, with the Kaiping coal mines as security. To protect this port from seizure by one of the Great Powers, which were then trying to "grab" whatever they could in China, the Chinese Government in April, 1898, declared it a "treaty" port, open to the ships of all nations.

Moreing saw the tremendous possibilities, and suggested to Gustav Detring the advisability of introducing foreign capital to develop the property. Detring was quite in accord with this which had been made possible by an edict issued on April 2, 1898, largely as a result of the efforts of Morgan on his previous visit. This edict created a Bureau of Control of Railways and Mines and authorized the introduction of foreign capital to the extent of 50% in Chinese mines, provided, always, that the control remained in the hands of the Chinese. This Bureau was divided into two sections, and Chang-Yen-Mao was made director of the section corresponding to the province of Chi-li. Moreing now played his trump card. Here are his own words:

"I propose that a Mines Department under a high Chinese official should be constituted with a European mining adviser."

Moreing had meanwhile ingratiated himself with Detring by "offering" to take up a million dollars worth of Ching-Wan-Tao bonds and, on Detring's recommendation the Bureau of Mines was created, and Moreing considerately offered to provide the mining expert. He made, however, one condition. The new expert should be paid a lordly salary and allowed to also represent the interests of Bewick Moreing & Co. This was also agreed to. By this time, Moreing had been back in London for some months. It was the end of 1898. He did not have to look around for the "expert" to send to China. He had him in mind all the time, the man who had helped him to "put over" the *Sons of Gwalia.*

Hoover arrived in Shanghai towards the end of February, 1899 and went on to Tientsin, where he met his new chief, Chang-Yen-Mao, and the latter's adviser, Detring. Since these gentlemen are very important for our narrative, let us pause to examine them more closely.

Chang-Yen-Mao was at this time a man of about forty-five, of outstanding physique, being over six feet in height, and of great strength. As a young man he had performed the remarkable feat of scaling the great wall of Pekin with the baby emperor Kwang-Hsu strapped to his back. The crowning of Kwang-Ksu enabled that resolute woman, the Empress Dowager, to remain the actual ruler of China, and she rewarded Chang by making him a Mandarin, and appointing him Chamberlain of the Court. He later became Director of the Northern China Railroad, and Director of the Chinese Imperial Mining Bureau, in which capacity he had Hoover "wished" on him. He was a shrewd man and acquired considerable wealth, but his honesty had never been called in question, even by the famous Dr. Morrison, Peking correspondent of the *Times,* who considered Chang an enemy of England.

Gustav Detring was a German about fifty-five years of age, who had come to Tientsin as a boy, and had made himself the greatest factor in building and progress of that city. For twenty-five years he was Commissioner of Chinese Customs and during that time was the adviser of the great Viceroy, Li Hung Chang. During this period he was practically the Foreign Minister of China. Members of the diplomatic corps could do little without coming down to Tientsin to see him. Mr. Detring was also for thirteen years Chairman of the British Municipal Council, a rare honor considering that he was a German. He was the founder of *Tientsin University,* and devoted his life to the interests of his adopted country.

On his arrival, Hoover was greeted with considerable deference in recognition of his great attainments. Was he not the miracle man who could conjure up minerals out of the ground? They gave him time to get his bearings, but in the end suggested that he do something for his enormous salary, which was in China two hundred and fifty times that of a day laborer. But it seems Hoover could do nothing without his fellow magicians. He had to wait till they came along. There was Newberry, the Australian, Agnew, the New Zealander, Jack Means of Stanford, who was a real geologist, D. P. Mitchell, another Stanford man, and his "crony" George Benton Wilson, the preliminary lawyer. Then a great expedition was organized to "prospect" in the provinces of Chi-li and Jehol. But this was not Western Australia, a British colony with established law and order. Hoover had great respect for his skin and would not go out without the protection of an escort of cavalry. According to Hoover's own report, the expedition visited some fifty districts in the province of Chi-li without accomplishing anything, much to the amazement of Chang, who could not understand how such a highly paid expert with such a costly expedition had not only failed to locate any deposits of minerals but had not succeeded in discovering anything at all. Had he not read in the papers of Finnegan's mare that kicked up the nugget at Kalgoorlie, which resulted in Pat Hannan discovering that fountain of gold, and of the Idaho jackass that located the Bunker Hill mine in that State? And yet this band of foreign devil magicians and miracle men could not find any gold or silver, which was being stumbled across by ignorant lowbrow Chinese peasants. Hoover returned to Tientsin that winter, and Chang, not knowing what to do with him, sent him to the Kaiping coal mines. That was exactly what Hoover wanted. He notified Moreing in London, and the latter at once sailed for China. But this business of traveling to the other end of the earth was rather expensive. So, before leaving, Moreing went into another huddle with Davis and Turner of the notorious *Anglo Continental Gold Syndicate,* and they floated a little company to pay expenses. This was the *Oriental Syndicate Limited,* registered in London on December 14th, 1899

"to adopt a certain agreement for the acquisition of certain concessions, rights, mineral properties, etc., and to deal with and turn to account the same."

They certainly intended to turn to good account that certain agreement when they got it. Ten thousand ordinary shares of one pound ($5) and ten thousand deferred shares of one shilling (25c) were issued, all to the *Anglo Continental Gold Syndicate,* and eighty-eight thousand and five hundred one pound shares kept "in the bag." The Bylaws of this syndicate contained the remarkable provision that after paying 100% dividend on the ordinary shares, the excess profits should be divided 50% to the ordinary shares, 40% to the deferred shares (that is sixteen times as much as to the ordinary shares, for the deferred shares only cost one shilling) and 10% to the directors. They were certainly figuring on making some profit out of that "certain agreement" which Hoover was to pull off for them. As a matter of fact they intended it to be all profit. Thus we have in December, 1899, Moreing again on his way to China.

Moreing arrived in China at a very inauspicious moment. This was in the beginning of March, 1900. The mother of the mandarin Chang-Yen-Mao had just died and, in accordance with Chinese custom, Chang could transact or discuss no business for 100 days. Moreing, accordingly, had to leave the whole execution of the scheme to Hoover and he left China in April for England.

Just at this very period a violent patriotic agitation directed against foreigners had broken out in Northern China. A fanatical sect known as the "patriotic harmonious fists," or Boxers, sprang into existence, claiming invulnerability, and openly declaring their intention of driving the foreign devils into the sea. In Chi-li the country soon swarmed with bands of Boxers, burning, pillaging and murdering missionaries and native converts. Towards the end of May the situation in Peking became so serious that, on the 28th, the Legations ordered up the Legation guards from Tientsin. They left on May 31st, four hundred and fifty-one strong, and arrived in Peking, ninety miles away, the same day. Immediately afterwards, marauding bands cut communication on the Peking-Tientsin railroad. Allied warships were rushed to Taku at the mouth of the Pei-ho and, on the night of June 9th, Admiral Sir Edward Seymour received a telegram from Sir Claude MacDonald, the British Minister at Peking, appealing for reinforcements. Within two hours Admiral Seymour left his flagship with a landing party and proceeded by rail to Tientsin. Here an exploring party was about to take out an engine to go ahead of the relief expedition to see if the line was clear, when Tong Shao Ye, assistant director of the Northern Chinese Railroad, and a notorious supporter of the Boxers, refused to allow the train to leave. Captain Bayly, R. N., of H. M. S. *Aurora*, Admiral Seymour's chief of staff, who was being left behind to organize the defense of Tientsin, came along and ordered the men to board the train. There were thousands of Chinese at the station, jeering at the troops, and with the huge crowd to back him Tong again interfered saying that, as director, he would allow no train to leave. Bayly's reply was characteristic of the man. "Fix bayonets," he ordered. "Man that train. And as for you, Tong," he added, "another word from you and I hang you to those rafters." This episode is recorded in the book *"The Fighting in North China"* by Midshipman Gips of H. M. S. *Orlando*, and in *"My War Experiences in China"* by Capt. Giepler of the German Navy. This Tong is the same ruffian who was later placed under arrest for aiding the Boxer maniacs in their attempt to massacre the women and children of Tientsin. An article published in the New York *Herald Tribune* of Sept. 15, 1929, purports to record an interview with Tong in Shanghai, in which he relates how his friend Hoover at great risk to his life kept a thousand Chinese from starvation during the siege of Tientsin. This is just one more of the Baron Munchausen tales propagated by Hoover's press agents. Save the chinese! Was it not in 1916, when he had hundreds of millions to spend for relief, that Chinese coolies were dropping dead of hunger at Hoover's mines in Burma, when a handful of rice would have saved them? He was too passionately preoccupied by the one great pursuit which he himself described a few years later in a letter he wrote when he was in Johannesburg on slave business, as "the great science of extracting the greatest possible amount of money from some other human being."

In the Spring of 1900 there were quite a number of Stanford college men in Tientsin. The *Tientsin University,* founded by Detring had been opened in charge of Dr. C. D. Tenney, an American missionary, of high reputation in China, and he had taken over from Stanford Noah F. Drake as professor of geology, and Van Norman McGee as professor of civil engineering. Hoover had already three Stanford men on his staff: Mitchell, Means and Wilson, and with the above five, his wife, and E. R. Lyman of Shanghai he formed a *Stanford Alumni Association* at his home, out on the Racecourse Road at Tientsin. Rose Wilder Lane describes with great gusto the noise and celebration attending this event, and how the college yell was given *fortissimo.* But the college yell was strangely absent in the subsequent fighting, and in the Stanford graduates as well, to their eternal discredit.

Tientsin was at that time a city of about a million inhabitants. It consisted of the native city surrounded by a great mud wall, and the foreign concessions on the other bank of the river Pei-Ho. The native city contained the Government mint and a great arsenal, strongly fortified, and defended by numerous Krupp cannon of the latest models. Across the river from the foreign side of the city was the Chinese Military College, to the west of it was the West Arsenal, and three miles, East of the city the East Arsenal, all strongly defended. At the mouth of the Pei-Ho were the great Taku forts.

The Boxer agitation had been particularly active in the province of Chi-li, and in May the Chinese Government, at the insistence of the European diplomats, had sent a force of some fifteen thousand men under Gen. Nieh towards Tientsin to suppress the roving bands. Things meanwhile had come to a crisis. The Boxers had laid siege to the European Legations in Peking and, as we have seen, Admiral Seymour had set out to relieve them with his little force of two thousand men, including a hundred and twelve Americans under Captain McCalla of the U. S. S. *Newark,* who was one of the outstanding heroes of the expedition. This little force met with unexpected resistance and was obliged to retreat, fighting desperately every inch of the way in the terrific heat, half crazed for want of water, and having to carry the wounded with them. On the afternoon of June 21st, the retreating columns found their way barred by the strongly fortified Hsiku Arsenal, 5 miles north of Tientsin. There was no course open but to attempt to take the arsenal. Seymour ordered: "Germans to the front," and the Germans did it, capturing the arsenal with enormous quantities of food, arms and ammunition, valued at thirty million dollars.

Meanwhile things had come to a climax at Tientsin. On the night of June 15th, 1900, the Chinese commenced burning and looting foreign churches and banks in the Native City. Bands of them approached the foreign settlements, sniping and burning houses in the outlying districts, especially in the French settlement. The alarm was sounded, and women and children were assembled and lodged in the cellars of the strongest buildings, such as the Gordon Hall, Astor House and the premises of Blow & Co. Next day the Chinese made a determined attack on the railroad station, but were beaten off, as it happened to be occupied by a force of seventeen hundred Russians, who had come up from Port Arthur two days before to join Seymour's expedition, and whose late arrival proved to be the salvation of Tientsin. The defending force was now two thousand, four hundred men, of whom seventeen hundred were

Russians, three hundred English and the others chiefly Germans and French, together with over a hundred local volunteers, chiefly English and German residents. Preparations had been made for a week or two previously in the way of throwing up barricades and fences, under the direction of Lieut. Wright with the help of the Chinese troops under C. F. Gammon, Tientsin agent of the American Bible Society, who certainly did his bit. With this force the inhabitants believed they could well cope with any attacks of the Boxers, when a new development arose. The commander of the Chinese forts at Taku had served notice on the admirals of the allied warships of the European powers lying at anchor outside the Pei-ho that he would allow no allied troops up the river and, knowing the dangerous situation in Tientsin and Peking, the admirals decided on strenuous action. On June 16th, they handed the commander of the forts an ultimatum calling on him to surrender the forts by 2 a.m. on the following day. The reply of the Chinaman was to open fire on the allied warships, and after a terrific bombardment of six hours the forts were reduced and taken by storm. As a result of this bombardment the Chinese regular troops at Tientsin believed the allies were making war on China and threw in their lot with the Boxers and, being reinforced by fifteen thousand Manchurian troops from Lutai, opened fire on the foreign settlements of Tientsin on the afternoon of June 17th. Then a terrible and unequal struggle began.

The defending force was only two thousand, four hundred men, including three hundred Japanese who arrived so fortunately on the 16th. On the morning of the 17th, a combined English and German force dashed across the river and captured the Chinese Military College, putting out of action a battery of three-inch Krupp guns mounted there. But in Tientsin Native City they had opposed to them thirty thousand Chinese troops, and an enormous horde of Boxer maniacs, equipped with one six inch and eleven smaller Krupp quick firing guns, which opened a devastating fire of remarkable accuracy against the foreign settlements. A veritable rain of shells poured into the town. The women and children (four hundred of them) and the non-combatant civilians (and to their credit there were very few) had mostly taken refuge in the cellars of the Gordon House. The Hoovers, who lived out on the Racecourse Road, made for the nearest strongly built house, which was that of Mrs. E. M. Drew, wife of the Commissioner of Customs, who threw open her house to refugees. Here they took refuge with a number of women and children until the arrival of the allied reinforcements on June 23rd.

Meanwhile, the situation was desperate. The defense was in the hands of Capt. Bayly of the H. M. S. *Aurora,* then a typical John Bull of fifty-two years, described by George Crowe in his book *"The Commission of H. M. S. Terrible"* as a "bluff sailor with a gist and a ringing laugh at the most anxious moments and a determination and vigor which carried his men irresistibly along with him." C. F. Gamman of the American Bible Society also wrote of him at the time:

"Capt. Bayly, the British Commander, is a man of the same stamp, both men that we may be proud of and in whose care we are sure of every attention and positive safety."

This man, who was a hero if ever there was one, has been basely traduced by Hoover's sycophant "liographers" because he did not hesitate to brand publicly the infamous cowards who were in hiding when four hundred women and children were in hourly peril of the unspeakable. On June 19th the situation seemed hopeless. There was no communication with the warships on the coast and no likelihood of getting reinforcements. Capt. Bayly was asked to take a chance and make for the coast. He refused. He preferred to fight, although he knew, as is shown by a letter he wrote at the time, that the chances were all against him and all in favor of the Chinese. However, as Mr. C. F. Gamman tells us he took the precaution of having lots drawn to decide the men who would have to shoot the women and children in case the Chinese were victorious.

But where was Hoover, "the hero of Tientsin" at this terrible time? Out, smiting the Chinese hip and thigh? No, living in the house of the English Commissioner of Customs. He was a young man at the time, his "real" age was only twenty-seven, a true fighting age. But all heroism is not necessarily physical, it might be argued. Perhaps Mr. Hoover's was a moral heroism? That same evening of June 19th, James Watts, a young Englishman, volunteered to carry the news to the sea and, accompanied by three Russians, he rode all through the night across open country and through all kinds of dangers to Taku, bringing the news of the desperate condition of Tientsin. Reinforcements of two thousand, four hundred men were at once disembarked from the warships and sent on to Tientsin, three hundred Americans and three hundred Russians in the van. They had to fight most of the way, and reached Tientsin on June 23rd, after suffering losses of forty killed and two hundred wounded. What rejoicing on their arrival! The last shell of the defenders had been fired that very morning!

By a strange coincidence, the Chinese did not bombard the settlements on that or the following day. The Chinese army had gone off to attack Seymour in the Hsiku Arsenal, and it was only after two days fighting that Seymour was relieved by a force of Russians sent out from Tientsin, and could return to that city. Mrs. Drew turned over her house to the American troops on their arrival on the 23rd, and Hoover and the other refugees there had to return to their homes. The inferno was over, but only for the time being.

As is usual in such cases, when the bombardment ceased the slackers who had been in hiding were very prominent, telling everybody how things should be run and strutting around as if they were the saviours of the situation. Capt. Bayly was so incensed that, in the words of Wm. McLeish, Secretary of the Municipal Council, he "issued some withering instructions about disarming the tenderfeet and do-nothings."

On June 25th the bombardment was resumed by the Chinese worse than ever, their shooting being more deadly and accurate. Report has Hoover making for the house of his employer the Mandarin Chang Yen Mao, which was a large red house in the British settlement, and the biggest and most prominent in the whole city. One would expect to be safe there, as this house, which was not hit once during the siege, was immune from attack by the Chinese on account of the high rank and position of Chang. Proof of this is the fact that it was proposed by the Volunteers to place Chang in the tower of the Gordon Hall, where nearly all the women and children were lodged, and mark the fact in large characters on the building, so that the Chinese could see it, for they would not dare shell it if they knew that Chang was there. Those brave men were not thinking of their own safety. They were thinking of the four hundred women and children whom it seemed impossible to save. They even asked Chang to send a message through to the enemy requesting them not to shell the Gordon Hall where the women and children were located. The messenger could not get through with the letter, and on returning was intercepted by the Volunteers, who found that instead of containing a request for the protection of the women and children, it simply asked them to stop the shelling until Chang and his party escaped. Mr. Detring was accused of the false translation, which he indignantly denied, and it is safe to say that a man of his high character could not be guilty of such a deed. It must have been some dastard attached to Chang who was responsible for the preparation of the false communication.

In spite of the reinforcements and the twelve pounder cannon brought up with them, the situation became worse, and on July 3rd Capt. Bayly ordered the settlements to be evacuated by all the women and children and all civilians unable or unwilling to bear arms and these were shipped down the river on the fifth.

Hoover, however, did not go with the refugees. He went along with Chang, who eventually obtained permission to leave and, on July 10th, sailed down the river in one of his own company's steamers, the *Peiping,* which was also safe from attack, accompanied by his mining "expert" Hu-hua, as Hoover was known in China, and by his adviser Detring, whose house had been destroyed during the siege. Meanwhile, urgent calls for fresh troops had been sent out by the allied nations to their Eastern possessions and, on July 11th and 12th, eight thousand men arrived in Tientsin, among them a detachment of the 1st regiment of U. S.

Marines under Col. Meade and one of the 9th U. S. Infantry under Colonel Liscom. Peking, which all this time had been shut off from the world, had to be saved also, and this could not be done if the Allied troops left a large Chinese Army and arsenal in their rear. The bold resolution was adopted, to attack the Native City of Tientsin. This battle, which took place on July 13th, 1900, is well described by Col. Naylor of the 15th U. S. Infantry in the 1925 yearbook of that regiment. He was one of the heroes of that desperate fight of six thousand men against a walled city defended by an army of thirty thousand Chinese with all the latest artillery in a temperature of over 100 degrees in the shade. They won, but what a price they paid. Colonel Liscom fell at the head of his troops. The Americans lost 33% of their officers, and 25% of their nen, fighting in that dreadful heat, parched with thirst, against a pitiless enemy. If the heroism which went into this fight was purely moral, the damage was entirely physical.

This battle ended the great siege of Tientsin, one of the most terrible of history. During the twenty-seven days of the bombardment, more shells fell in the settlenents than in Ladysmith during its famous four months' siege. The siege of Tientsin is also notable for the many men who took part in it, who afterwards became famous. The World War English admirals Beatty and Jellicoe, who were both badly wounded; the American generals Brewster and Smedley Butler, who was also wounded, the German admiral Von Usedom, the gallant Russian general Wogack, and "the hero of Tientsin."

I notice that even the New York *Daily News* in its recent review of Hoover's career, characterized by Walter Winchell as an attempt to publicly wash Hoover's dirty linen, credits "the hero of Tientsin" only with trying to rescue a cow.

Tientsin had now been relieved, and Hoover, "the hero of Tientsin" was down at Tong-ku with his employer Chang and Detring. Things were in a bad way at the Kaiping mines, which had been abandoned during the fighting. This was the great opportunity that Hoover had been waiting for so long. The Russians would seize the mines, he cried to Chang. Why not put them under British protection by forming a British company? It seemed a practical suggestion, and Detring, who was a practical business man, was in favor of it. Chang, however, demurred. He was responsible to the Empress, and he feared her displeasure if he had anything to do with the foreign devils, whom she so thoroughly hated. In the end, however, he left it all in Detring's hands and went on to Shanghai to join his family which had preceded him. Hoover now resumed the arguments with Detring, and Detring, seeing no other way of saving the mines than by putting them under the protection of England, consented. He would give a Deed of Trust for the property to Mr. Moreing, who would form an English company in accordance with the new Chinese Mining Regulations of June 1899, which provided for control always remaining in the hands of the Chinese. He sent up to Tientsin for J. B. Eames, a young English lawyer who happened to be there at the time and who, like every other red-blooded young man, had served as a volunteer during the siege. Eames came down to Tong-ku and drew up the Deed of Trust. And here is where Hoover played his trump card. Why make out the Deed of Trust to Moreing? It would have to be registered in China.

Moreing was in London. So why not make it out in his own name, and thus save time? Detring did not like to do this, for, after all, Moreing was a man of position in the financial world, and Hoover was not. Yet he thought Hoover might be trusted. Was he not a trusted employee of the Chinese Government, and was he not an American from the land that has always professed friendship for China? After considerable discussion the Deed was drawn up on July 30th 1900, and given to Hoover a few days later.

The Deed of Trust conveyed to Herbert Hoover, his heirs and assigns, all the vast properties of the native *Chinese Engineering & Mining Company,* with the exception of those situated in the Treaty Port of Ching-Wan-Tao, on condition of his forming a new British company with a capital of one million pounds, of which three hundred and seventy-five thousand pounds was to be issued in fully paid shares to the shareholders of the native Chinese company. The new British company was to provide a hundred thousand pounds ($500,000) for working capital, which sum was to be paid into the Tientsin office of the *Chartered Bank of India, Australia and China* not later than February 28th, 1901. The new company was to automatically come under the new Chinese Mining Regulations of June 1899, according to which management would remain in the hands of the Chinese. Hoover had authority to convey the property to the new company when formed in accordance with these conditions. The enormous value of the property thus conveyed can be gauged from Hoover's own report of June 1900, in which he estimates the coal available at five hundred and twenty-five million tons, which, at a fair valuation of only fifty cents a ton would make the coal alone worth two hundred and sixty-two million, five hundred thousand dollars, without taking into account the other properties and buildings of the company.

Hoover had played for high stakes and won. He had the Deed in his own name to deal with as he thought fit. If Moreing did not come across, someone else would. Hoover did not want Chang Yen Mao, who was in Shanghai, to know that he had the Deed, so he and his wife sailed by the first steamer the S/S *Tsintau* from Tong-ku to Shanghai, as Mr. and Mrs. Clark. On arrival in Shanghai, he cabled to Moreing on August 8th: "I have the deed" and registered it in Shanghai.

Now Hoover was actually born in the United States and was accordingly entitled to call himself an American citizen, although he had never voted or paid taxes. Almost right across the street from the Astor House Hotel in Shanghai was the American Consulate at 12 Kiukiang Road. Did Hoover register his Deed of Trust over there? Oh, dear no, he went right down to the Bund, to the Consulate of his Britannic Majesty, and registered the Deed right there. How he could have done this without making a declaration that he was a British subject is unexplainable. Mr. Bourne, the British Consul, was also a Judge and knew the law, and he certainly would not have registered a Deed of Trust for any American. Any lawyer knows that. Having accomplished this precious formality, Hoover took the first steamer from Shanghai for Europe, leaving on the S/S *Weimar* August 18th and arriving in Genoa on September 29th. He then rushed overland to London, where he arrived a few days later.

Great was the rejoicing among the three "financiers," Moreing, Davis and Turner. Here was Hoover with the "jools." Their admiration, however, turned to dismay when they learned that the Deed of Trust was not in the name of Moreing, but in that of Herbert Hoover, and that it was only to be had for a consideration and a very big consideration too. Moreing had little dreamed that the raw youth he sent out to Australia three years before was so soon to beat him at his own game.

A conference was held. There would be no trouble in financing the working of this enormously valuable property. The difficulty was to get around the Chinese Mining Regulations, which prescribed Chinese control. For this, the support of the British Government was necessary. Moreing, who had a back door entrance to the Foreign Office through one or other of his "guinea-pig" mining company directors, at once went there with Hoover and explained the situation. Here was one of the greatest steam coal deposits in the world, only sixty miles by rail from the ice free port of Ching Wan Tao, where a new harbor had just been completed. What if it were a "Treaty" port open to all nations? The mining company owned all the adjacent land and buildings. Any ships entering the port would have to be unloaded and loaded by the mining company's employees. They wanted to "take" that mining company and put it under the British flag. Give them the support of the British bayonets, and England could have one of the greatest coaling stations in the world, controlling the whole North Eastern Chinese coast, and of inestimable value in case of war with Russia or with the United States of America. The foreign Office was amazed. It had not known that Ching Wan Tao was ice-free all the year round, owing to a local warm tidal current. The English may be slow, but not where their interests are concerned. Immediately a cable was flashed to China, and on October 3rd, 1900, a few days after Hoover's arrival in London, a British landing party from H. M. S. *Aurora* occupied Ching Wan Tao. Moreing, however, received no definite promise from the Foreign Office regarding the other venture. He thereupon "approached" Mr. Geo. Bussy, the editor of the *Westminster Gazette* and W. T. Madge, editor of the *London Globe* and these papers, especially the *Globe,* started a campaign calling on the Foreign Office to take action if the mines were to be saved. On October 10th, Moreing had an interview with Lord Salisbury, the British Foreign Minister, who definitely promised him the support of the British Empire, and on October 12th, 1900, Moreing cabled to Drummond & Co., lawyers in Shanghai, to notify Detring that he ratified the agreement made with Hoover. This was all very well as far as Moreing was concerned. But he was still figuring without Hoover, who held the Deed of Trust, and who could be depended on to dictate his own terms of settlement.

The conspirators now had the support of the British Government. Their next step was to devise a plan to fool the Chinese. Under the arrangement made by Detring with Hoover, Chang Yen Mao was to remain Director General for life of any new company that was formed. This would never do. They accordingly decided that if they could not bamboozle Chang with promises, they would make a separate agreement with him, which they would never recognize or put into effect once they got possession. They formed a new company, which was registered in London on December 20th, 1900, with a nominal capital of a million shares of one pound ($5) each, and a paid up capital of seven one pound shares, in all thirty-five dollars, one of those companies that a Lord Chief Justice had described as "seven undischarged bankrupts." They drew up By-laws for the company, according to which one of its objects was to carry into effect a certain memorandum, which did not then exist, but which was the agreement they intended to make with Chang in case promises did not serve to secure a transfer of the property. However, on careful examination of the Deed of Trust, which had been drawn up by Mr. J. B. Eames, a snag was found. The Deed specified that the property was to be assigned by Hoover direct to whatever new company was formed, on the conditions being complied with. This would make Hoover, in effect, a trustee for the contemplated new company, and, as such, he, and incidentally the others, could not, according to English law, make any promotion profits. This would never do; it would have to be all profit. It was absolutely essential that the Deed be altered. Moreing wrote a letter on November 9th, 1900 to Detring, requesting his consent to modifying it so that the property could be assigned by Hoover to Moreing on the conditions being complied with, giving a fraudulent pretext for the change. By the end of November all the plans had been laid and, with the Bylaws of the new company and the Deed of Trust in his pocket, Hoover dashed back to China by way of the United States, arriving in Shanghai by the S/S *Nippon Maru* in the first week of January 1901.

In the interval, the British Government had shown the importance it attached to the Kaiping coal mines coming under British control. As a result of the desperate fighting in North China there was an acute coal shortage in the great cities owing to the closing of the mines. In October 1900 they were reopened under the protection of Russian troops, and the British officials

T. H. Kingsley, the Superintendent, and C. E. Burt, the chief engineer, returned to their posts. The British Blue Book China No. 7 (1901) shows us what England will do when she has her back up. The English politely asked the Russians to clear out of the mines, and when the Russians replied that they had troops there only for the protection of the mines, the English Foreign Office cabled on November 3rd 1900 that England would send plenty of troops to protect the mines, and more if necessary. It amounted, in diplomatic language, to a threat of war, and the Russians had to give way. Moreing and Hoover had shown the British Foreign Office that, in the words of the Tientsin & Peking *Times* "the Kaiping mines and the port of Ching Wan Tao were strategic keys to the military control of North China." This was a bone that the British bulldog would not let go.

While Hoover was on his way back to China, Moreing's associate, Edmund Davis, got in touch with Leopold II, King of the Belgians, the notorious ruler of the Congo Free State, who had extensive interests in China. It was the custom of Leopold to promote to positions in China men who had distinguished themselves for toughness in the Congo, the abominable atrocities which shocked the civilized world when exposed by Sir Roger Casement and American missionaries in 1903. One of these, Emile Francqui, had been promoted to be Belgium Consul in Hankow. This is the same Francqui who shortly afterwards tricked the Americans out of the Canton-Hankow railway concession, and who was in charge of the distribution of the Belgian "relief" during the World War. Another of Leopold's proteges was Emmanuel de Wouters whom Leopold had succeeded in having appointed as legal adviser to the Tsung-li-

Yamen (the Chinese Parliament). He was a shrewd and skilled negotiator and had considerable influence with the famous Viceroy Li-Hung-Chang, through whom he obtained valuable railroad concessions for Belgium in the face of British opposition. Leopold was offered a share in the spoils for his co-operation and the royal brigand accepted. Francqui and De Wouters were ordered to "stand by" and help out Hoover. Hoover had the keys, but was not yet in the treasure vault. The transfer of the property had yet to be obtained.

Hoover, as we have told, arrived in Shanghai in the first week of January 1901, and went on to Tientsin. It was bitterly cold that winter. Famine prevailed throughout North China. Millions were dying of starvation. Everybody, white or yellow, who had a little surplus, gave till it hurt to relieve the terrible distress. If Hoover did anything to alleviate, or even help to lighten, this distress, it is not on record.

Chang Yen Mao was not then in Tientsin. He was in his palace in Peking where he had had as guest for the past three months the Viceroy Li Hung Chang, who had been called to the Capital to help in the solution of the terrific problems arising from the enormous penalties being imposed on China as a result of the Boxer rising. However, Hoover was impatient and had Detring request Chang to come down to Tientsin. Meanwhile he had had prepared a deed of conveyance and transfer by Mr. White Cooper, a Shanghai lawyer, which he submitted to Detring. This deed of transfer contained no reference to the conditions of paramount importance to the Chinese, namely control by the Chinese and protection of Chang's interests, and, on Detring calling his attention to this, Hoover wrote Detring a letter on February 9th, 1901, in which he stated that "the Chinese Board would have in itself the entire management of the company's property in China and that His Excellency Chang would be Director General of the Company for life."

A very important point to remember at this stage of the negotiations is that under the Deed of Trust, Hoover became trustee for the new *Chinese Engineering & Mining Company Limited* the minute it was registered on December 20th 1900, and, as such, could not take any promotion profits. This was the big fly in the ointment, but it was skillfully removed. Hoover had J. B. Eames the lawyer who drew up the Deed of Trust on July 30th 1900, insert the words "agent of Moreing" after Hoover's name. Of course to do this he had to have Detring's consent, Detring was not averse to their making a reasonable promotion profit. But he little dreamed what this gang had prepared. When Eames made this alteration, Hoover carefully concealed from him that the agreement had been ratified and the new company already formed, thus making Hoover trustee, for the new company. All was now set to deal with Mandarin Chang Yen Mao.

Chang came down from Peking to Tientsin, and they all went into conference. Chang and Detring on the one side and Hoover and De Wouters on the other. Hoover had brought with him as interpreter Dr. C. D. Tenney of the Tientsin University. The deed of transfer was at once put before Chang to sign, but as it did not contain any protection for the interests of Chang or the Chinese owners, he promptly refused. They pleaded with him, assured him that everything would be just as he wanted, but Chang was a shrewd gentleman and wanted all this embodied in the Deed of Transfer. He began to suspect Hoover's honesty. Hoover was nothing if not tenacious. For three days running he came back each day with the deed of transfer, pleading with Chang, but without result. On the third day Hoover lost his temper and threatened the man who had been his employer, who had befriended him and saved his life. He announced that if Chang did not sign Hoover would have him broken by the American, British and Belgian Governments. Finding Chang still impervious, Hoover used to Chang a filthy, disgusting expression, in Chinese which, in the subsequent lawsuit, even an interpreter would not venture to translate. Realizing that Chang was not to be cajoled, Hoover now put over the big coup that he and his pals had prepared in London.

On the fourth day of these long and heated discussions, as they were later on called by Judge Joyce in the Chancery Court, Hoover pulled the ace from his sleeve. His lawyer, Mr. White Cooper of Shanghai, who was also present at these conferences, produced a Memorandum agreement which contained all the points that Chang insisted on, and which wound up with the pious wish: "The Company would be managed in such a spirit as to make Chinese and foreign interests harmonize on a fair basis of equality and to open an era of co-operation and protection that would enrich the Government and the people." And it was explained to Chang that their insistence on his signing the deed of transfer was to enable them to register it in England and that this Memorandum agreement was the genuine and governing document. Even Detring fell for this trap, and advised Chang to sign, as he feared the Russians would seize the mines again. Accordingly on February 19th, 1901, Chang Yen Mao signed the

Deed of Transfer of these vast properties to the new English *Chinese Engineering & Mining Company Limited.* Simultaneously, Chang and Detring for the Chinese, and Hoover and De Wouters for the firm, signed the Memorandum agreement. Now look at Clause 3 of the Memorandum of Association of this new English Company formed just fourteen months before. It reads: 3. The objects for which the Company is established are:

> (a) To enter into and carry into effect, with such modifications (if any) as may be agreed upon, the agreement mentioned in Clause 3 of the Company's Articles of Association of Clause 3.

Now the above mentioned agreement was never produced at any time and what was evidently referred to was this Memorandum agreement which Hoover intended to put over and did "put over" on Chang on February 19th, 1901. This is what the plotters had planned in advance, to obtain possession of these vast stores of wealth by means of a document that they could, and, as a matter of fact, did, repudiate. For these enormous properties Hoover had given Chang "a scrap of paper."

But this was not all. To complete the deal, in accordance with Hoover's Deed of Trust, the new English Company had to deposit by February 28th, 1901, the sum of a hundred thousand pounds for working capital in the Tientsin office of the Bank of India, Australia and China, which formality they had conveniently forgotten. Now this company, as we have seen, had no half a million dollars, its total paid up capital being just thirty-five dollars, just the price of a case of whisky. Here is where old King Leopold, who did not care particularly by what means he made his money, came to the rescue. On the very last day, February 28th, 1901, his bank, the Banque d'Outremer, cabled the half million dollars to the Bank of Tientsin. Hoover took the deed to the property, and King Leopold withdrew his money by cable the very next day.

Believing that everything was on the level and above board, Chang Yen Mao had returned to Shanghai at the end of February, arriving there on March 2nd. Hoover, meanwhile, after having the Deed of Transfer registered, took possession of the mines under the protection of British troops and hoisted the British flag. Only a few weeks previously, on February 17th, 1901, the United States, which was opposed to the policy of "grab" in China, had expressed to China its sense of the inexpediency and even extreme danger of considering private territorial or financial arrangements at least without the full knowledge and approval of the Powers. Mr. Hay, U. S. Secretary of State, sent a copy of this memorandum to all the powers, including England, but at this very time England was bamboozling the United States and placing under her own domination the great Kaiping coal mines and the ice-free port and coaling station of Ching Wan Tao, through the instrumentality of Herbert Hoover.

When Detring, on July 30th, 1900, had given Hoover the Deed of Trust, he had imposed on Hoover the verbal condition that he should have no connection with the new company when formed. In spite of this, Hoover went ahead and took possession of the property and made himself and De Wouters managers, a great combination. Hoover's apologists in this Chinese business have made much of the fact that the new company made a considerable profit during the first year after taking over the mines. But they said nothing about these humanitarian gentlemen taking advantage of the coal famine to "gouge" the public into paying sixteen dollars a ton for coal, which, according to Hoover's own report of June 19, 1902, was produced by contract labor, the contractor receiving about ten cents per ton for slack and about twenty cents for lump coal, the filling costing about four cents per ton extra. What became of these enormous profits of that first year's working has always remained much of a mystery, as the Company's accounts certainly did not show them. Hoover had introduced "efficiency," should we not rather say "deficiency"? In the hundreds of propaganda articles published at great expense throughout the world in 1928 to explain away Hoover's connection with the "taking" of the Kaiping mines, much stress is laid on the fact that Hoover abolished "squeeze" at the mines (it is to laugh, as the French say) and also padded payrolls, although he himself tells us that the mines were worked by contract labor, and the contractor, of course, had to pay his own men. He also tells us in the above-mentioned report:

> "The disregard for human life permits cheap mining by economy in timber and the aggrieved relatives are amply compensated by the regular payment of $30 per man lost."

This does not sound at all like the Hoover appealing for Belgium, but rather like the mining expert who, three years later in Australia, told the world that "men were cheaper than timber."

When Hoover, in violation of his promise to Detring to have no connection with the new Company, had taken over the management with De Wouters, he also took over the Kaiping coal mine buildings in Tientsin which, as you have seen, were located in and occupied great part of the American concession obtained from China in 1861, and hoisted the British flag over it. The United States had never exercised any jurisdiction over this concession, but had not abandoned their claim to it, and on February 21st, 1901, General Chaffee, the American commander in Peking received a petition from the American merchants in Tientsin to resume occupation of the concession, pointing out that Americans would be badly handicapped without the concession, as they would have to pay wharfage to a foreign power and also to China, and asking him to take the matter up with Mr. Conger, the American Minister. Negotiations were opened with Li Hung Chang, who offered to return the concession to the United States, but the most strenuous and determined opposition was made by the new *Chinese Engineering & Mining Co. Ltd.* (Herbert Hoover, General Manager). Eventually, on October 14, 1901, Mr. Conger made a formal demand on China for the return of the concession, but the British Government had meanwhile intervened to protect its protege and on October 23rd, nine days later, the Taotai turned the "American" concession over to England, which changed the name to the *British Southern Extension.* And this was in the reign of Roosevelt!

Senators who have recently had their offices burglarized may well have wondered how this could be possible. But there is nothing impossible to unscrupulous people. When England gave the protection of her troops to Herbert Hoover in the first days of March 1901 to take possession of the Kaiping mines, she probably knew as well as he did that the new English *Chinese Engineering & Mining Company, Limited,* had not paid one single penny for that enormously valuable property, and she wanted her *quid pro quo*. What about that ice-free port and coaling station of Ching Wan Tao? The Deed of Trust to Hoover and the deed of conveyance and transfer had made no mention of the all-year ice-free port of Chin-Wang-Tao or the harbor and buildings there or the five miles of railroad track connecting the port with the main line. This was something the Chinese Government had an interest in and did not want to let go. Indeed it was their intention to make it a Chinese Naval Station. Hoover wanted those deeds, but Liang Cheng and Yen Fu, whom Chang had left to represent him in his absence, very properly refused to give them up. Now we have it on the authority of no less a person than Herbert Hoover, in his letter of March 12th, 1901, to Moreing, that he broke open the safe and "took" the deeds by force. On behalf of the new English *Chinese Engineering & Mining Company,* Hoover took all of this property at Ching-Wan-Tao, and this port, which was made a Treaty Port in 1898 open to all nations, including the United States, became to all intents and purposes a British naval and coaling station and has flown the Union Jack ever since. England never forgets a favor done, and this undoubtedly explains the fact of Hoover's hidden influence with the British Government and his immunity during all the subsequent years.

Hoover stayed in China in charge of the Kaiping mines until September 1901. During these six months he played fast and loose with the property. There was no one to say to him nay. He did what he liked. His first step was to discharge the two European officials Kingsley, the superintendent, and Burt, the chief engineer. He even went so far as to seize Burt's furniture, which Burt had to take Court action to regain. The

Chinese shareholders in the old company began to realize they had been fooled. The three hundred and seventy-five thousand shares they were to get in the new company were not forthcoming. A storm was brewing, and Chang, who had had to leave for Germany on a mission with Prince Chung, would soon be back. Hoover's course of action lay terribly clear before him, and he acted promptly. He left China, and never returned.

He was now a rich man. How much had he made out of this Chinese "deal"? Wilbur J. Chamberlin, a correspondent of the *New York Sun*, who stayed at Hoover's house in Tientsin in March 1901, tells us that he cleared half a million dollars by it, and we think that is a fair estimate as regards the money end. There was however something much more important that he fought for and obtained, and that was a directorship in the company and a partnership with his former employer Moreing. Hoover held the whip hand. He had not let go of the Deed of Trust, and Moreing had to give in. The partnership was worth a fortune. But, after all, with a man of the peculiar abilities of Hoover, the firm should travel far. And we accordingly find Moreing, in September 1901, dissolving his partnership with T. Burrell Bewick and Edward Hooper and taking in as his new partners Herbert Clark Hoover and an ex-convict, also of peculiar ability, named Anthony Stanley Rowe.

On his way back to England, Hoover stopped off at Stanford to show his old college teachers what a credit he was to the institution, and arrived in the early days of November 1901 in London, where he was to make his home for the next fifteen and a half years.

The new English *Chinese Engineering & Mining Company* had indeed obtained possession of the Kaiping mines, the largest and most important transfer of property ever made in China, by the deed of conveyance signed by Chang Yen Mao on February 19th, 1901. They had not, however, given one penny consideration for it. But even with the amendment, no promotion profits could be made except through the Oriental Syndicate, to comply with Clause 3 of the Memorandum and Articles of Association, and to do this the Deed of Trust would have to be assigned by Hoover to Moreing, and by Moreing to the *Oriental Syndicate,* and by the *Oriental Syndicate* to the new *Chinese Engineering and Mining Company.* Hoover held the Deed of Trust and would not let go till he got his share. They held a special meeting of the Company on December 9th, 1901, to make him a director, which brought with it a salary, but this was not enough. A dispute evidently broke out among the plotters regarding the division of the spoils, and it was not until May 2nd, 1902, fifteen months after the property was taken possession of, that the agreement as to the division of the spoils was made. By this agreement, Moreing transferred the rights under the Deed to the Oriental Syndicate for seventy-nine thousand, five hundred shares in that syndicate out of a total of a hundred thousand; and by a separate agreement, filed at the same time, the *Oriental Syndicate* transferred to the new *Chinese Engineering and Mining Company* for nine hundred ninety-nine thousand, nine hundred and ninety-three shares of that company out of the total capital of a million shares. Now the other seven shares already issued were in the name of clerks, so that the *Oriental Syndicate* simply "took" all the capital stock of the new company. The Oriental Syndicate, as we

know, was Moreing, Davis and Turner, the trio that
planned the "business," and what did they give in exchange? Nothing. Moreing, under his agreement with the
Oriental Syndicate, got 79½% of this, and out of this
had to pay Herbert Hoover, and he later swore in Court
that after he had settled with the other members of the
firm, he had only nineteen thousand shares of the *Oriental Syndicate* left.

How much Hoover received for carrying out his end
of this extraordinary transaction is not quite clear. But
it is on record that he transferred seventeen thousand,
five hundred shares of the new Company in 1902 and
over eight thousand in 1903. So that he must have held
out for a large portion.

Observe that this firm of financiers, did not wait for
the above agreements, which apparently gave them title
to the property, before selling the shares in the new
Company, which shares, until the agreements were made,
were not legally worth the paper they were printed on.
They issued and sold six hundred and twenty-five thousand shares in 1901, holding back the three hundred and
seventy-five thousand shares the Chinese were supposed
to get, in case the latter ever put up a fight for them.
These shares were one pound ($5) shares and were
mostly sold at a premium, so that the six hundred and
twenty-five thousand shares sold must have netted about
four million dollars. Did this money go into the coffers
of the Company? Oh, dear, no! That money, every
penny of it, went to the members of the firm. Of course,
investors who bought shares imagined that the money
they put up was to provide working capital for the new
company. Not so. These birds knew a trick or two.
After they had sold the shares, which at the time they
were sold were legally so much scrap paper, they issued

— 86 —

two and a half million dollars worth of 6% Debentures for working capital, thus watering the value of the shares they had already sold by one half. These debentures were easily placed, on account of the enormous value of the property. Indeed, the Chairman of the Company, W. F. Turner, tells us at the Meeting of the Company held in London on July 16, 1901:

"The whole of the debenture issue has been placed privately, without any cost whatever to the company."

You may well ask how investors would buy shares without looking up the title of the Company. The answer is that they do it all the time, relying on the bonafides of the statements fed to them. That is where promoters reap their harvest. Moreover people who could plan so far ahead were not apt to overlook very much. Article of Association No. 104 of this new Company read:

"Except by the authority of the Board or of a General Meeting no member shall be entitled as such to inspect any books or papers of the Company other than the Register of members and of mortgages."

It looks as if the boys had really intended to also fool the Chinese out of the three hundred and seventy-five thousand shares they were entitled to receive, for we find that on October 31st, 1901, nine months after the mines had been taken possession of, the six hundred and twenty-five thousand shares had been issued to the insiders and mostly sold. But not one single share had as yet been issued to the Chinese. There was a subtle reason for this delay. They had agents in China picking up at bargain prices, from Chinese who began to despair of ever getting anything, the scrip of the old Chinese Company, which was to be exchanged for the new shares, and which new shares, on account of the enormously high prices ruling for coal, were soon at a considerable premium.

This is the story of how Herbert Hoover "took" the great Kaiping coal mines of China for himself and his friends, and the ice free port and coaling station of Ching-Wan-Tao, for England. He had arrived. We find him at the end of 1901 established in his home in London, a gentleman of position, a partner in the important mining firm of Bewick Moreing & Co. with Moreing and Rowe, and a director of the Chinese Engineering & Mining Company, Limited, with Moreing, Davis and Turner, whom we are learning to know, and with the Congo slave drivers Thys and Francqui, his wartime partner in the Belgian "relief," whom we will know better soon.

CHAPTER THE FOURTH

WELCHING.

THE curtain was drawn on the first act of the Chinese drama. The plotters had come out on top. Hoover had laid the foundation of his vast fortune, and in its founding, as in that of most other great fortunes, there was something to make one shudder.

London's Big Ben struck the hour of midnight. Scotchmen took another drink to lubricate their throats as they sang *"Auld Lang Syne"* on the steps of St. Paul's. It was New Year 1902. But Hoover was not there to join in the festivities. When did he ever take part in any? He was on the high seas, bound for Australia. He was now the boss of those bounders down there who had dared to laugh at him and give him his first hair shirt. He would show them. Was he not now the "engineering" partner of the great firm of mining engineers, Bewick Moreing & Co. (none of the members of which, by the way, was a mining engineer), with full control of all the Australian properties? He was going down there to reduce wages, or, as his partner Rowe expressed it: "to conduct a campaign against present high rates of working costs." But this, as we shall find, was a small part of his programme.

Whitaker Wright and Horatio Bottomley had been the "financiers" who had done most to float West Australian mining companies. Wright, the magnificent, and Bottomley, the beneficent, were men of magnetic personality and much ability. They secured large followings among the public, who went gambling mad. Wright and Bottomley, as we have already told you, relied for their profits on Stock Exchange manipulation, and the inevitable crash came. The end of 1900 saw the collapse of Wright's *London & Globe Finance Co.*, bringing down with it in its fall over thirty Stock Exchange firms. Wright was shown to have issued a false balance sheet. He was prosecuted, brought back from America, and sentenced to seven years penal servitude. He committed suicide in the dock, dying, as he had lived, dramatically. In 1901 Bottomley's *West Australian Market Trust* went to the wall. He, too, like Wright, was a "philanthropist," and, although there were a good many irregularities about his companies, he always managed to escape prosecution. It was only in 1921, when he was a Member of Parliament with a large following in the House of Commons and was being considered for a Secretaryship of State that he was at last exposed and proved to be a heartless swindler of the unfortunate widows and orphans of the World War. He, too, received a sentence of seven years penal servitude. Indeed, but for his quarrel with Bigland, he might today have been Prime Minister of England. He just happened to be found out. They all slip up sometime or other. With these big dogs out of the way, there was more meat for the other promoter, and that was Moering.

Wright had floated two enormously successful mines in the Kalgoorlie field of West Australia, the *Ivanhoe Gold* and the *Lake View Consols*. This latter mine was enormously rich. In 1899 it had paid 250% in dividends and, as the "insiders" held nearly 30% of the stock, on which they had paid up only 25% of its nominal value, they actually received in that year 1000% dividend. The directors of all Wright's companies were "dummies" of his, who obeyed the master mind. On his downfall, they elected one of his friends to the chairmanship of both companies. This was a stockbroker named Francis Algernon Govett. With all Wright's genius, he could not beat the Stock Market in the shares of his own mines, and in the boom year of 1899 his finance company, the London & Globe, actually lost nearly $4,000,000 in dealings in shares of the Lake View Consols. The reason for this was, of course, that there was leakage of information from the mines. With Moreing, this was not possible. His system was a closed circuit. He was the promoter, who controlled the financial companies, which floated the mining companies and named the majority of the directors. Bewick Moreing & Co. appointed the mine managers, "yes" men, who would blow hot and cold as instructed. The first reports from the mine came to them and gave them a tremendous advantage in Stock Exchange operations. Then they had their field agents, who picked up abandoned properties or ones they could obtain for a trifling sum and these were sold for large sums to the companies they controlled, or, if important enough, floated as separate companies with capitals out of all proportion to the sums paid for the properties, the differences representing the promoter's profit. They were enabled to thus play fast and loose with the companies they controlled by means of an ingenious clause they inserted in the Bylaws of these companies, known as the Waiver Clause. This clause actually purported to reverse the relations between the directors and shareholders by making the shareholders trustees for the directors, thus enabling the directors to use the company's capital in any way they saw fit. This Waiver Clause was supplemented by another, known as the Discovery Clause, which we have shown adopted in the *Chinese Engineering and Mining Company,* and which prevented the shareholders from having access to the books and papers of their own companies.

Hoover, now the "engineering" partner of **Bewick Moreing & Co.**, was on his way to Australia in the first days of 1902 accompanied by his wife and F. A. Govett, the new chairman of the *Lake View Consols.* It would be hard to imagine a greater contrast than that between these two. Hoover, the rube, uncouth, uncultured, half baked, half educated, who imagined that he was a "mining expert" because he had had a college diploma in geology thrust on him, but with all the secretiveness and cunning of a peasant woman, and Govett, the sophisticated city stockbroker, born into wealth, a man of refinement and education, and moreover, jovial, a good fellow, a regular man about town. They were, however, really complements, the one of the other. *Abyss cries to the abyss.* There was a common bond between them which fastened them to each other with ties of steel, and this was the mutually shared belief that people who invested in their companies were idiots and not entitled to any consideration whatever. What a combination! Hoover in charge of all the West Australian mines controlled by Hoover Moreing & Co., and Govett, the stockbroker, on the Stock Exchange! They joined hands, this strange team, and their co-operation was only interrupted by death, some twenty years later.

Of course it was contrary to the rules of the Stock Exchange to enter into business connections with an "outsider." But greedy people are not worried by rules or laws. Are not some of them even reputed to have robbed the ferryman on the voyage across the Styx? Now Whitaker Wright was a rascal. But he was generous. The villagers where he lived erected a memorial to him, which still tells the world that "he loved the poor." His shareholders in his mining companies got what dividends were coming to them, in the Lake View Consols 250% in

1899 and 12½% per month, that is at the rate of 150% per annum in 1900. This was something Govett could not understand. Something would have to be done about it.

When Hoover and Govett arrived in West Australia, their first call was on Sir Arthur Lawley, the new Governor, in Perth. He had come over in May, 1901, from Rhodesia, South Africa, where he had been Administrator of Matabeleland, and where Bewick Moreing & Co. had an office at Salisbury. Lawley had endeared himself very much to these mining people by trying to introduce 'forced labor,'' otherwise slavery, into Matabeleland, and they thought him just the man for the Governorship of West Australia, one who would aid them in their fight to break the power of union white labor there, which still managed to secure a living wage for the white miner. In return for the coaling station of Ching Wan Tao, the British Government was under an obligation to Moreing and Hoover, and the deal was arranged. Lawley obtained the Governorship of West Australia. We have seen how Hoover, when out in West Australia a few years before, had acquired a profound hatred of white labor and had gone so far as to openly advocate in the Press the removal of the restrictions on Asiatic labor. He had hoped for much from Lawley, but was disappointed, as the Government then in power in the Colony, was opposed to anti-labour legislation. There was no way then of reducing costs by lowering wages, as Hoover had hoped for, although, as we have shown you in the first chapter, they were barely at the subsistence level. Some other plan would have to be devised. This was the importation of contract Italian and Austrian labor to break the power of the unions, and the adoption of a new system of accounting to make it appear that the working costs had been reduced. This consisted in giving the working costs per ton of 2000 pounds instead of the English ton of 2240 pounds, which already made a reduction of 10%, and by not including as working costs the development work, diamond drilling or depreciation, thus giving the dear public the impression that Bewick Moreing & Co. were the most efficient and cheapest managers in the field. How true that was will be shown in the scandal of the *Golden Horseshoe Estate.*

After calling on Lawley in Perth, Hoover and Govett went right on to Coolgardie, which God had cursed with sand, drought, flies and gold. They at once visited the Lake View mine. Now the late manager of this mine, H. E. Calahan, had estimated the ore reserves in 1900 at over 300,000 tons and was dismissed for being too optimistic. The new general manager, Mr. Hartman, was consequently prudent. His report of September 1, 1900, estimated the ore reserves above the 500 ft. level at 65,000 tons, value $32 to the ton, 55,000 tons, value $8 to $15 to the ton, and unlimited quantities value $2 to $8 per ton. In a supplementary report on January 15th, 1901, he stated that the ore bodies were of greater extent than anticipated and suggested increasing the number of crushing stamps. In his report at the end of 1901 he estimated the ore reserves of a value of more than $10 to the ton at 178,797 tons. They asked Hartman how he came to make such a report, and he naturally replied because the ore was there. But, no; they knew better. The report went out immediately that there were only 50,000 tons of ore reserves in that mine. When John Hays Hammond, the great American mining engineer, reported on the Camp Bird mine in Colorado, he spent weeks examining it and took over 4,000 samples. Hoover did not have to take any samples or even look

— 94 —

at the mine. In any case, they were out to break the values of the shares of the *Lake View Consols,* and thus by trickery secure absolute control, which Wright had not been able to do with an expenditure of millions. Right away, on January 31st, 1902, Govett cabled to London to defer payment of the monthly dividend of 12½% that had been declared for December, stating that the reports from the mine were wrong and that there was terrible mismanagement. It did not matter that Mackinnon, the consulting engineer, agreed with Hartman, or that Hewitson, the noted mining expert, estimated the ore reserves at 180,000 tons, almost identically the same figure as Hartman. Hoover and Govett had changed all that. They made it only 50,430 tons. Hartman was discharged, and the management of the mine given over to Hoover Moreing & Co. W. A. Prichard, a classmate of Hoover's at Stanford, was put in charge. This meant goodbye to dividends for the shareholders. The shares, which had stood as high as ten and a quarter pounds ($52.50) collapsed to one pound, eleven shillings, sixteen pence ($8.50), less than one-sixth, within six months. It is also very evident that the insiders on this tremendous scheme knew what was going to be pulled off, for by the time Govett's cable arrived on January 1st, the shares had already fallen from ten and a quarter to four and five-eighths pounds, less than half. How honest this deal was, can be judged from the fact that millions of tons of payable ore have since been taken from the old *Lake View.* After that time, the *Lake View Consols,* under the control of Govett and his gang, especially after Hoover joined it as a director, became just a private bank for them. They speculated with the shareholders' money. If their purchases were good, they kept these "plums" for themselves. If they turned out to be

"duds," they became the property of the shareholders. This is not supposition. Govett himself later callously admitted it.

Hoover was nothing if not active when it was a question of making money. Within the space of a week of arrival in the goldfields he had wrecked the share values of the *Lake View Consols* and obtained the management of that great mine. He then made a tour of inspection of the other mines under the control of his company. First of all to the enormously rich *Hannan's Brownhill* we have mentioned, and of which Hoover always seems to have had the illusion that he was at one time manager. Adjoining the *Hannan's Brownhill* was another small mine, the *Hannan's Oroya,* which was then in debt and which had not even been properly tested by boreholes. Here was a chance for making some money. Hoover suggested an amalgamation of the Brownhill with the *Oroya.* This was done by buying up shares of *Oroya* at one pound till they reached three and three-eighths of a pound and selling *Brownhill* shares from three and three-quarters of a pound they fell to two and three-quarter pounds. Then the raw deal was pulled off. The capital of the *Brownhill* mine was raised from 140,000 to 450,000 one pound shares and two-thirds of these shares were paid for the *Oroya* mine, which was unproven, whilst the shareholders of the fabulously rich *Brownhill* mine only received one-third of the shares in the amalgamation. This meant a profit of a couple of million dollars for the insiders. That the *Oroya* eventually turned out to be a good mine does not change the face of the deal as it was made at the time. Then out to the mine he has the illusion that he discovered, the *Sons of Gwalia,* and for which he predicted such a wonderful future less than four years before when they were "putting over" the new company on the London market. This time not so good. He reported by cable only 30,000 tons of ore blocked out above the 6th level. The Company, which was as we know controlled by Hoover Moreing & Co., thereupon issued a gloomy circular and prices dropped heavily. Of course Hoover knew there was nothing wrong with the *Sons of Gwalia,* which has produced millions of tons of payable ore since then.

At the meeting of the *East Murchison United* in March 1902, a cable arrived from the great expert Hoover. These cables, by a curious coincidence, always arrived when the General Meetings were being held. Well, Hoover, who had prophesied only a few years before that this would be one of the great gold mines of Australia, was a little more modest this time. He cabled that he had examined the mine and took a favorable view of the prospects. This is the kind of report a quack doctor gives about a patient when he is figuring on "splitting up" with the undertaker. Poor *East Murchison* was then on its last legs, and was interred a few years later. No, not interred, but abandoned, for Hoover believed in letting the dead bury its dead, and letting creditors come to see what they could scrape out of the remains.

At the second ordinary General Meeting of the *Cue Consolidated Finance Co., Ltd.,* one of Moreing's finance companies, held in the first week in March, 1902, C. A. Moreing, the Chairman, told the trusting shareholders:

"We have bought the *Morning Star* near Mount Margaret and Waroonga South at Lawlers."

He did not have to give the trusting shareholders any information about the *Morning Star.* That beautiful name was enough. But he thought fit to give them some particulars about the more plebeian *Waroonga South.*

— 97 —

This is what he told them:

"H. C. Hoover cables February 24th—property 64 acres. Geological formation similar to Sons of Gwalia. At No. 1 level, ore body 200 feet long, 12 feet wide. Developments at No. 2 level show grade improving with depth.

"100 ft. level—14 feet of ore averages 19 dwt. ($19). Between 100 ft. and 200 ft. levels estimated ore in sight 20,000 tons worth 19 dwt. ($19)."

Now, if this means anything, it means that this property had hundreds of thousands of tons of ore, what was exposed being of an average value of 19 dwt. ($19 to the ton), and improving with depth. And what was the reality? The *Waroonga South* did not belie its name. It was just a "waroonga," a wash-out. The ore did not run more than 6½ dwt. ($6.50 to the ton) and it was worked for two years at a tremendous loss to the *Cue* shareholders. Needless to say, the investors in this company never got a penny return on their investment. The *Morning Star* did not shine very long. This constellation turned out to be nothing but a rushlight. One thousand, one hundred and twenty-three tons of ore was all that it ever produced. Not enough to keep one of these gents in liquor for a year.

Hoover returned to London in the first week of May, 1902, looking remarkably well. He needed to. There was lots to be done. The amalgamation of the *Brownhill* and *Oroya* mines had to be rushed through. Then there was trouble in China. The shareholders in China of the old native *Chinese Engineering & Mining Company,* a good many of whom were Europeans resident in China, realized that they had been flim-flammed, and were raising the deuce. They had not received their 375,000 shares until the end of 1901 and then these were found to be "bearer" shares, thus preventing them from having any vote or say in the Company's affairs. They saw that the remaining 625,000 shares had disappeared, that the hundred thousand pounds working capital had not been put up, but that five hundred thousand pound debentures had been issued against the mine, on which interest would have to be paid at 6% before there would be any profits available for dividends. Hoover, the bold trustee, who had "taken" these mines, constituted himself as spokesman for the new English company, of which he was now a director and one of the largest shareholders. On June 27th, 1902, he wrote a long letter to the *North China Daily Times* in Shanghai, defending the new company and proving that it was really an English company and not, as many had supposed, under the control of Belgium. Incidentally, he mentioned in his letter that the shareholders had nothing to grumble about, for the land taken over by the new company was much greater than that held by the old Chinese company. He was of course, referring to the deeds he had taken by what we will mildly call force. The native Chinese for their part saw that they had been fooled in every way. Not only as regards their shares. But also with respect to the management of the Company, which was supposed to be in the hands of a local Chinese Board. Chang Yen Mao, too, had been cheated out of the position promised him as Director General for life. And, worst of all, England had "taken" the port of Ching Wan Tao, which was not included in the Deed of Transfer, and which China had intended to convert into a Naval Station. The Deed of Transfer, as we have seen, had itself been obtained by Hoover on the strength of the Memorandum agreement signed by him on February 19th, 1901, and afterwards

— 99 —

repudiated by both Moreing and the new English Company. In subsequent law proceedings, as we shall see, Hoover swore that when he executed the Memorandum he believed it was binding and always did everything in his power to enforce it. Thus far no one has yet sustained this claim. Mr. T. R. Wynne was appointed General Manager of the new *Chinese Engineering & Mining Co., Ltd.,* on Hoover's return from Australia, and arrived in China in August, 1902. After arrival there, as was later testified at the trial before Judge Joyce, he received a letter from Hoover telling him to pay no attention to the Memorandum. What more proof is required of Hoover's real intentions in this matter? Wynne was a hard boiled little man. For fifteen years he had been agent and general manager of the *Bengal Nagpur Railroad* in India. This, however, was too much for him. He threw up the job and returned home, in December. It was a big job carrying a large salary. But some men have principles, and some have not. Before leaving China, Wynne referred to Hoover's report on the Kaiping mines as "very interesting as a fairy tale."

When Wynne resigned, the position of General Manager was offered to Colonel Browne, also of the Royal Engineers, who was in the service of the *Chinese Northern Railroad,* but Col. Browne, being familiar with the circumstances of the case, very properly refused.

Meanwhile important developments had occurred. The accounts up to February 28, 1902, of the first year's working of the new English *Chinese Engineering & Mining Company, Limited,* the thirty-five dollars company that had swallowed up 625,000 out of the 1,000,000 shares, were submitted at the annual meeting of the company in London on September 28th, 1902, and did not reach China until November. It was seen from the accounts that there was no mention of the hundred million pounds supposed to have been put up as working capital, nor of any of the money received for the 625,000 shares sold having been paid into the treasury of the company. The accounts too, only showed a profit of eighty-three thousand, six hundred and two pounds when coal was selling as high as sixteen dollars a ton, which only cost about fifty cents a ton at the pit's mouth. Protest meetings of shareholders in the old Chinese company were held in Tientsin, Shanghai and Hong Kong. The local Chinese and Anglo-Chinese Press bitterly attacked the new company. Before things had come to this pass, however, the gang in London had decided that something must be done, and their idea of arranging matters was by buying off. Accordingly, Moreing left London at the beginning of November for Genoa where he caught the S/S *Koenig Albert* for Shanghai. He had with him some 54,000 shares in the new company and a sum in cash as an inducement for Chang and Detring.

While Moreing was on the high seas, things had come to a crisis. Ever since Hoover had "taken" the mining property, the Chinese had been appealing to the Censor Wang to memorialize the Throne to have Chang Yen Mao give an explanation of the transfer of the Kaiping mines. But Wang hesitated to do so, as Chang was a very powerful man. And then, China was not in a position to dispute with Hoover's new British company, which had four regiments of British soldiers at the mine headquarters. These British troops, which had originally been sent there to protect Hoover when he took possession of the mines in March, 1901, had been there eighteen months and were withdrawn in the Fall of 1902. In their absence, the Chinese decided on a bold step, and on November 17th, 1902, a detachment of fifty Chinese troops

— 101 —

appeared at the mine headquarters at Tongshan, hauled down the Union Jack, and hoisted the Chinese Dragon flag. The Chief Engineer, a Belgian named Manet, attempted to hoist the British flag again, when the Chinese officer significantly pointed to the fact that he and his men were armed. Manet telegraphed to the British Minister in Peking, and Sir Ernest Saton immediately put a hundred and fifty British soldiers aboard a train in Peking and proceeded to Tongshan, hauled down the Chinese flag, and ran up the Union Jack again where Hoover had hoisted it twenty months before. That is how England acts when her interests are at stake. Manet, who was an engineer, had not come all the way from Belgium to be a puppet for their ilk, and he at once resigned and returned home. Hoover, who, as you have seen, was the spokesman for, and actual managing director of the new thirty-five dollar company which controlled these vast properties he had "taken" for it, at once replaced Manet by—whom do you think? None other than his old chum, preliminary-lawyer Wilson, making him Engineer in Chief of these enormous mines employing over ten thousand workmen.

The replacement of the British flag did not settle matters. The Chinese had more courage now. Old Li Hung Chang had died in November, 1901, and the new Viceroy of the province of Chi-li was the great Yuan Shi Kai, the real founder of modern China, who was afterwards Emperor. Yuan Shi Kai was an intimate friend of the Censor Wang, and he had the latter send a memorial to the Empress denouncing Chang. The Empress issued a Secret Edict ordering Chang to give a detailed report of the manner in which he had been fooled out of these great possessions. This order was immediately complied with Chang, who at the same time had his representative at Tongshan, Mr. Yang Shang Ching, order the Chinese miners to stop working. At the same time Mr. Yang issued a proclamation which he had inserted in the Chinese papers *Sin Wan Pao* of Peking and the *Wa Wo Pu* of Tientsin, explaining the situation to the Chinese and adding that he personally had always been suspicious of Hu-Hua, as Hoover was called in China.

Now Chang Yen Mao was a very important personage. He had been a favorite of the Empress, who admired his manly strength and had made him Chamberlain of the Imperial Court. He was at this time Reader of the Imperial Chancery, Director of the *Northern Chinese Railroad,* Director General of Mines for *Chi-li* province. He was a Mandarin of the first class and held the decoration of the Peacock's Feather. Altogether a personage of great importance. The Empress Dowager did not feel like taking any action against him. But Yuan Shi Kai was insistent, and eventually Chang Yen Mao was degraded, stripped of all his ranks and titles and ordered to recover for China the great properties he had been defrauded of by Hoover, or else lose his head on the executioner's block. This was the kind of decree there was no arguing about. Chang, through Detring, got in touch with the London firm of lawyers, Hallams Sons, Coward & Hawksley, and ordered them to take legal action. There was no other way. China was not in a position to take back the mines by force. At this time, one of the firm, Moreing, had arrived in China with the inducement money. It was too late. Meanwhile Hoover, who appears to have received some seventy thousand shares in the new company, as his part of the bargain, was selling out as fast as he could. Within six weeks (Sept. 24, to Dec. 8) he disposed of twelve thousand, five hundred shares.

This year 1902 would seem to have been a pretty busy one for Hoover. Yet he managed to take time for an exploration trip to British Columbia in August. On his return, he began to take a great interest in the affairs of the West Australian gold mine, the *Great Fingall Consolidated*. This was a company which had been floated in London by Moreing during Hoover's absence in China in 1899. It was an amalgamation of two mines, which had been "engineered" by Rowe, and was so successful from the promotion standpoint that it resulted in Rowe winning his partnership with Moreing. The *Great Fingall Consolidated* was closely controlled by Hoover Moreing & Co., who nominated the entire board of directors, all "dummies," although Hoover, Moreing and Rowe individually had practically no shareholdings in the company. On February 3rd, 1902, for example, Moreing held only five shares in the company, Rowe twenty and Hoover none, that is in their own names, for it was the custom of these people to hold shares in the names of secretaries, clerks, stockjobbers and others, just as they do today. Rowe was the secretary of this company, and proudly considered himself the "parent" of it. Hoover was the "engineering" partner, and, as such, was the first to receive the cables that used to come in secret cypher from the company's manager. Rowe was a fairly young man, thirty-seven years of age, the same age that Hoover pretended to be, and they became closely attached and visited at each other's homes. Hoover at that time was living in Hornton Street in Kensington, London, in the fine big gray house he had rechristened *The Red House* in remembrance of Chang's *Red House* in Tientsin, where he had lived during the fighting. Rowe had been convicted of embezzlement in 1885 and served his sentence. After his release he obtained employment with a jeweler named Streeter, whom he also robbed. Here, suddenly, he was in charge of mining properties in which the public had invested millions of pounds sterling.

The reports from the *Great Fingall* mine were coming in uniformly favorable and satisfactory. In August, 1902, the one pound shares stood at eight pounds, and at this price they were very cheap according to the earnings indicated by the reports from the mine. Then in September the market price slipped back to seven and a half pounds. Here was a chance for making some easy money. Armed with their "inside" information, Hoover and Rowe began to buy shares of the *Great Fingall*. Now there was a clause in the partnership agreement of Moreing, Hoover and Rowe, which stipulated that whatever speculation was done was to be done by the firm and not individually. But they speculated in *Great Fingalls* right under Moreing's nose. They bought the shares, but, strange to say, the market did not advance. They bought more. The price dropped further still. They did not realize until it was too late that there were people "bearing" the market, people who had much longer purses than they had. They were caught in a trap. Rowe resorted to forgery of share certificates of the *Great Fingall* and of the *Hannan's Brownhill*, of which he was secretary. This, in itself, was not a crime against the law at that time, for by a curious omission, the Forgery Act of 1861 contained no section which applied to the forgery of a certificate of shares. However, Rowe borrowed money against these forged certificates and that was a crime. He simply issued certificates and signed the names of two of the "dummy" directors who were never on the job. He was already forced to do this on September 26th, and again on October 15th and

again on November 24th, when he borrowed fifteen thou-
and pounds from Lionel Robinson, a stockbroker, through
an intermediary. The sums thus borrowed against forged
certificates amounted to half a million dollars. Even
this was not sufficient to save the situation. Hoover
started selling out his illgotten shares in the *Chinese
Engineering & Mining Company,* and finally in November,
Hoover and Rowe in desperation had the "dummy" directors of the *Great Fingall* declare a fifty per cent cash
dividend in hopes of boosting the market and saving
their skins. This was too late. Lionel Robinson, who
knew what was going on in the Stock Market, had his
suspicions. After making the loan of fifteen thousand,
he sent a clerk to examine the books in the offices of the
Great Fingall, which, bear, this in mind, were right in
he offices of Hoover, Moreing & Rowe. The clerk found the
entries to be all right, but Robinson was still suspicious
and sent a clerk a few weeks later, on December 15th,
who noted that the entries first made had been erased
with a knife. Robinson consulted his lawyers and on
December 21st sent a registered letter to each of the
directors of the *Great Fingall,* whose addresses were in
the offices occupied by Hoover and Rowe, to inform
them officially of what he had already informed the office
informally on December 15th. Rose Wilder Lane, who
had evidently access to a lot of inside information, in her
biography of Hoover written for pre-election propaganda,
slipped up badly at this point. She describes in some
detail how Hoover had gone with his wife and Mr. and
Mrs. Rowe and their children to a Christmas pantomime
on Boxing Day (December 26th) and how Rowe had
disappeared on the following day. Was Hoover unaware
that Rowe was a forger? Did he not learn it Dec. 21,
from the registered letters of Lionel Robinson? He

should have learnt it on December 15th, when the discovery of the erasures was made. He might have known it before then, for they had been gambling together. What was he doing with such a man? On December 26th Rowe absconded.

There was an aftermath. Edgar Storey, a Liverpool colliery proprietor, had sold Rowe in September 3,000 shares of *Great Fingall* for joint account of Rowe and Hoover at seven pounds per share. This transaction, like millions of similar ones that are put through every day in all parts of the world, was by word of mouth. On September 29th, Rowe paid Storey fifteen thousand pounds on account, leaving an unpaid balance of six thousand pounds. This amount was not paid, and Storey sued Hoover for it. Hoover repudiated the debt. Storey issued a writ against Hoover on January 17th, 1903. Hoover did not enter his defense until February 20th, and the defense was a general denial. The case was originally set down for trial by a Judge in chambers, but Hoover balked at this, and on April 27th, requested trial by a special jury, which in the City of London corresponds to a jury of Wall Street men familiar with financial transactions. Now Edgar Storey, was no stranger to Hoover and Rowe. He was one of the largest shareholders in their *London & Western Australian Exploration Co.* He knew who he was dealing with. If he sold the shares by word of mouth, that is how this business was regularly conducted, especially by people who knew each other as well as these did. Then Storey was no "shyster." He was a wealthy man, a man of position. On hearing his evidence and that of Hoover, the city jury decided in favor of Storey without leaving the jury box, awarding him the six thousand pounds he claimed, with costs. There was no getting around the fact that the shares were transferred to a joint account of Rowe and Hoover. Did Hoover pay? No, he did not. He appealed on the technicality that there was no written contract to show that he was legally liable. This is what is called in England pleading the Gaming Act. It was only a debt of honor. The Court of Appeals had no option but to allow his appeal. He had "welched" on his debt. If he had been a member of any Exchange in the universe, he would have forever been barred for this. While this appeal was being heard in November 1903, Rowe, who had been arrested in Canada and brought back in September, was sentenced to ten years penal servitude. He collapsed in the dock. Just five days before Rowe arrived in England under arrest, Hoover found it advisable to sail for Australia at the other end of the world. The "hero of Tientsin" abandoned to his fate his former partner and gambling associate, the man whose food he had eaten and wine he had drunk. Rowe took the "rap" and Hoover went scot free.

Rowe left a wife and five children in poverty, as all his property was seized by his creditors. An interesting sidelight on what a racket these mining promoters had is evidenced by the fact that the Receiver of his estate found that Rowe, who had only been a secretary, was earning from twenty-five to thirty thousand dollars a year and had three hundred thousand dollars in the bank before he started the gambling game with Hoover. He had furniture valued at thirty-five thousand dollars, and coaches, horses and wine valued at fifteen thousand dollars. Another curious commentary on the fact that one can sit at the same Board of Directors, or in the same Cabinet, with a man without knowing his real character is provided by the following extract from the speech of Colonel Parry Nisbet at the General Meeting of the *Talisman .Consolidated Gold Mining Company,* on December 9th, 1902:

> "Most of you know my friend Mr. Rowe personally and, if so, you will think with me that he is a director we could not possibly spare from the Board."

Within three weeks, Rowe was a fugitive from justice, a pariah.

CHAPTER THE FIFTH

MORE DIRTY WORK IN AUSTRALIA

ROWE had done his forgery act and flown the coop. Moreing was on a bribery mission to China. And Hoover, the honest partner, the hero of the Kaiping mines, was left to weather the storm alone. God may be omnipresent, but the devil is certainly ubiquitous. The firm was now reduced to Hoover and Moreing, and Moreing was in China. The situation was very bad. Hoover must have plunged heavily, for we find him soon afterwards leaving the big *Red House* in Hornton St., and going to live at 39 Hyde Park Gate in an apartment in the name of his wife. The henroosts, too, had to be visited. At a meeting of their *London & Western Australian Exploration Company* on December 19th, 1902, we find them writing off about $750,000 for depreciation, which is generally a euphemism for "subtraction." Not only that, but the books were made to show that 40,000 *Sons of Gwalia* shares and 6,000 *Cosmopolitan Proprietary* shares belonging to the above company had been sold, and that there was a little "discrepancy" of $200,000 or so. Of course, this kind of finance was nothing new to these gentlemen. In the Summer of 1902, they had already "written off" the total $700,000 standing to the credit of the Profit and Loss account of the *Sons of Gwalia* company. The *Great Fingall* shareholders, however, were greatly worried. Share certificates in their company to the extent of $435,000 had been forged. To these people Hoover made a characteristic gesture. After consulting his lawyer, and you admit that he needed a good one, he magnanimously declared that his firm would make

good any losses the *Great Fingall* company might suffer.
Great applause. Of course, his lawyer had advised him
that the *Great Fingall* company was not responsible for
Rowe, and he was taking no chances in making his
"sporting" offer. His fingers had been burnt to the
bone. Most of the ill-gotten wealth from the Kaiping
seizure was gone. To a memorial being erected by his
graduation class at Stanford, he was able to contribute
only five dollars, and yet this may have been a tremendous sum for him to give away, as in all the twenty
years he lived abroad he is not known to have ever given
a penny to church or charity.

Moreing returned from China in the middle of February. He had done his little act in the approved
manner, put his presents worth half a million on
Detring's desk, and remarked what a nice day it was.
Detring, however, was not such a fool for Moreing as he
had been fo Hoover. He deposited the shares in a bank
and made a declaration before the British Consul of the
circumstances under which they had been given.

Moreing was back in London and, like the daring
soul he undoubtedly was, decided to turn adversity to
account. Taking advantage of the apparently magnan-
imous offer of Hoover, he put a greater stranglehold than
ever on the *Great Fingall* company, and sold to it the
West Fingall, a worthless property, at a price estimated
to be half a million dollars, just to repay him for the
trouble he had had. He also appointed as its secretary
another employee of his, T. W. Wellsted, whom he took
into partnership. No more geniuses like Rowe for him.
He had all the peculiar talent he required in Hoover.

We have shown you what a busy person Hoover was
during the three months he spent in West Australia in
the beginning of 1902. Among several other things

he had done for his firm was to acquire the management of some more mines, the *Cosmopolitan,* the *Golden Age,* the *Bellevue.* It meant for his firm expansion and a greater field of action, but for the poor mines it meant a lingering death under Doc. Hoover, and for the shareholders, positive disaster. Once he touched a mine, it was as if the palsy seized it. The management of these new mining properties was obtained by an insistent and insidious campaign carried on to show that Hoover Moreing & Co. (in other words, Hoover, as he had sole charge of the West Australian properties) were the most efficient and cheapest managers on the field. The low working cost figures they presented were obtained by excluding development, diamond drilling and depreciation, which other mines included, and by importing cheap contract labor and making economies in the working of the mine as regard height of stopes, supply of timber, etc., with utter disregard of the life of the miners. Men were cheaper than timber.

And how he hated white labor! At a dinner of the Council of West Australian Mine Owners in London on July 15th, 1903, he made another violent attack on the white workers of Australia. He could not understand why a man should be paid seventeen to twenty dollars a week when it only cost him eighteen dollars a week for his board. This in a climate where it was a crime to let a man live, let alone work, and work under the horrifying conditions prevailing there, in the terrific heat, without proper ventilation or sanitation, always in the firing line, one might say, and ever absorbing the poison gold!

By pull, by bribery, by buying into companies, Hoover's firm, in the Spring of 1904, controlled the management of some twenty-five gold mines in West

Australia, which then became mere gambling counters in their hands. They obtained large salaries, too, for managing the mines, they monopolized the sale of mine supplies, forcing the mines they managed to purchase from them at their own extravagant prices, and charging a salary and a commission for this service as well. They kept secret reserves of gold in all these mines, and these secret reserves had a habit of secretly disappearing. How much these secret reserves might amount to can be estimated from the report of the artist Julius Price of the *Illustrated London News* who relates that he saw in a reserve storeroom at the *Hannan's Brownhill* mine what he estimated to be from twenty to thirty tons of gold. And how gold disappeared is explained by the Minister for Mines in the Western Australian Parliament in July 1906 when he said:

> "Gold stealing is practiced not only by miners but by persons in higher positions where facilities are greater."

And the men. Concerning them, Hoover had one consideration. He knew that there was no better instrument for reducing wages to the very lowest level of subsistence than the contract system and imported cheap labor. Italians came in streams, attracted by what appeared to them in their own country as high wages, but what was in reality only the barest of livlihoods under the most terrible of conditions, and practically a death sentence as well. Under the contract system they had to work desperately hard to earn a living, and if they saved enough in a few years to return home it was generally to die within a short time in the prime of life from the dreaded "miner's complaint." The Royal Commission on Immigration appointed by the Government of Western Australia to look into the question held thirty sittings during June and July 1904, and on page 7 of their report state:

"Other witnesses gave evidence as to the Italians arriving at Fremantle, commonly proceeding at once in batches to Day Dawn and Kalgoorlie, and that they were usually met on landing at Fremantle by certain persons who took railway tickets for them and appeared to direct their movements."

Now Hoover's firm had its big supply depot at Fremantle. On pages 8 and 9 of the report we read:

"We find that there has distinctly been preference shown to Italians in some mines especially the *Great Fingall* mine at Day Dawn, the *Peak Hill Gold* mine at Peak Hill, the *Long Reef* at Lennonsville, the *Morning Star* at Mount Magnet during the time Bewick Moreing & Co. had an option thereon, the *Sons of Gwalia* mine at Leonora, the *Lancefield* mine at Laverton, the *East Murchison United* mine at Lawlers and possibly to a certain extent the *Ivanhoe, Associated* and the *Great Boulder Main Reef* mines at Kalgoorlie."

All these mines mentioned except one were under the management of Hoover. To what an extent Hoover used this alien contract labor is shown from the following on page 10 of the Royal Commission report:

"During Messrs. Bewick Moreing & Co's option on the *Morning Star* mine at Mount Magnet, preference to Italians was very decidedly shown, the evidence of Mr. Coon, under manager of the mine, is that some 30 Italians were sent there on Messrs. Bewick Moreing & Co. (Hoover's firm) taking charge, and only one British worker, a tool sharpener, was employed."

Now, there was no objection to Italians, as such. The trouble was that they were obliged to work for contractors, who swindled them out of their pay and kept them in a constant state of distress, thus striking a blow at Union labor and hitting the small neighbourhood storekeeper. At Hoover's *Sons of Gwalia* mine, 60% of the workers were foreigners. The result was that the population of that community fell off from 2,000 to 500 in three years, as the Italian and Austrian immigrants were obliged to live under the most squalid conditions, in order to save a little to send back to their families in Europe. The employment of men absolutely ignorant of the English language, and having to handle explosives constantly in the course of their work, was a great danger to the English speaking workmen. The Commission's report states on this point:

"Besides the very general concurrence of opinion on the part of witnesses that danger was likely to arise by reason of men in a mine being unable to understand one another's language, direct evidence was given to us of instances where danger had actually been encountered due to this cause."

The imported contract labor was not nearly as efficient as the British and Australian workers. The Royal Commission report states that the latter were much more able and skillful miners. The real reason for importing the Italians was to break the back of Union labor and bring these saucy Australians to their knees. The Commission report finds on page 13:

"We are disposed to draw the inference from the facts of the case and from the statements of these witnesses that the favour shown the Italians was designed to counteract the advantage gained by the Workers Unions before the Australian Court by rendering it more difficult for their members to obtain employment with the design of forcing them in the long run to abate their terms."

Under Hoover, the importation of blackleg labor continued, and the men "sweated" to death in that terrible climate under the contract system, dying in the prime of life from "miner's complaint." These men were being murdered in the lust for gold, sacrificed on the alter of greed. As Dean McCullagh said at the funeral of one of these poor victims:

"At the present time there is a terrible responsibility resting on the shoulders of someone."

The influx of this Italian contract labor threw thousands of union workers out of employment. In April 1904, there were a thousand men unemployed in the small town of Kalgoorlie alone. The "brass check" system was adopted. Every worker became a marked man. If he casually dropped a remark about dangerous conditions or shortage of timber in the mine where he worked he was at once dismissed, and not only dismissed but deprived of a livelihood on the field as a miner. He had either to change his name or leave the country, and leaving the country was not so easy. They were out there in the Australian desert, some five hundred miles from the coast. These miners were in a worse condition than convicts. They earned a bare subsistence in a most dreadful climate, and worked in perpetual danger. Absolutely nothing was done for their protection or safety. The mine inspectors were bribed. They inspected the big mines only twice a

year, and sent the mine managers notice a few weeks
before their arrival, so that everything might be "dressed
up" when they came. When the inspectors did give
orders, they were ignored by Hoover's managers. Here
is Mr. Scaddan, afterwards Premier of Australia, talking in the West Australian Parliament; referring to a
mine inspector's report:

"In his report dated November 1904, the inspector stated in relation to the *Lake View Consols* that he gave orders in November 1903, to
limit the height of the stopes to 10 feet, and that
in March 1904, the stopes were still over 10 feet
and still dangerous. In the *Golden Horseshoe*
in 1904, stays were ordered, and the orders were
ignored. In the *Ivanhoe* mine in 1904, special
orders were given to limit the height of the various stopes to 14 feet, but these orders were absolutely ignored. In the *Oroya Brownhill* mine,
orders were ignored on several occasions."

These were all mines under Hoover's control at the
dates mentioned. And were these Australians any more
to him than Chinamen, or than the gladiators of
Nero? Well could these miners chant on their way
to their work, in Latin, if they knew it as well as
Hoover: *"Ave, Hoover, morituri te salutant."* In 1901,
before Hoover came down to take control, out of 17,879
workers employed in the gold mines in West Australia
175 had been killed or injured, and in 1905, when
nearly all the mines were under his control out of
17,792 men the number killed and injured had gone up
to 304, an increase of 80%. The men worked in an
atmosphere of perpetual fear, never knowing when
some of the roof would fall in for want of sufficient

timbering. Here is a letter said to be from Robert J. Grant, the Canadian mining engineer, who afterwards was mysteriously converted by Miracle Man Hoover into Food Director in Colorado and subsequently into Director of the Mint in Washington, which position he still holds, but who was then in the employ of Hoover as manager of the *Cosmopolitan Proprietary* mine:

"It has simply come to this, that so far as I am concerned I will not continue after the end of June, as I should only be laying myself open to a charge of manslaughter. The mine is getting very shaky, and in two months' time things will be much worse, and with no development work going on there will be no ore left to crush. I do not think for one moment that your mine is done as a gold producer—far from that; but I say that it is worked out for the present, and this is directly attributable to the want of mining timber. All that I can say is that you are directly to blame for this state of affairs, for I had not been here any length of time before I wrote on this subject, and letter after letter has been written without even getting an acknowledgment. On the question of dividends you have certainly kept up your reputation as letter writers, as I have letters on this subject nearly every week, but on a vital question such as mining timber, I have been unable to get a reply. I can only say that I am disgusted at the way in which the London office has treated my cables and correspondence. All they seem to care about has been the payment of dividends. The payment of this last dividend, and the want of mining timber, have been the downfall of your mine."

Men were cheaper than timber.

The worst feature of these intolerable working conditions under Hoover was not the danger from premature explosion of dynamite charges by the foreign blackleg labor, or from rock tumbling down the excessive stopes or falls of earth from the untimbered roofs or from being dropped down 1,500 to 2,000 feet into the bowels of the earth without adequate safety appliances. It was in the degradation of white manhood from the abominable check system where men did not dare to open their mouths when they knew that the lives of their comrades were in danger, and from the system of search adopted in some of these mines, where white men were obliged to strip naked and jump over barricades. Yes, we have heard the words "the dignity of labor."

Other mines were won over by the unusual methods above mentioned to place themselves under Bewick-Moreing management and were thus condemned to a lingering death. Here are some of their names, the *Vivien, Burban's Birthday Gift* and *Lancefield* in 1903, and in the beginning of 1904, the *Paringa,* the *White Feather Main Reefs* and the *Merton's Reward.* Emboldened by this success, Bewick-Moreing & Co. schemed for and obtained the management also of the great *Golden Horseshoe Estates* in March 1904, and of the equally important *Great Boulder Perseverance* in April 1904. But these are stories that must be told separately.

The importation of alien blackleg labor had meant the ruination of the small retail merchant, and the monopolization of practically all the mines, forced to buy their supplies from Hoover's firm, was putting all the machinery and supply houses out of business. A

wave of indignation and protest spread throughout the
Colony. Meetings were held in all the chief mining
centers. Even Norman Keenan, Mayor of Kalgoorlie,
who was lawyer for the Hoover firm, sent a protest to
the Premier of Western Australia. Walter James, the
Premier, who was not a radical, but a conservative, in
his speech of March 25th, 1904, in Her Majesty's
Theatre in Kalgoorlie, said:

> "He hoped they would have sufficient energy and
> invention to find some means of preventing the
> gold industry of the State being monopolized by
> any one company or any one firm.

A motion for an investigation by the Government
was introduced in the Western Australian Parliament.
Hoover, however, as he had done in China, went boldly
to the front, and by lobbying among the members of
Parliament and subsidizing the Press even endeavored to
have the mining legislation changed so that the mining
companies he controlled would have the fee simple of
their holdings. Here are a few statements from speeches
made in the Western Australian Parliament, which
will give an idea of these activities. Mr. T. H. Bath,
after referring to mining experts as "boodlers", said:

> "Some of these mining experts and promoters
> became respectable and now they have the boiler-
> plate audacity to get up and talk about Western
> Australia hampering mining conditions, and
> labor conditions being detrimental to the interests
> of the British investor."

At a later date, Mr. Bath spoke as follows:

> "We have insidious proposals for the removal
> of many of the conditions which have been in-
> serted in the mining legislation of this State;
> and these appear, while they are carefully veiled,

side by side with the Press interviews with Mr.
Hoover, who is the representative of Bewick
Moreing & Company in this State. Mr. Hoover's
remedy for all the ills to which the mining industry is heir is that mine-owners should be
granted the fee simple of their holdings."

Mr. W. T. Eddy, speaking in the House at about
the same period, said:

"One thing suggested to him was that Mr.
Hoover and his people were throwing out sug-
gestions as to what the prospector should do by
way of opening up good shows for these capitalists to purchase later at a low price."

The Minister for Mines, however, put a dampener
on the greed of Hoover when, in his speech of December 19th, 1905, he said:

"A great stir has been caused by the speech
of Mr. Hoover, who drew attention to the necessity of greater security for title, etc. * * *. But
not for one moment should we dream of hand-
ing over the fee simple of a mineral area."

Hoover, in his greed, had even wanted the Government to surrender its rights to those mining properties
and give them over to him and his friends in fee simple.
He failed in this, but all the rest was his. He had
made his firm an octopus, which controlled the richest
mines of the State, and the sale of all supplies to
them. It controlled the lives of the miners. It controlled the output of the mines, the secret reserves. It
controlled the mine managers themselves and made them
blow hot or cold as required by these gamblers on the
London market. These mine managers did not have
to be engineers. They were mostly college mates of
Hoover's. All they had to do was what they were told.

CHAPTER THE SIXTH

THE GOLDEN HORSESHOE ESTATES

"*O cives, cives, quaerenda pecunia primum est; virtus post nummos.*"

Our readers will pardon us for quoting Latin again. But this was written by Horace, the Roman poet, with whose works Mr. Hoover, the Latin scholar, must be very familiar, nearly 2,000 years ago, and is still very much to the point. It means, freely translated: "Greed and money first, and all the rest after."

The seventh annual meeting of the shareholders of the *Golden Horseshoe Estates Company, Limited,* was held in London on April 27th, 1905, under the presidency of Sir John Purcell, K.C.B., director of the National Bank. His speech was widely published in the Press. We offer you the following extract from it:

"Now, gentlemen, I turn to the dismissal of Messrs. Bewick Moreing & Co. (Hoover's firm) from the office of general managers of our mine; and the observations I am about to make in regard to this will, I venture to think, throw light upon the report of the auditors and explain the position which, in the course of their duty, these gentlemen have taken up in regard to our accounts. You will remember that at our meeting twelve months ago, I had announced that we had appointed Messrs. Bewick Moreing & Co. to be our consulting engineers; that they were to take over the management of the mine; and that we had entered into an agreement with them to that end. This agreement was based upon a letter addressed to us by the firm on February 23, 1904. Shortly stated, in that letter the firm undertook that if we employed them they would by the following December 31 reduce our working costs to 25s. per ton, exclusive of expenses incidental to the smelting of concentrates and ores. But to enable them to carry out this proposal of theirs we were, on our part, to agree to an expenditure of £12,000 for certain alterations in our plant which they deemed necessary and in this connection, in the course of discussions following upon their letter, they assured us by the mouth of Mr. Hoover that they had a complete knowledge of our mine and plant, which they had duly inspected. They stipulated for a fee of £1,000 per annum and 1 per cent. upon dividends, all of which was to be returnable if they failed to carry out their undertaking as to reduction of costs. They added in the letter referred to that it was their practice to purchase stores in bulk for all companies under their management, and that the savings were duly returned to the companies. Later on, it was explained to us that they ran a department for working the arrangement in question. Well, gentlemen, it was clear to your directors that if Messrs. Bewick Moreing & Co. could accomplish all that they professed in their letter to be within their power, this would mean a very considerable addition to the revenue derived from the mine; and, in the result, an agreement was duly entered into embodying the foregoing, as well as an undertaking from Messrs. Bewick Moreing & Co. that the costs of 25s. per ton were to cover development on the same standard, and to at least the same amount as in 1903.

We declined, however, to have anything to do with the co-operative stores arrangement. Here it might be as well that I should explain why this seemingly advantageous proposal was not accepted. You will bear in mind that, according to the terms of the agreement, if Messrs. Bewick Moreing & Co. failed to bring about the promised reduction to 25s. per ton, then, they were to have no title to any payment for their services. Well, obviously it was my duty to see that the promised reduction was fairly and squarely carried out, and therefore it was incumbent upon me to take care that, at the close of the year, i should be in a position to satisfy myself on the foregoing head by a comparison of figures on a like and equal basis. Hence it was that I would have nothing to do with this co-operative scheme, and I specifically laid it down by word of mouth to each one of the members of the firm, and clearly, in writing, in the first official letter addressed to their colonial partner at the mine, that all accounts and all returns should be made to our London office on exactly the same lines and in the same form as previous to the agreement; and, further, in accordance with the agreement, all telegrams, letters, etc., from the mine should be sent direct to the registered office of the Company. This particular requirement I shall have to refer to again later on. Here, perhaps, I may mention that not long after we got to work we were approached by the firm to join in a co-operative foundry business and also in a co-operative insurance business; but all this I, with the concurrence of my colleagues, declined to entertain pending results as to costs at the end of 1904.

But to proceed. It was soon borne in upon me that, having got their foot in, they were laying themselves out to be the masters of the mine. This I was determined not to allow; I need not say that I was loyally supported by my colleagues. Hence it was that I unceasingly persisted in endeavoring to enforce obedience to the orders of the board. My efforts, however, were fruitless. I found that the instructions of the board as to accounts and returns were not being complied with. Invoices and receipts for moneys as between employer and employed were not forthcoming. Then the auditors complained that they were not being supplied with proper vouchers. A copy of their letter was sent to Messrs. Bewick Moreing & Co., but without result. They still failed to furnish the required invoices and vouchers. In April the firm informed us that 100 unnecessary men had been dismissed, making a saving, as was stated to me by Mr. Hoover, of £3,000 a month. Later on, when the returns reached the office, it was found that 45 men had been reinstated at the end of May, and at the end of August the number of men employed was 50 more than when the firm took charge of the mine. Developments were not being maintained as guaranteed. On a comparison it will be seen that whilst the footage done in 1903 was 10,180 feet, it dropped in 1904 to 6,754; and a report will show the state into which the development work had drifted during the months from April to August. Again, we had the firm applying for some £40,000 over and above the figure of £12,000 which, in the first instance, they assured us, from their intimate knowledge of our plant,

would be all that was needed. This application the directors declined to entertain until more particulars were obtained from the mine. When these arrived it appeared that £20,000 only was needed, and this latter included a sum of £15,000 for a new engine. We consented to allow an additional £5,000, but we refused to spend the money asked for in respect of the engine, which we believed was unnecessary; and that we were right in this view is proved by the fact that our manager distinctly states that not only does he not require it, but that such an engine would be a source of constant trouble. Cable information reached us from Paris to the effect that, contrary to the specific terms of the agreement, a certain person was allowed to go down the mine and sample it. This was indignantly denied by Mr. Moreing in London and by his representative at the mine. We have, however, in our possession a sworn affidavit proving that this person was actually at the time stated taken through the mine by Mr. Moreing's representatives, and that he was furnished with assays and the then latest plans. In fact, this person was given information which was not at the moment in the possession of the directors. According to his own statement, made before the Australian Commission on the Boulder Deep, this person is an employee of a company whose business it is to deal in mining shares, and he is also, I understand, a writer for certain financial newspapers. This person was, no doubt, following his vocation in pursuit of suitable knowledge for the purposes of his employers. But, to say nothing of the fact that they acted in direct contravention

of their agreement, I leave you to judge as to the propriety of the conduct of our then managers in opening our mine to a person whose business lay in the particular direction indicated. You will gather, gentlemen, from the foregoing that matters were not proceeding smoothly. We tried, however, to place them, if possible, on a better footing; and accordingly, in April, a letter was addressed to the manager of the mine calling for certain explanations and certain particulars so as to enable the board to form a clear estimate of the position. We were without an answer to this letter until the middle of July, and then we obtained it only through the mere chance of a copy of a reply, dated June 4, having no doubt accidentally got into the usual weekly correspondence despatched to us from the mine. It was at once suspected that the original had, contrary to the terms of our agreement, been sent under cover to Messrs. Bewick Moreing & Co. in London, and that it had been kept back by that firm. On applying to them the fact had to be admitted. This letter, under the hand of Messrs. Bewick Moreing & Co.'s representative at the mine, clearly showed that, according to the view of their Australian partner, the firm could not carry out the promised reduction in costs to 25s. per ton, whilst keeping developments up to the same level as in 1903. After this, we came to the conclusion that the time had arrived when steps should be taken to obviate serious difficulties. In the result, on September 7, the directors had an interview with Mr. Moreing, when, after a full discussion, it was suggested to that gentleman that his firm should retire from the management of the mine. He promised to meet the directors on the following morning and to give a definite answer. He failed to do so. His partners—Messrs. Hoover and Wellsted—did, however, attend. They declined to surrender the mine— Mr. Hoover adding that we would have to force them out. This we regarded as an idle threat, but, as will be seen presently, it proved not to be so. Immediately after the interview we wrote a formal letter to Messrs. Bewick Moreing & Co. dismissing them; and we, at the same time, cabled to their representative at the mine to hand the mine over to Mr. Klug pending the arrival of Mr. Sutherland. In the course of a few hours we learnt that Messrs. Bewick Moreing & Co.'s partner, acting on instructions (as he stated) from his firm, declined to surrender the mine and it was not until our solicitor on the spot put a power of attorney into force that we obtained possession of the property. Upon obtaining possession we found that mullocking and timbering had been neglected, so much so that twice over, formally by letters (found in our office at the mine), the Government inspector of mines had warned Messrs. Bewick Moreing & Co.'s representative of the consequences and danger to the workmen arising out of this neglect. We had no intimation whatsoever of this state of affairs, and if the mine had been shut down I leave you to imagine what an opportunity such an incident would have afforded market operators. In other respects, too, as regards plant and the like, the mine had not been satisfactorily worked. Here let me contrast the foregoing with the state of the mine when it was handed over to Messrs. Bewick

Moreing & Co. by Mr. Sutherland. On this point I will read to you the *ipsissima verba* (very words) of the Government mine inspector. He writes to Mr. Sutherland under date March 18, 1904, as follows: "In the course of the last 15 months, during which I have been discharging the duties of a Government inspector of mines on the East Coolgardie Goldfields, I have on numerous occasions inspected the *Golden Horseshoe* mine, of which you have had the management throughout that period. Upon such occasions it has been a source of satisfaction to me to notice the careful and miner-like methods that have been followed in the conduct of operations, and the care that has been exercised for the safety of those persons who have been employed in and about the mine. It affords me pleasure to be able to say that in those respects I believe you are leaving the mine in as satisfactory a position as it has been at any time during my tenure of office on this goldfield."

But, gentlemen, this was not all. Next we learn that Messrs. Bewick Moreing & Co., by their representative, had placed in the hands of their own bankers a quantity of our gold, of the value of some £14,000, on the ground, forsooth, that we owed them money for stores. Needless to say we were quite ready to pay any sum properly due to them upon the production of proper vouchers. These have never been produced. On the advice of our solicitors in Australia we commenced an action against Messrs. Bewick Moreing & Co. on December 17. The writ was served on December 21, and the case was duly proceeded with upon the opening of the Australian Courts at the end of

February. After discussions, however, between our legal adviser, Mr. Crisp, and Mr. Abrahams, as representing Messrs. Bewick Moreing & Co., we recently agreed, on the advice of Mr. Crisp, to the following arrangement—namely, Messrs. Bewick Moreing & Co. at once to surrender our gold, when in exchange we were to hand them £10,000 on account of any claim under the agreement and on account of their out-of-pocket expenses and of any money due for stores, etc., subject, however, to the verification of figures by our Australian auditors, Messrs. Davey, Flack & Co., who are to have free access to all the books of Messrs. Bewick Moreing & Co., so as to enable them to adjust figures. We agreed with our legal adviser that an adjustment on these lines, rather than a recourse to the law courts, was in the best interests of the Company, and so the matter is being dealt with. I have now put before you the main grounds upon which your directors considered it their duty to remove Messrs. Bewick Moreing & Co. from the charge of your mine, and it seems unnecessary for me to labor the matter further. Gentlemen, I am bound to admit that in the light of subsequent events we made a great mistake in employing Messrs. Bewick Moreing & Co. at all. But, without doubt, we should have been guilty of a still greater error had we not, so soon as our eyes were opened, acted as we did. I can only assure you that, as in the initial step, so also in that which followed, the sole object of your directors was to deal with the position in the best interests of the shareholders. This much I would like to add. I desire to give expression to our very great appreciation of the extraordinary

efforts made by Mr. Sutherland and by our underground manager, Mr. Morgan, to overcome the
very serious difficulties, both above ground and
below, which had to be met with when they were
replaced in charge of the mine. It is solely to
these officers and to other members of our old staff
on the spot, who loyally supported them, that
everything at the mine is now in good working
order. I now turn to another matter. Gentlemen,
we are told that West Australian gold mining is
under a cloud; and truly, it is idle to shut our eyes
to the fact that it has been disgraced and dis-
credited by a series of squalid scandals which have
robbed it of public confidence. Then, at times,
we hear and we read a good deal touching Westralianism, followed by more or less sapient sug-
gestions and nostrums for crushing it; as, for instance, allowing free inspection of mines, appointment of local directors, and the like. Well, gentlemen, for myself, I can only say this, that if
Westralianism means underhand and ungentleman-
like tricks and dealings to gain control of mines
for market purposes; if it means intrigue and
manipulation on the part of market operators who,
for their own base purposes, attempt to corrupt
mine managers and companies' confidential officials, above and below ground, to the end that they
may betray their trust; if it means the employment of touts; if it means the dissemination and
the sedulous circulation among shareholders of un-
truths, arranged for the purposes of dishonest
speculators; if it means coquetting with shareholders of a speculative turn, and caballing to
supplant directors honestly doing their duty to

their co-partners, and who are at the same time endeavouring to raise the gold mining industry of Australia out of the mire of being but the mere counter for gambling on the Stock Exchange; if, gentlemen, Westralianism means all this, then I say that the criminality involved in such base proceedings rests, not with horny-handed toilers on the fields of Kalgoorlie, but with kid-gloved gentlemen in London, who fatten on this so-called Westralianism. * * *"

Mr. Treasurer, a shareholder, asked: There is one question I should like to refer to, and that is the suppressed letter of Messrs. Bewick Moreing & Co. You have referred a good deal to the development work and the cost of it. I should like to know whether you can tell me what Messrs. Bewick Moreing & Co.'s estimate for development was, as that appears to me to be one of the salient points of the cost.

The Chairman: With regard to the question which has been put by Mr. Treasurer, I may say that in the suppressed letter of Messrs. Bewick Moreing & Co.'s colonial partner he put the cost at 30s. per ton, exclusive of development, and he put the development at £6 per foot, and you will remember that 25s. was to include development.

Mr. Treasurer: Ours is £4 per foot, I understand.

The Chairman: Yes.

Mr. Helby said he noticed in the Chairman's remarks that he referred to Mr. Hoover; he presumed he was one of the members of the firm of Messrs. Bewick Moreing & Co., and was the same person referred to by Mr. Justice Joyce in the case of a Chinese company as having taken possession of certain deeds by force. He would like an answer to that question.

The Chairman replied that Mr. Hoover was a member of the firm of Bewick Moreing & Co. and was the same gentleman.

Mr. Helby: I think we ought to be very thankful that we have an Irishman at our head instead of a Chinaman. What you have said must have been most interesting to the shareholders who are not speculators, but who are investors, and I think we must thank you and your colleagues very heartily, indeed, for the manner in which you have dealt with the matters in question. It accounts now very clearly for the manner in which the shares of this Company were manipulated in that period.

The above report of the meeting of the *Golden Horseshoe Estates* was widely published in the English press. The Bewick Moreing & Co. referred to was Hoover's firm, consisting of Hoover, Moreing and the secretary, Wellsted, and this Australian business was in direct charge of Hoover. The Australian representatives of the firm mentioned, who were thoroughly exposed, were Prichard and Loring, both classmates of Hoover at Stanford. It is the story, in Sir John Purcell's own words of the attempted sacking of this enormous gold mine on the same lines as the Kaiping mines, and, on Hoover's failure to make himself "master of the mine," of mine wrecking, sabotage, gold taking, stock manipulation, and the usual inhuman disregard of the lives of the workers.

The great London newspaper, the *Times* had to say on this matter:

"We advise those of our readers who are interested in Western Australian mines to study carefully the speech made by Sir John Purcell at the Meeting of the *Golden Horseshoe Estate Company Ltd.,* today."

We advise all who are interested in the career of Mr. Hoover to go and do likewise.

CHAPTER THE SEVENTH

RACKETEERING IN BILLIONS

RACKETEERING is a recent phase of American life, but is apparently an imported product. We have seen it practiced in its various forms in the report of the *Golden Horseshoe Estates*. The reader may well ask how this could be possible. It is very simple. The firm of Bewick Moreing & Co. was impermeated with the respectability derived from association with a bishop's brother. Then, it had gotten off to a flying start with the *Hannan's Brownhill,* a mine so rich that all the incompetence in the world could not wreck it. Then came the stock-in-trade of the firm, an ungodly amount of bluff. When Hoover joined the firm in 1901, not one of the three partners was a qualified mining engineer. A great many of their managers (we have seen the example of preliminary lawyer Wilson) were of the same category. The public, however, as if determined to live up to Barnum's famous dictum about "suckers," generally take people at their own valuation. This is how Hoover and some of the others in the firm became great "mining experts." It is exactly like a firm of quack dentists setting up a huge electric sign to tell all and sundry that they are the "biggest and best dentists in town." How was it done? As it is done in almost any other business. Naturally they had to spend money to keep themselves before the public in a good light, and one has only to peruse any of the mining publications of that period to learn what "eminent" and "expert" engineers they were, but it was the public who paid the piper. It is almost impossible to find a single issue of any of these mining or so-called "financial rags" without a glowing account of Hoover's firm, while the name of the really eminent large London firm of mining engineers and managers, John Taylor & Sons, which had been in business for over a hundred years without a scandal, is scarcely or never mentioned. All these sugar coated pills had, of course, to be paid for, but this came out of the plunder. Occasionally, however, an editor's indignation got the better of him, as when the *Mining World* referred to the rascalities in West Australia as playing with marked cards and loaded dice.

We have already seen that Hoover was the "engineering" partner of this firm of "experts", who performed the miracle of reducing costs by simply doctoring the accounts. There were, however, other mining properties to be looked after, besides those in West Australia. Hoover's firm had interests in South Africa, where Moreing had been Chairman of the great *Van Ryn* mines, and where it had in 1902 floated that rawest of deals, the *Geduld Deep*. It was also interested in mines in Egypt where there was no gold, and in mines on the Gold Coast of Africa, where the Governor of that Colony, Sir Matthew Nathan, had admitted that the mining concessions were not worth the paper they were written on. People who remember the notorious Hoover "rubber pool" may be interested to know that his firm was also in the rubber plantation business in Ceylon. In electric power, too, and right here in the United States *St. Lawrence River Power Co.* The name seems somehow familiar. It was sold in 1902 to the Mellon crowd, but the Moreing Hoover boys still retained an interest in it.

Rather varied interests, you may think. But nothing is too much for a miracle man. Hoover was the "engineering" partner, and, as such, had charge of the mining properties. We have seen some of the methods he used to obtain a monopoly of the gold mining industry in West Australia, but that was far from being all of them. In the same *Golden Mile* at Kalgoorlie where the Golden Horseshoe Estates were located, there was another great gold mine of the same capital importance (about $15,000,000) and Hoover "wanted that too." This was the *Great Boulder Perseverance*. He was negotiating for the management of both at the same time. He had secured the *Golden Horseshoe* on the bare pretense that he could reduce working costs, but this argument would not go with the *Perseverance,* which had perhaps the best manager in the field. That was Ralph Nichols, who was a real mining engineer, a graduate of the *School of Mines* of Columbia University, who had been Superintendent of the *De Lamar* mines at Pioce, Nevada, and had also had charge of the *Moffit* and *Smith* mines at Leadville. In 1898 he had been employed by Frank Gardner to take charge of four mines Gardner had promoted in West Australia at a total salary of $25,150 a year, of which $15,000 was for managing the *Perseverance* mine and $4,000 for the management of another mining property that had so far yielded no results, the *Boulder Deep Levels.* In December 1903, Ralph Nichols left for a vacation in the United States leaving his brother Harry in charge, and Hoover, who happened to be on the same steamer returning to England suggested to Nichols an arrangement by which Hoover's firm would take over the management of the *Perseverance* mine. Nothing was decided, but Hoover, on his arrival in London, notified the directors of the *Perseverance* that he had made an arrangement with Nichols. It was just for the purpose of forcing Nichols' hand.

Meanwhile developments had occurred in the *Boulder Deep* mine. On March 7, 1904, a lode of mineral had been struck at 900 feet. It was nothing of importance, of low value and "patchy," but it was something to be "exploited." The *Boulder Deep* one pound ($5) shares were at that time worth only ten shillings, six pence (60c). This company was absolutely controlled by Frank Gardner, who was a notorious gambler, the other directors of it being Gaskell, his private secretary, Bramall, his accountant and Zebina Lane, his consulting engineer. Gardner was at this time in financial difficulties. He had put up his holding of 170,000 shares in the *Boulder Deep* mine which had only a market value of $100,000 as security for a loan of $400,000 from the *Perseverance* mine, of which he was also chairman. He was still "in the red" and something would have to be done about it. Who could save him? Who but Hoover, the miracle man of finance?

Ralph Nichols returned to London from America on March 25, 1904, and the same night about 11. p. m. Hoover and Gardner called on him at his hotel, and made a deal with him. The management of the *Gardner* mines was to be placed in the name of Hoover's firm, although Ralph Nichols was to remain sole manager. In return for this, Nichols would receive an assured salary of $30,000 a year, an increase of about $5,000. And what did Hoover's firm gain by such an arrangement? All reports from the mines to be sent to them twenty-four hours before being sent to the boards of directors of the companies. This was what Hoover wanted, the advance information for Stock Exchange speculation.

The agreement Hoover signed with Ralph Nichols on March 25th, specified that all reports and information from the mine were to be sent to Hoover's firm (that is Hoover himself, as he was the first to get all cables) twenty-four hours before being sent to the London offices of companies concerned. Within four weeks, Hoover signed the agreement between his firm and the *Great Boulder Perseverance Company* approving the arrangement with Nichols as far as the *Perseverance* mine was concerned, but containing the important condition that all information obtained and discoveries made at the mine should be transmitted direct to the *Perseverance* Company's office in London and not through Hoover's firm. Hoover completely disregarded this condition and the reports of the ore estimates made by Hoover's class-mates Prichard and Loring, as well as other important information, were cabled direct from the mine to Hoover in London. It was another case of marked cards and loaded dice. He had the advance information with which to beat the market. He insisted on Ralph Nichols selling all his shareholdings, and when Mr. Nichols stipulated that Hoover's firm should not gamble either, Mr. Hoover assured him that they were not going to deal in the shares. But was this not what Hoover had bought his way into the mine for?

To obtain the management of this great *Perseverance* gold mine, Hoover's firm had to buy out Gardner who was chairman of that company. They advanced him $20,000 in cash, and took up a large quantity of his *Perseverance* shares. Moreing said it was 38,500 shares they bought from him. Hoover, in a letter of April 8, 1904, said it was 60,000 and in a cable of May 10, 1904, to the Australian office said 40,000. It is really quite hard to know which figure to believe, but it is certain that one lot of 40,000 shares was traced to them, this being held in the name of Mr. Roberts of their bankers, Roberts & Lubbock. They had thus invested nearly half a million dollars to get control of this mine, and what for? The purchase arrangement with the gambler Gardner provided that the profits were to be split 50-50. And yet, Hoover had told Ralph Nichols that his firm were not going to deal in the shares.

The occurrences at both of these mines were investigated in the second half of 1904 by the Western Australian Government, which appointed a Royal Commission of three members for this task. These investigations showed that the *Boulder Deep* mine had been "salted," and recited the irregularities at the *Perseverance* mine, but fixed no responsibilities. The *Financial News* of London, referring to this, after quoting the *Kalgoorlie Miner* and the *Western Mail* to the same effect, goes on to say:

> "One point which is almost universally commented upon in the West Australian papers is the suppression in the report of the names of individuals."

Mr. Downey, the chairman of the Royal Commission of three, was a lawyer for Hoover's firm, and this easily explains what the newspapers could not understand.

And what had happened to require the Government to intervene? When the gambler Gardner had made his deal with Hoover, he practically made his London headquarters at the office of Hoover's firm. His accountant, Walter Bramall, who was also a director of one of Gardner's other mines which came under Hoover Moreing management, moved right into their offices at 20 Copthall Avenue. Then the game began.

First, let us take the *Boulder Deep*. On May 3, 1904, Harry Nichols, the temporary manager in the absence of his brother Ralph, received a cable to dismiss Mr. Cullen, the purchasing agent, at once. And then, as if by a miracle, quite suddenly, the assays of the samples of ore taken from the mine began to show extraordinary high values. This information was cabled by Harry Nichols to Gardner, who told him to keep it a secret and, if enquiries were made, to report "everything very discouraging."

The shares of the *Boulder Deep* began to rise in the London market. Not fast enough, however, for the boys. Someone was reported to be selling. This was taken to be Michael Flynn, who had been for six years underground manager of the mine, and on May 18th, Harry Nichols received a cable to remove Flynn and replace him by one of Hoover's men. Thus the racket went merrily on, and the *Boulder Deep* shares which in March had stood at sixty cents, had reached by the beginning of June the price of ten dollars a share! An advance of 1,500%! What had occurred to account for this? The mine assayer, Harold Vickers, was salting the samples and reporting high assay values where none existed. Zebina Lane, a director of this mine, in his sworn evidence stated:

> "Somebody, probably in London, has paid the officials at the mine to do it."

There is little doubt about this, for, on Ralph Nichols' return to the mine on June 1st, he started re-sampling the mine on June 6th and, before his samples ever reached the assay office, prices began to tumble. The "insiders" in London knew right along that it was a swindle. Who were these insiders? Harry Davies, representative of the *West Australian*, swore at the en-

quiry that he knew something was wrong, as Lionel
Robinson anticipated both the rise and fall in the
price of the shares. Zebina Lane, too, swore:

> "After I got to London, I made enquiries and
> found it was Robinson that was doing all the
> dealing and running the stock."

And who was Lionel Robinson? He was the London
stockbroker who had brought about the downfall of
Hoover's forger partner Rowe, and whom we will find
in the following years associated with Hoover in the
notorious Australian Smelting Corporation and the
scandal of the Zinc Corporation. Robinson was the
man who was running the market for this *Boulder Deep*
swindle.

There is no knowing, however, the volume of the
gambling that took place. Robinson filed a sworn
declaration with the Royal Commission of Enquiry
showing his dealings in these shares *but only for clients
in Australia.* No mention whatever of the hundreds
of thousands of shares that changed hands through his
firm in the London market. And this escaped the eagle
eye of E. P. Downey, Chairman of the Commission, and
lawyer for Hoover's firm!

The evidence taken at the enquiry, however, shows
that Vickers, who was salting the samples, passed the
information to a man named Chappell, who sent it to
Ducker, the stockholder agent in Sydney of Lionel
Robinson. Chappell in turn communicated it to a
mysterious firm he referred to as "Herbert & Co.," which
has never been identified.

It is a more than remarkable fact that although
Hoover had made arrangements with Gardner and
Ralph Nichols on March 25, 1904, to take over the
Boulder Deep mine, and although Harry Nichols,

brother of Ralph, who evidently distrusted Hoover, had cabled in April that he would leave the job at the end of the month, and although Ralph Nichols himself arrived at the mine on June 1, yet the Hoover people did not "officially" take over the mine until June 11th, when Ralph Nichols had proved that it had been salted. What a feather in the cap of honest Hoover and his "experts," who had "discovered" that the mine had been salted! Remember that Hoover's agents, Pritchard and Loring, had already been down that mine towards the end of May, and do not forget that Hoover's firm at that very time were in a gambling partnership with Gardner in the shares of the *Perseverance* mine, and that Gardner and his gang were right there in the Hoover firm's office. What a joke this must have been to them that they discovered the salting! Hoover improved on it by cabling to the mine that the responsible parties should be rigorously prosecuted. Which was probably good for an extra round of drinks. It was cleverer than any of the detective stories Hoover had ever read. How he would have laughed, if he could have laughed. But Hoover cannot laugh.

The *Boulder Deep* shares dropped in a few days to one-eighth of their value. They dropped before the salting was ever discovered, showing that the "insiders" knew and that it was all a plot. And mining stock speculators, who were generally small people, lost millions of dollars in this rawest of swindles.

Now all these mines we are talking about were in the *Golden Mile* at Kalgoorlie, as close to one another as houses in a street. As a matter of fact, the *Lake View Consols*, managed by Hoover's firm, was right next door to the *Boulder Deep*. The *Great Boulder Perseverance* was just a little distance away. This was

the mine in which Hoover had arranged with the
gambler Gardner to take up 60,000 shares or so of
Gardner's holding in return for the management of
the mine. At the same time he encouraged Gardner
by offering to let him have half the profits on the
resale of the shares. This was another of Hoover's
little jokes. When he got into a good mine as we have
seen in the *Golden Horseshoe,* and the *Lake View* it
was to wreck the value of the property with the object
of gaining control of it. This was conclusively proved
at the Government enquiry into the affairs of this mine
a few months after the one into the *Boulder Deep*
scandal, when Pierre Ledoux, engineer for a Belgian
investing company, swore that as soon as he heard
that Hoover's firm was to have the management of the
Perseverance mine, he advised his people to sell 24,000
out of the 40,000 shares they held in that company.
Ledoux knew their racket. He remembered the deal
Hoover had pulled off a few years ago earlier with the
Lake View Consols, when he wrecked the value of that
nine by over $5,000,000 overnight, by issuing an estimate
of ore reserves that was afterwards proved to be conclusively wrong.

Now, on April 20, 1904, Hoover had signed the
agreement with the *Great Boulder Perseverance Company,* by which his firm was to take over the management of that great mine, but leaving Ralph Nichols
still in charge as local manager. This agreement was
to say the very least questionable, for it contained a
clause to the effect that all information must be sent
direct from the mine to the *Perseverance* company,
which clause Hoover never intended to carry out, and
never did carry out, for had he not already, on March
25th, signed a different agreement with Ralph Nichols,

whereby all information would be cabled to Hoover's firm twenty-four hours before being sent to the *Perseverance* company? This was a cold, calculating, deliberate act calculated to give the Hoover boys an opportunity of playing the market with advance information illegitimately obtained.

Hoover lost no time about swinging his band into action. On April 21st, a cable was sent to his Australian manager and classmate, Prichard, an "expert" of about the same attainments as himself, to take control of the *Perseverance* mine at once and sample the mine. On May 18th, Prichard cabled to Hoover his estimate of ore reserves as 354,462 tons, containing 282,567 ounces of gold, a reduction of 30.9%, as Prichard put it, from Ralph Nichols' estimate of December 31, 1903, which was 401,677 tons containing 483,110 ounces of gold. This will give an idea of what an engineer Prichard was, as the difference indicated was over 41.5% and not 30.9%, as any schoolboy would have figured out. Was this report given out to the shareholders? Bless you, no. The Hoover crowd still had that big bundle of shares to get rid of.

On May 18th, the *Perseverance* shares stood at 22 shillings. By May 30th, they had dropped to 17 shillings. Someone was selling. On May 31st, thirteen days after receipt of Prichard's report, it was sent out to the unfortunate shareholders, who had meantime been kept in the dark, while the "insiders" speculated. Prichard's report of May 18th was sent out to the shareholders on May 31st. But not as it was received. The report said nothing of a reduction of ore values of 41.5%, nor even of 30.9% (as Prichard had given it). It had been changed to 25% by Hoover's own hand.

The market was now weak; Hoover's firm held a

large block of shares and stood to lose money. This was not in their Credo. They decided to go boldly to the front and wreck the values of that great mine, just as they were doing at that very moment in the *Golden Horseshoe,* just a few minutes walk away. W. J. Loring, whom Hoover had entrusted with the *Golden Horseshoe* "job," was ordered to come into the *Perseverance* and re-sample the mine. He knew his "business." On June 20th he cabled that the ore reserves were only 139,329 tons of a value of $2,000,000 as against Ralph Nichols estimate of reserves worth $10,500,000, just a little difference of $8,500,000. This cable reached Hoover's office in London in the morning of June 20th (Australia being some hours ahead of England) and was not issued until the night of June 22nd to the shareholders, who did not receive it until the 23rd, three days later. In the meantime, while the shareholders were in the dark, Hoover's firm sold 38,500 shares on the 21st, and there is no knowing how many more, as they had the market at their mercy. The shares dropped 30% in these three days. This is not all.

When Loring cabled his report on June 20th, he asked if he might publish it in Australia. Hoover replied that he was on no account to do so. The Australian shareholders were also to be kept in the dark until the Hoover Moreing crowd had made their "killing."

Of course, Hoover and his "experts" were thrown out of the *Perseverance* mine as they were out of the *Golden Horseshoe,* that they had also tried to wreck. Ralph Nichols was reinstated as manager and, as had happened with the *Lake View* mine, it was found that his original estimate of ore reserves was correct, and that the estimate of the Hoover firm was inaccurate, if anything. Michael Flynn, who had been underground manager of the *Perseverance* mine under Ralph Nichols for six years and who knew the mine inside out, swore at the Government enquiry that when he saw their estimate he knew "there was a nigger in the fence."

Hoover and Moreing tried to explain their conduct by pretending that they had acted in good faith, and had taken a heavy loss on the shares they sold. Moreing put in a declaration that this loss was about $135,-000. Hoover, in a letter to his Kalgoorlie office, had said it was $200,000. On the other hand, Prichard, Hoover's Australian general manager, who was in London in July, wrote to Loring that the loss on the shares was $65,000. What is one to assume from these three contradictory reports of one simple figure? Independent of the fact that gambling in the shares of the company they managed was sufficient to condemn them, it is very evident that the Hoover Moreing crowd lost no money at all. They were not in business for that. This was rather conclusively proved by the fact that Hoover had cabled on May 10, 1904, to Prichard and Loring, a cable confirmed by himself by letter of May 13th, informing them that in order to obtain the management of the *Perseverance* mine he had had to buy 40,000 shares at twenty-seven shillings, six pence ($6.50) per share for account of the Australian branch of his firm. If there had been any loss, the Australian branch of the firm would have had to settle it, and there was nothing to settle.

An important fact brought out at this Government Enquiry was that the statements of output from all these mines managed by Hoover's firm were false. Secret reserves of gold were kept, which were used to balance the output and make it appear to the public that the mines were producing uniformly, and only the "insiders" knew the actual production from month to month. It is the advance information thus obtained that gave the Hoover firm such an enormous advantage in gambling operations. That is what they were mining "managers" for.

As in the case of the *Boulder Deep,* the Royal Commission of Enquiry into the false estimates given out by the Hoover firm fixed no responsibilities and, as in that case, the explanation lies in the fact that Mr. Downey, the Chairman of the Commission, whom we have seen to have been a lawyer for the Hoover firm, represented the Council of West Australian Mineowners, whose secretary was Bramall, the accountant of the gambler Gardner, and whose offices were right in the offices of Hoover's firm in London

And yet the press, with these things before it, could not understand how the guilty parties escaped. The London *Morning Post,* which is a very conservative paper, commented:

> "None of those responsible for the scandals of
> Westralianism have been brought to book, and
> the whole industry is still under the stigma."

What did Hoover and Moreing care about Royal Commissions enquiring into their rackets? They were above the law. Was it not only three years before that Hoover had "taken" the ice-free port and coaling station of Ching Wan Tao for England? Was not Ching Wan Tao the outlet for the Kaiping mines, and the key to the military control of North China? A jewel in the crown of England worth more than the Koh-i-Noor! No, these men could not be prosecuted. Listen to what F. A. Govett, Hoover's stockjobbing associate, had to say on this point when interviewed by a representative of the *Mining Journal:*

"With regard to the recent Royal Commission when it was found rather difficult to get information, do you know whether any application was made to the English Government for assistance?" he was asked.

Govett replied: "I don't think so, but it would have been perfectly useless."

Govett knew. They could have stolen the Crown Jewels and gotten away with it.

CHAPTER THE EIGHTH

SLAVERY IN THE 20TH CENTURY

"THEN, as we have seen, Hoover, by his curious methods, had succeeded in obtaining the "management" of the *Golden Horseshoe* and *Perseverance* mines, he had established a practical monopoly for his firm in West Australia. The Hoover firm had become an octopus, racketeering in the stock market, racketeering in the mines, racketeering in the sale of mine supplies, racketeering in human lives. They had now in the Summer of 1904 thirty-two mines under their "management," all under the control of "expert" Hoover, practically all of which were condemned to an early death at his hands. For Hoover was never an engineer, and the stories of most of these mines are monuments to his incompetence erected at the cost of the unfortunate investors. Readers may well ask how this was possible. They may equally well ask how the Congress of the United States in August, 1917, gave the absolute control of 45,000,000 American farms to this same Hoover, who was just as ignorant of farming as he was of engineering. The Spanish proverb says: "A donkey loaded with gold passes through every gate."

We shall now leave West Australia for a while and journey to the Transvaal in South Africa. In the Winter of 1899, the mine owners there, on the authority of Sir J. B. Robinson, who was one of them, urged on by their abominable greed, forced a war on the Boer Transvaal Republic, because President Kruger would not let them have all they wanted. You remember reading of that terrible campaign, where Kruger, with a handful of farmers, held out for over two and a half years against all the might of the British Empire. Hundreds of thousands of lives were lost, a billion and a quarter in treasure wasted, in order that these Park Lane millionaires might have their way. And what was it they wanted? Nothing, but to dominate white labor. The mines in South Africa were worked by black "Kaffir" labor and, as these laborers were only suited for unskilled work, a large percentage of white labor was required for such jobs as those of foremen, overseers, mechanics, carpenters, etc. This brought a considerable influx of white people into the Transvaal and these white people organized for their protection. This was anathema to the mining magnates. Just as Hoover had tried to do in West Australia, these other capitalists (for Herbert Hoover, Esquire, was now in the capitalist class), decided to break the back of white labor in the Transvaal. An enterprising gentleman we know, who had mining experience in China, suggested the importation of Chinese laborers. This gentleman had proved himself in California to be a complete failure as a miner. But that did not matter. He would like to get these South African "brothers" some Chinese. During the Boer War the Kaffirs had been earning fairly good wages from the British military authorities, and, when it ended in May, 1902, they felt little inclination to return to the mines to be murdered. For that was the fate in store for them in these mines. The official average death rate for the year 1903 being 71.25 per 1,000, and the death rate for the month of July 112 per 1,000, and this without taking into account the thousands of boys who returned to their homes every year only to die. Talk about warfare, where was there warfare as deadly as this? Human life was being sacrificed, after a purgatory of toil and torture, for a wage of fifty cents a day. Even this was too much for the mine barons. They could get Chinamen for half the price. And with the Chinamen would come Chinese overseers, artisans and mechanics to displace high-paid white labor. It was useless that Mr. F. H. P. Creswell, manager of *The Village Main Reef* mine, had proved that unskilled white labor could be economically employed on account of the white man's greater output. They wanted to eliminate the white man altogether. Here is a letter from Mr. Percy Tarbutt, a director of *The Village Main Reef* mine to Mr. Creswell:

23, St. Swithin's Lane, London, E.C.
3rd July, 1902.
"My dear Mr. Creswell,

With reference to your trial of white labour for surface work on the mines, I was not present at the Board meeting, when a letter was written stating that the Board did not approve of the suggestion, and on receipt of the last mail I called another Board to reconsider the matter, in view of the fact that the local Board had already commenced to adopt your suggestion. I have consulted the Consolidated Goldfields people, and one of the members of the Board of the Village Main Reef has consulted Messrs. Wernher, Beit and Co., and the feeling seems to be one of fear that if a large number of white men are employed on the Rand in the position of labourers, the same troubles will arise as are now prevalent in the Australian Colonies, i. e., that the combination of the labouring classes will become so strong as to be able to more or less dictate not only on questions of wages, but also on political questions by the power of the votes when a Representative Government is established."

The South African magnates decided on the introduction of the Chinese. This was not, however, so easy to bring about. The Transvaal then had the status of a Crown Colony. It was governed by a Legislative Assembly of twenty-four, of whom thirteen were nominees of the British Government, and any enactment passed by the Legislative Assembly required the approval of the British Parliament. The Legislative Assembly was presided over by the High Commissioner, who was the Governor of the Colony, Lord Milner. It required a man more in sympathy with ideas of slavery to put through the dirty job. Strings were pulled at the Colonial Office, then presided over by Joe Chamberlain, the statesman who had boasted that the Boer War was a "feather in his cap." Sir Arthur Lawley, the man who had tried to introduce a form of slavery when Administrator of Matabeleland in Rhodesia, who had been sent to Australia to influence labor legislation, and who was a fine public speaker, was the man for them, one in sympathy with the "cause." As Governor of the selfgoverning Colony of Western Australia, he had a very nice position, a magnificent mansion, a salary of $20,000 a year, and extra allowances for entertaining. In 1901 he had received $150,000 for this purpose and an extra $100,000 for a new ballroom for his mansion. What a lovely job! And yet he gave up all this for the position of Lieutenant Governor of the war bankrupted Transvaal Colony at a salary of $10,000 a year. There was certainly a nigger (or rather, we should say a Chinaman) in that woodpile! He left Perth in West Australia by the S/S *Sophocles* on August 14, 1902, arriving in Durban, Natal, on August 31st and proceeding direct to Pretoria, the capital of the Transvaal. Soon afterwards, he was sworn in as High Commissioner to preside over the Legislative Assembly. That he was considered of more importance than the Governor is shown by the fact that when $150,000 was voted for a new house for Lord Milner, $200,000 was voted for a house for Lawley. With Lawley in the saddle, an aggressive and insistent campaign was initiated for the purpose of influencing public opinion not only in South Africa, but also in England, in favor of the importation of Chinese labor. Meetings were held all over the country, addressed by officials, some of whom had been bribed and others subjected to political pressure, with the object of showing that there was not a sufficient supply of Kaffir labor and that the importation of the Chinese was necessary for the salvation of the mining industry.

This was denied by Sir Godfrey Lagdon, the Commissioner for Native Affairs, by Mr. W. Wybergh, the Commissioner for Mines, and by the South African Press. At this, the mine owners became "tough." Lawley dismissed Mr. Wybergh, Mr. Monypenny, the editor of the Johannesburg *Star*, was forced to resign and the whole staff of the Johannesburg *Leader* was fired. The other newspapers had to fall in line. Employees were forced to sign petitions stating that calamity would befall if the Chinese did not come. Clergymen, not always to be bought over to such an ungodly cause, were purchased. The Chinaman was needed to save the Transvaal! This opinion was solemnly endorsed by the Transvaal Chamber of Mines, two very prominent members of which were Ernest Williams, who had been Hoover's boss for a while in West Australia and was now manager of the Hoover firm's prize South African venture, the *Geduld Deep*, where they had taken advantage of the name of a rich mine to float a worthless property, actually introducing the shares on the London market at a premium of 150%, and William L. Honnold, consulting engineer of the

Transvaal Coal Mining Trust, which had had its London offices with Hoover's firm. This is the same Honnold, who was afterwards prominent in the Belgian Relief and in some of Hoover's more recent activities.

The propaganda campaign was carried on even more extensively in England, many of the leading newspapers and even several pious bishops referring to the necessity of saving the Transvaal by means of the Chinaman. The saviour John Chinaman, however, was not intended to come as an angel Gabriel, but in the role of an "indentured laborer." As Lawrence Sterne wrote: "Disguise thyself as thou wilt, still, Slavery, said I—still thou art a bitter draught."

Meanwhile, Joe Chamberlain, the British Colonial Secretary, came down to the Transvaal in the Winter of 1902 and in January, 1903, put through a deal with the mine owners, whereby he offered the Government support to the scheme for introducing the Chinamen in consideration of the mine owners subscribing $150,000,000 in three yearly installments towards a loan for the reconstruction of the Transvaal. Immediately afterwards the Transvaal Chamber of Mines sent two agents, Skinner and Noyce, to China to investigate the possibilities. Meanwhile, the campaign of propaganda for the introduction of Chinese labor was persistently and extensively carried on in the Transvaal and in England at enormous expense and twelve months elapsed before it was considered that the time was ripe to outrage the feelings of all humanity. Chamberlain, who, like a true politician, was facing both ways, had gone on record as being opposed to the importation of Chinese into Africa, and had consequently to resign in order to save his face, his place as Colonial Secretary being taken in September 1903, by his private secretary Alfred Lyttelton. Lyttelton was a lawyer who, from 1899 to 1901, had been chairman of the Transvaal Concessions Commission and was thus personally known to all these mine magnates. He was the one who was to "deliver the goods." The British Government had been already compromised by Chamberlain.

Eventually, on February 10, 1904, Lawley rushed through the Transvaal Legislative Assembly an Ordinance prescribing the conditions under which Chinese were to be employed in the Transvaal gold mines, and, under the pretext of saving time, it was cabled scrapwise to the British Parliament for its approval. It was only a few months before, that the British Government had called the attention of the whole world to Sir Roger Casement's report on conditions in the Congo:

> "The most terrible slavery exists. The administration is atrocious, and if there is not speedy intervention it will be too late."

The soldiers of King Leopold of Belgium, to satiate his greed for money to satisfy his concubines, were massacring, torturing, and mutilating the natives of the Congo who did not bring in enough rubber. The Belgian soldier Lacroix, in his confession published in the *Niewe Gazet* of Antwerp, said:

> "I will go before my Judge for having killed 150 men, cut off 60 hands, crucified numerous women and children, and cut off the sexual parts of many men and hung them on the fences."

It was customary for the Belgian officers to hand out cartridges to the native soldiers in their employ and for every cartridge they spent, they had to bring in a man's hand. One of these Belgian officers on duty in the Congo at that time, who had especially distinguished himself in this kind of "zeal" for King Leopold was Emile Francqui, the man who had helped to tricked the Americans out of the Hankow-Canton railroad concession in China in 1901, and who had at the same time "stood by" in case Hoover needed any further help in the "taking" of the Kaiping mines. This is the humanitarian Francqui who had sole charge of the distribution of the Belgian "relief" during the World War, for which Hoover did the buying and shipping. At the time we are writing of, February, 1904, Francqui was a director, in company with Hoover, of the Chinese Engineering & Mining Company, for which Hoover had "taken" the Kaiping mines. He was not the only Belgian slavedriver on the directorate of that company. There were others, including Colonel Thys. But the big four who were running the company were Edmund Davis and his twin soul, Turner, Moreing and Hoover, and of these four, Hoover was the one in charge. He directed the affairs of the company. He was its spokesman, all important reports going out on behalf of the company bearing the scrawl "H. C. Hoover." He had as chief engineer of the company his nominee the preliminary lawyer Wilson.

In December, 1903, the British Government had protested to all civilized nations against the atrocious conditions in the Congo, and here it was in the months of February, March and April, 1904, debating the putting into force of Lawley's Ordinance for the importation of Chinese, one of the most inhuman documents the world has ever seen. The Chinese were to be imported to the Transvaal as unskilled workers. They were not to be allowed to practice any trade. They could hold no property or rights of any kind. They were to live in compounds, apart from the rest of humanity. They were to work ten hours a day on two meals a day and for a minimum wage of twenty-five cents a day to be paid after thirty days work. They must not leave the compound without a permit, and no permit could be given for more than forty-eight hours. They could be transferred from one employer to another, just like a horse or a cow. There were tremendous fines for the slightest infraction of the regulations, and these fines were to be deducted from the twenty-five cents a day wage. In other words, they would be enslaved so much longer until the fines were paid. These penalties were also independent of any other punishment (flogging, torture, etc.). After three years, the Chinaman, if still alive, was to be shipped back to China. In case of death from accident, the compensation was to be fifty dollars, and in case of serious accident twenty-five.

Of course, all liberal-minded people were opposed to this damnable Ordinance, which was nothing but slavery pure and simple. All the great selfgoverning British colonies protested. In the House of Lords, men of vast experience like Lord Carrington, Lord Coleridge, Lord Stanmore, Earl Spencer, and the Bishop of Hereford protested bitterly. In the House of Commons, John Burns, General Seely, Lloyd George and Sir Henry Campbell-Bannerman were equally violent in their indignation. However, the British Government had been sold out by Chamberlain to the mine owners of the Transvaal, and Lyttelton, with a big party majority behind him, forced the measure through. To do so, he used every artifice and device of the accomplished party hack, lying, misrepresentation, suppression of facts. Parliament was told that the Chinaman would receive a minimum wage of fifty cents a day, that he could bring his wife and children at the mine owner's expense, and that the compounds, instead of being "cages" were going to be "garden cities," where John Chinaman could grow his own fruit and vegetables. It was going to be a little paradise for them in South Africa. Lyttelton did not tell Parliament that there was no intention whatever of allowing the women and children to come with the Chinese, or that these young men in the prime of life would be herded in compounds not half an acre in size, two thousand men to a compound, where there was hardly standing room for them, these compounds being enclosed by the huts where the Chinese were to live, twenty in a hut, twenty-seven feet by nineteen and a half and twelve feet high, sleeping on wooden shelves, two men to a shelf. Lyttelton did not tell Parliament that twenty-five cents in the Transvaal was not worth more than five cents in China, nor that it would take a month's wages to buy a new suit of jeans. He said nothing about the miners having to climb ladders as much as a thousand feet to the surface after ten hours of heartbreaking toil in an atmosphere of perpetual rain. He said nothing about having to work alongside of Kaffir convicts. He said nothing about the armed guards. He sold his conscience, as many other politicians do, for the sake of his party.

While Parliament was debating, the Transvaal mine-owners were acting. They sent two agents, Perry and Hamilton, to China to organize recruiting at Hong Kong, and Tientsin, and other places. They were not meeting with great success, despite the great unemployment in North China as a result of the fighting in Manchuria. The local Chinese authorities were opposed to the scheme. They saw that it was tainted with slavery. At this juncture, Hoover arrived back in London from Australia in February 1903. Over at a certain tavern at the corner of Throgmorton Street where he used to meet his South African "friends," he heard the grumbling about the unwillingness of the Chinese to come over to their "garden cities." Why had they not consulted the miracle man? They could have the whole empire of China if they would pay for it, all but the port of Ching Wan Tao. How many did they want, a million? No, only two hundred thousand. Shucks, that was easy. What if they did not want to come? He did not laugh. He cannot laugh. He chuckled.

April 18, 1904, the *Chinese Engineering & Mining Company, Limited,* sold into slavery 200,000 fellow human beings. These were Chinamen. But still they were fellow human beings. Their only misfortune was that they were poor. They had parents and wives and children or sweethearts whom they loved, just as we do ours. But good-bye to all that. They were going to be sent down there in slave ships through the tropics, crowded worse than chickens in a coop, not as men, but, in the words of the Bishop of Hereford, as "animated implements" which when done with were to be re-exported again dead or alive. They were coming down from the Chinese summer to the South African winter to work over a thousand feet down in the bowels of the earth in perpetual moisture, ten hours a day and then, with feet of lead, climb up the ladders to the surface. Semi-starvation, toil, the whip, the torture, promiscuity, sodomy, bestiality. It was a hot day in hell when that contract was signed. But Satan must have shuddered. This was too much like competition.

With the exception of the few thousand Chinese already recruited in Hong Kong, a good many of whom were convicts, the Chinese Government wanted to get rid of, Hoover's *Chinese Engineering & Mining Company* now had the monopoly of the recruiting and shipping of the Chinese slaves to South Africa. Before the

Ordinance was ever approved by the British Government, they were advertising widely throughout the provinces of Shantung and Chi-li. But in the advertisements no mention was made of the fact that the wages were only to be six dollars per calendar month, that the Chinese would be confined to compounds, that they were not allowed to take their wives and children, that the work was underground in the bowels of the earth, or that they might not trade or own any property. These advertisements were, as Lloyd George said in the House of Commons, fraudulent.

Buildings were erected at Ching Wan Tao to house the Chinamen who came enquiring about the "garden cities" in the Transvaal. Once they got there, they were not allowed to escape, the walls were eighteen feet high. These men were crimped, shanghaied. Was not Hoover's company getting ten dollars for every Chinese they recruited and twenty-five dollars for his passage to South Africa? Oh, yes. They attended to the shipping, too. The ships were chartered by one of their directors, G. Todd Symons, a shipbroker. All the ships chartered were regular tramp twin-deck iron steamers of about 3,000 tons, some less,—the *Ikbal*, the *Cranley*, the *Swanley*, the *Tweeddale*, the *Inkum*, the *Sikh*, the *Katherine Park*, the *Courtfield*, the *Brinkburn*. Under the convention made between England and China regarding the shipment of these Chinese, they were to be shipped according to the regulations of the Indian Emigration Act of 1883. Under this act, not more than a thousand men could be shipped by the above type of vessel. You can imagine that this number was good and plenty. Indeed, it would be hard to ship a thousand pigs in a ship of that size. These gentlemen, however, paid no attention to treaties or conventions.

They shipped these Chinese slaves under the Hong Kong Chinese Emigration Ordinance of 1889, under which they could obtain licenses to carry two thousand or more Chinese in one of these iron tubs. Apart from its terrifying inhumanity, this also was in itself illegal, as the Hong Kong Chinese Emigration Ordinance of 1889 did not apply to this kind of traffic.

The first Chinese shipped were those recruited by the Transvaal Labour Commission, at Hongkong, 1,054 of them, who left Hongkong on May 25, 1904, by the S/S *Tweeddale* and arrived in Durban, South Africa on June 18th. These men were sent to the *New Comet* mine on the Rand, where they were met by W. L. Honnold, the friend of Hoover, who was afterwards prominent in the Belgian "Relief." The rest of the Chinese slaves were all recruited or pressganged at the Hoover *Chinese Engineering & Mining Company* stations, the new general manager, Major W. S. Nathan, who was reported in the press as having been indefatigable in recruiting, having evidently been specially brought over from the Transvaal for that purpose. The first shipment of these was made from Taku, near Tientsin, by the S/S *Ikbal,* a twin deck iron vessel of 3,400 tons. Her departure was somewhat delayed by an attempt at escape by some of the Chinese who were crimped. But there were armed guards. Oh, yes, armed guards with guns to see that they arrived safely at their "garden cities." The S/S *Ikbal* eventually sailed on June 30, 1904, with 2,020 Chinese slaves, accompanied by Mr. Baldwin of the *Chinese Engineering & Mining Company,* and, of course, the armed guards, and the doctors, and the crew. It would take someone very good at arithmetic to figure how they packed them into that old iron tub, 2,020 of them. Just imagine the horror of it! It was mid-summer, the heat over 100 degrees in the shade, and on an iron vessel headed for a four weeks voyage through the tropics. The slave ships of old had nothing on this. Standing room only in that blistering sizzling heat, and four weeks of it! What excuse could there be for it? The excuse of the twenty-five dollars per head passage money that went into the coffers of Hoover's *Chinese Engineering & Mining Company*. They arrived at Durban on July 26, 1904. Oh, no, not all of them. 1,969 of them. There were fifty-one missing. What did that matter? They were only Chinamen. The Hoover firm had insured them for a hundred and twenty-five dollars a head against all risks, including falling overboard and jettison, and, dear reader, if you do not know what "jettison" means, it is the nautical expression for "throwing overboard." What became of them? Who knows or cares? Hoover's company collected the insurance money and all was serene. You remember the following from Whittier's poem:

"All ready?" cried the captain,
"Ay, ay," the seamen said;
"Heave up the worthless lubbers—
The dying and the dead."
Up from the slave ship's prison
Fierce, bearded heads were thrust—
"Now let the sharks look to it—
Toss up the dead ones first."

On arrival in Durban, the 1,969 survivors were herded into a compound, finger printed like convicts and given brass tags, and then shipped in sealed railroad cars like cattle to the Transvaal, a thirty-hour journey. The first batch of them arrived on the Rand on July 31st, 1904. They were fine big strapping fellows from North

China, young men in the prime of life, many of them over six feet in height. They had left their homes and folks and hopes behind and had come here thousands of miles to suffer, many of them to die. Their bones would never lie with those of their ancestors. It was pitiful to see these sturdy big chaps marching off to their unknown fate before the eyes of the slave trader who had sold them. Oh, yes, he was there to meet them, to witness his own handiwork. He had slipped away quietly from London and sailed by the S/S *Carisbrook Castle* on July 9, 1904. His name does not appear on the passenger list of that vessel, but he arrived by it at Cape Town on July 27, 1904, and proceeded direct to the Transvaal to meet the first installment of the boys sold into slavery and see that they were directed to the mines that he was interested in.

And what was the fate in store for these stalwart young Chinese? We read in the *Star* of Johannesburg:

"At the Geduld the coolies will, for months to come, in mining work be employed on shaft sinking, which means that most of the time they will be working in water and in an atmosphere of perpetual rain."

This was in the cold South African winter, and these boys had just arrived in their cotton jeans from the hot Chinese summer. They had to work a ten hour shift on two meals a day, rice with scraps of fish or meat and tea. They had to sleep twenty to twenty-five in a room on wooden planks, with only one cotton blanket for a covering. And the nights were cold, bitter cold, in the Transvaal! There was no dodging work, either. Working with a hand drill, the Chinaman had to drill thirty-six inches of rock a day, including the removal of the stone he broke down, or else have a reduction made in his "wages" of twenty-five cents a day. This, in the Transvaal, was not enough to buy a package of cigarettes. For infractions of the rules, or not performing sufficient work he was tried by the Superintendent of Inspectors under the Ordinance and apart from flogging or torture, subject to heavy fines, so that many of these unfortunates, at the end of thirty days toil, were actually in debt to the mines. After their heartbreaking work, they had to climb by ladders to the surface from the bowels of the earth, which in itself was inhuman torture. They were not allowed to leave the precincts of the mine, and, if they did, were subject to arrest by any white person. We have all read of the horrors of slavery in the Southern States. But never anything like this. The American slave had his home and his family and a great deal of personal liberty, and, if a good worker, was well taken care of. These Chinese were brought over in the prime of life to be broken on the wheel within three years for the purpose of grinding out ever greater profits for the monsters of greed who owned them.

There is a story from ancient Egypt of a slaveowner who said to a newly-purchased slave: "Now you are mine, I have bought you." "That is your business," answered the slave. "But, will you try to run away?" asked the master. "That is my business," the slave replied. So it was in the Transvaal. In spite of the compounds, in spite of the guards, in spite of the floggings and tortures that awaited them if caught, many escaped. Houdini had nothing on some of these Chinese. Their ingenuity knew no limits when it was a question of regaining freedom. It is told of one of them who made a dash from the compound that he was caught by the troopers and dragged back at the end of a rope. After taking his punishment, he again escaped, this time hidden under the tarpaulin of a delivery wagon. Caught again and put to the torture, he again escaped and this time succeeded in reaching a native store, where he purchased some shoe polish and red ochre and converted himself into a fullgrown Kaffir. They escaped in spite of all vigilance, and, not being allowed to work elsewhere than at the mines, were obliged to form themselves into marauding bands, which roamed the country, plundering the farmhouses of the Boers, whose arms had been taken up by the British after the war. These occurrences were carefully suppressed in the local Transvaal press, which was owned or subsidized by the mineowners. But the news gradually leaked out to England, where the moral conscience of the people had already been aroused by the horrible stories from the Congo. Some of the great Liberal newspapers in England sent correspondents to the Transvaal to investigate, and they sent home reports to make the blood run cold. A violent agitation started to remove this infamy and it resulted in orders being sent out to suspend recruiting and shipping. A general election was fought out in England, largely on this issue, and the Conservative party was overwhelmed at the elections for having degraded the Nation by lending its protection and prestige to the ruthless enslavers of a people. The new Liberal Government immediately ordered the repatriation of these slaves to China. But they counted without the mineowners, who put up a determined opposition, refusing to post up the repatriation notices, and, when obliged to do so, putting up queer translations. The mine owners would have to bear the cost of sending them back, and this amounted to about thirty-five dollars a head, which they wanted to save. Edmund Davis, Hoover's fellow director on the Board of the *Chinese Engineering & Mining Company,* and one of the original plotters for the 'taking' of that enormous property, actually went to see the Kaiser and offered to sell him the Chinese for the German colony of South West Africa. The gall, audacity and inhumanity of this is something unbelievable. Hoover's firm had recruited and shipped over 50,000 of these unfortunates. After all, it was not such a bad business. There was a profit for the company of about twenty-five dollars a head. "Cruel as death, insatiate as the grave," are the words of the poet Montgomery, who attributes the ruthlessness of the slave dealer to his greed. "He buys, he sells,—he steals, he kills for gold."

CHAPTER THE NINTH

In the Name of the U. S. A.

LET us now go back a little. The crash of the notorious Whitaker Wright's *London & Globe Finance Company* had a sequel. The direct cause of his downfall had been the "ratting" of some stockbrokers who had conspired with Wright to make a corner in *Lake View* shares and had "let him down." The Official Receiver for the *London & Globe* sued these stockbrokers on behalf of the estate. In the course of this famous action tried in June 1902, some remarkable evidence was produced. It seems that Wright's accountant, Mr. Worters, before retiring on account of illness, had submitted him a draft balance sheet showing that the *London & Globe* was "in the red" to the extent of $500,000, but that after Worters' retirement another balance sheet was submitted on December 5th, showing a balance to the credit of the *London & Globe* of over $2,250,000. Wright's assistant accountant was David Anderson.

This gentleman, who could make liabilities appear as assets, was too much of a treasure to go without a job. Hoover grabbed him at once. Indeed, he never let him go and, when Hoover separated from Moreing in the beginning of 1908, the first condition he stipulated was that he should have Anderson. The Hoover firm of "expert" engineers was now well equipped. It included in London the partners, Moreing, Hoover and Wellsted, none of whom were qualified mining engineers, Dennis, another Stanford man who, like Wilson, had become an expert mining engineer by taking a degree in law, and Anderson the accountant. They called themselves mine managers and engineers, but were really, as Moreing described the firm, a large "financial" institution, and the word "financial," as we know, covers a multitude of sins.

Among the many companies floated by Wright's *London & Globe Finance Company,* there was the *Victorian Gold Estates, Limited,* founded in 1896 to exploit *Deep Leads* in the State of Victoria in Australia. *Deep Leads* (pronounced "leeds") were ancient underground river beds or gutters, hundreds of feet below the surface, buried by flows of lava or basalt, the courses of which could not be determined by the trend of the present watercourses owing to the drainage lines being altered by flows of basalt or deposits of newer layers of sand and gravel. At the end of 1900, the *Victorian Gold Estates* was divided up into two companies, the *London Valley Goldfields* and the *Moolort Goldfields,* with a combined capital of $7,500,000, all of which was lost to the unfortunate shareholders on the crash of the *London & Globe.* This was a "business" that appealed mightily to Hoover. Investors might come and want to see their lots in Silver Falls City. Drillings could be made of ordinary mine workings. But who could dispute about what there was or was not in underground river streams down there four hundred to seven hundred feet below ground level?

The *London & Globe* had held a large number of shares in the two above mentioned companies, as well as two thousand acres of adjoining claims. Through the good offices of Hoover's stockbroker associate, Govett, who was one of the Whitaker Wright crowd, Hoover's firm purchased these assets from the Official Receiver for a small sum and, in May 1903, floated the

London & Globe Deep Assets, Limited, with a capital of a million dollars in shares of one dollar each, so that the small people might bite. The shares acquired were, of course, worth nothing, and the two thousand acres of claims, which had never been proved in any way and which were given the fancy name of "Option Blocks," were worth just as much. In July, 1903, Hoover's firm reconstructed the *London Valley Goldfields* company and the *Moolort Goldfields* with a capital of $800,000 for each, "milking" the old shareholders by giving them partly paid shares in the new company. Indeed, at the meeting held on June 29, 1903, to arrange the reconstruction of the properties, Hoover spoke of their great value, although he had never even seen them. This incident alone is sufficient to show what this miracle man is capable of. They followed a similar procedure with the *Victorian Deep Leads,* another of these Whitaker Wright properties, which they reconstructed in exactly the same way in September, 1903, with a capital of $1,600,000. All these companies, although the properties were located in Victoria, were registered in New South Wales, so that Hoover and his gang could make use of the Waiver Clause in the By-laws, which had been declared illegal in England, and which would permit them to play fast and loose with the companies' funds without responsibility to the shareholders.

They had not done so badly, so far. They had taken in $1,000,000 in the *London & Globe Deep Assets Co.* for the so-called "Option Blocks," a property never proved and never worked, and another $600,000 or so from the partly paid shares issued to former shareholders in the other three companies. They now saw a chance of making a "killing."

— 170 —

Hoover brought over to Victoria from the United States a great geologist, Waldemar Lindgren, Chief of The U. S. Geological Survey, Western Section, the man whose pick he used to carry when on his vacations from Stanford. On September 11, 1903, six days before the arrival back in England to stand trial of his gambling partner, the forger Rowe, Hoover left England for Victoria to meet Lindgren.

Lindgren was, and is, a great geologist, and a very fine gentleman. But he had no idea that Hoover, no longer the raw rube he had known as a boy ten years before, was now a very sophisticated product. Lindgren brought his pick with him. But he did not require it. What was needed there was the "dowser" or twig, which many geologists have more faith in than in their so-called science. They went over the ground together, Lindgren and Hoover, with that miraculous twig. It was the Australian summer, the weather was quite hot. Again and again the thirst-quenching flask of firewater usually carried on such occasions was produced. The twig began to wiggle.

They were then on the Moolort property. They continued on to the adjoining Loddon Valley. For some reason or other that twig would just not stand still. On to the *Option Blocks,* which had never even been tested to see if there was a watercourse there or not. "All payable," the recorder set down. And last of all came the *Victorian Deep Leads.* By this time the twig had been thrown away. "Five miles of this lead should yield a profit of seventy-five dollars a foot." That meant a profit of almost $2,000,000 for a property where they never found one single grain of gold.

Lindgren, Chief of the U. S. Geological Survey, Western Section signed that report. Under ordinary circumstances this would be almost incredible. How could he estimate or imagine or suppose what was down there hundreds of feet underground, where there was no knowing how the watercourses ran or what they contained, except by diamond drilling foot by foot? He had been hoodwinked. He could only say, like Ralph Nichols in the *Perseverance* case: "They got me to do it."

A new company was now floated, under the high faluting name, *The Australian Commonwealth Trust*, with a capital of $1,250,000, to finance these "deep lead" companies, and a glowing prospectus was issued giving the report of the great expert Lindgren, Chief of the U. S. Geological Survey, endorsed by the self-appointed "expert," Hoover, telling the public of all those fabulous millions lying in the "deep leads" and only waiting to be pumped out. It also told of the $35,000,000 or so of gold that had, in bygone days, been extracted from the *Madame Berry Lead*, which was ever so many miles away, and actually printed and issued a map calling the whole system of 25 miles on which these claims were located the "Madame Berry Lead System," which was untrue. The prospectus did not tell the public that the large amount of gold won from the *Madame Berry* was obtained some fifty years before, and in shallow workings only a few feet deep, not hundreds of feet down in underground rivers, or that the Whitaker Wright companies which had had these properties for years had never won an ounce of gold from them, and that there was little prospect of their being able to do any better.

Indeed, the only asset they had of any value was the name Lindgren, Chief of the U. S. Geological Survey, and this was exploited to the limit. His report was printed in booklet form and widely circulated. Even a book, with maps, and containing his report, was published and put on the market. The *Lodden Deep Leads* (*Victoria*) *Limited*, another of these swindling "deep lead" propositions, which had been founded by the notorious Horatio Bottomley, joined hands with them and moved their offices, as Gardner's accountant had done, persistent campaign of misleading statements in the press, which lasted for years. Paid "puffs" appeared regularly, even in leading papers whose names have become symbols of business honesty and conservatism throughout the whole civilized world. What the value of this Bottomley company was can be gauged by the statement made by Mr. Crole Rees, one of the shareholders, at its meeting in June 1904, when he said that although the property was capitalized at three million dollars, he did not believe it was worth two hundred and fifty dollars. The result of this persistent "ballyhoo" was that in 1906 they actually forced the shares of the Australian Commonwealth Trust by their false reports and statements to a premium of nearly 300%, and the other companies to a lesser extent. How did they accomplish this? They had at that time been "working" the properties for three years and had not produced a single grain of gold. But at every meeting a trayful of gold nuggets was passed around, and invariably reference was made to the report of Lindgren of the U. S. Geological Survey. They were trading on the name of the United States.

Encouraged by the avidity of investors, anxious to throw their money down the "deep leads," the Hoover firm actually floated another company in December,

1906, the *Berry United Deep Leads,* with a capital of $1,250,000. A glowing prospectus, again featuring the report of the Chief of the U. S. Geological Survey, was issued. They took in the public's money to the extent of $250,000 in this "ramp" and issued a further $200,000 in debentures, although they knew by this time, as they had known right along, that the whole business was an absolute failure and fizzle.

Things had by now become so outrageous that the Victorian Government felt obliged to intervene, and decided to issue a special bulletin owing to the, as expressed by the *Australian Trading World,* flagrant misrepresentations in a section of the English press. The *Australian Mining Standard* of Melbourne, writing on this, said:

> "Consequent upon the wildly speculative and, in a large number of instances, misleading statements published in the London press in regard to the possibilities and prospects of the newer deep lead mining in certain parts of Victoria now largely controlled by Messrs. Bewick Moreing & Co., mining engineers, Mr. Stanley Hunter of the geological branch of the Victorian Mines department has written some explanations thereto."

In April, 1907, the Government of Victoria published and distributed in England and in Australia this report of Mr. Hunter which, in reserved language, shows up the promoters. In it he showed how facts were misrepresented. He referred to the opportunities for mismanagement. He called attention to the statements frequently appearing in the London papers, and which were obviously intended to mislead. The *Money Market Review,* in commenting on these swindles, wrote:

"It is evident that what the speculating public has to fear is not the lie direct, but the lie oblique; not the frank falsehood, but the suave misrepresentation, the deceitful deduction, the insidiously misleading inference."

It was, however, too late. The British public had already been bled to the extent of many millions. They had parted with their money on their faith in the U. S. Geological Survey.

Practically all this money had been pumped out of the pockets of British investors. The Australians had been warned by their newspapers. The great Australian paper, the Sydney *Bulletin* had occasion more than once to refer to these "promoting and gambling concerns" and their "crusade of lying." This paper also remarked on one occasion:

"Bewick Moreing aren't specially sensitive about losing other people's money, and they may do it at *Loddon Valley*."

And on another:

"With such concerns in the field, the garden variety of shareholder needs safeguarding. And publicity is the best safeguard available."

They knew what was going on down there in Victoria.

And what was done with all these millions, of which the shareholders never recovered a single cent? Ask Hoover and his friends. Spent on working the "deep leads"? Don't imagine it. The records of the Victorian Government show that the Option Blocks, for which the public had subscribed $1,000,000, was never worked at all. On the *Moolort Goldfields* and *Loddon Valley Goldfields* properties together, $410,000 was spent, and this included $40,000 borrowed from the Victorian Government, and never repaid. The working, too, was a record of inefficiency and mismanagement. At *Moolort,* Whitaker Wright's old company had sunk a shaft. Hoover had a beam engine pump set up there at great expense, and then it was found to be unsuitable and had to be "junked." He then had Cornish pumps installed and they pumped and pumped and pumped for nearly three years and then found that they were nowhere near the main "lead" at all. The great "expert" geologist didn't know how to locate it. He was just learning at the expense of the shareholders. Did he tell this to the shareholders? Bless your innocence, no. The trayful of gold nuggets was passed round at the company's meetings, and the shareholders were called on to put up more money. Such was the gall of this crowd that, a few months after the warning of the Victorian Government, we find them jacking up the shareholders of the various companies for more capital, the *Loddon Valley Goldfields* for $400,000, the *Moolort Goldfields* for $575,000, the *Victorian Deep Leads* for $400,000. They even had the audacity to apply for a loan of $100,000 to the Victorian Government, which lent then $40,000 against a mortgage on their machinery. Soon afterwards, they packed up, bag and baggage, and ran away, leaving the machinery in the hands of the Government, which only obtained $16,500 for it!

The *Victorian Deep Leads* is a story of similar disaster. Not one grain of gold was ever produced, except from the pockets of the English investors. This, too, was abandoned to its fate. And this was not all. They had a last flutter in November 1907, when they founded the *Prentice* and *Southern Deep Leads,* with a capital of over $1,000,000. Furthermore there was a "deep lead" property, the *Duke,* which was paying divi-

dends, and Hoover's firm obtained the management.
Adieu to dividends for evermore. From then on, the
story of the *Duke* was disaster. Another of these "leads"
they managed for other people was the *Cathcart,* and we
have the Chairman of that company's report to the effect
that Hoover's boys made a "terrible mess of things."
They actually lost the "lead," and it was only found
again when the Hoover crew ran away from the State,
abandoning all the properties and leaving the creditors
to collect their debts from that trayful of gold, if they
could find it.

Not one red cent of all their millions ever came back
to the unfortunate investors in the *Deep Leads of Victoria.* Hoover and his gang had pumped them dry, not
with Cornish pumps, but with the propaganda circulated
over a period of five years under cover of the Geological
Department of the United States of America.

CHAPTER THE TENTH

MANDARIN CHANG SAVES HIS HEAD AND HONOR

WE have seen how, in 1903, the Mandarin Chang Yen Mao was deprived of all his honors and titles by the Empress and ordered to recover for China the Kaiping mines and the port of Ching Wan Tao under penalty of losing his head, and how he instructed lawyers in England to take action in the law courts. This was the only remedy open, for China was not then in a military position to take back the mines by force in face of the might of England, which backed this outrage for the sake of the coal and coaling station and port. What importance was attached to them can be seen from the speech of Mr. Gibson Bowles, M. P., in the British House of Commons on February 2, 1904:

> "With regard to China and Japan * * * in any naval war, coal is the determining factor and we hold the coal."

The London lawyers instructed were, however, in a terrible quandary. They knew that England would not haul down the British flag from these mines, even if held by thieves. They were consequently afraid of presenting a claim of fraud and demanding the return of the properties. They felt obliged to claim only the enforcement of the Memorandum agreement of February 19, 1901, signed between Chang and Hoover, which had never been put into effect, and which was obviously never intended to be put into effect.

On May 7th, 1903, a writ was issued on behalf of Chang Yen Mao and the old Chinese company against Moreing, Bewick Moreing and Company (of which Hoover was a partner), and the new *English Chinese Engineering & Mining Company, Limited,* claiming a declaration that the memorandum agreement signed between Hoover and Chang was binding. Hoover was not specifically named as a defendant (although he was a defendant as member of Bewick Moreing & Co.), due to the fact that the alteration he had had made in the Deed of Trust given him by Detring made him appear as the agent for Moreing. But as this was an equity case, and, by permission of the Court, the pleadings were amended to include a charge of fraud on the part of Hoover, he, as Trustee, thus really became the main defendant in the action. It has always been maintained by Hoover's paid propagandists that he was only an innocent witness and not a defendant in that famous lawsuit, but the facts are just the opposite. Any equity lawyer will understand this. Besides, here is an affidavit of Hoover himself to prove it:

I, Herbert Hoover of 20 Copthall Avenue in the City of London a member of the firm of Bewick Moreing & Company of the same place one of the above mentioned Defendants make oath and say as follows:

1. I have read what purports to be an affidavit of Thomas Henry Kingsley sworn herein on the 31st of October, 1904. Mr. White Cooper who is referred to in paragraph 6 of the said affidavit acted in the matter in the first instance upon my personal instructions as solicitor for the Defendant Charles Algernon Moreing and continued to act in that capacity until the month of February, 1901, when he accepted the retainer of the Oriental Syndicate Limited and the Defendant Company for whom he and his firm have ever since to the best of my belief continued to act

down to the present time in relation to the matters in question in this action and it was in his capacity as Solicitor for and on behalf of the said Oriental Syndicate and the Defendant Company that he prepared the documents of the 19th of February, 1901, referred to in paragraphs 11 and 12 of the Statement of Claim and accordingly on behalf of the said Charles Algernon Moreing I should object to his giving any evidence in the matter on the ground of privilege and as I verily believe that the Oriental Syndicate and the Defendant Company would take the same objection.

2. With reference to Dr. Tenney I say that this gentleman was personally employed by me as my Interpreter for the purpose of checking the Interpreter who was employed by the Plaintiff Chang and that he took no part in any of the negotiations prior to the signature of the above mentioned documents save in so far as he checked the interpretation of the Plaintiff Chang's Interpreter and the transcription of certain of the documents. To the best of my recollection he was only employed in the matter as aforesaid at the very last stage after all the negotiations had been definitely concluded and was only present at the interview immediately prior to the signing of the documents for a few hours. I verily believe the said Dr. Tenney could not give any material evidence in the matter except as to the accuracy of the translations and which as I verily believe are not in dispute and I submit that it would be a waste of time and expense to take his evidence on Commission or otherwise and that if he were really required as a witness

and his expenses paid and had been applied to by the Plaintiff's he would have been willing to have come over to attend the trial.

3. Ever since the institution of this action which involves the most serious allegations against myself personally and which commenced as far back as the 7th of May, 1903, I have through the Defendants' solicitors been urging and endeavouring that it should be either brought on for trial with all possible dispatch or dismissed for want of prosecution but the Plaintiffs have consistently up to the present time succeeded by their tactics in frustrating my efforts and every step that has been taken by them since the delivery of the Statement of Claim down to and including the setting of the case down for trial has been in consequence of orders of this Honourable Court which I have been forced to apply for by reason of their dilatory procedure and I verily believe that the present application for the examination of witnesses in China has been made in furtherance of a desire and intention on the part of the Plaintiffs to keep the act on foot as long as they possibly can without bringing it on for trial and I verily believe that the effect of an order for such examination would be to inordinarily delay the proceedings and thus effectuate the said object.

4. In the month of September last fully believing that the trial of this action would take place at the end of October or the commencement of November or that it would be dismissed for want of prosecution, I arranged with the representatives of several important Companies

for whom my firm act as Mining Engineers to
proceed to Australia with my family for the purposes of the business of such Companies and accordingly in the aforesaid belief I booked passage
for myself and my family by the S/S *Mongolian*
which will sail for Australia on or about the
22nd of December and it is absolutely necessary
that I should fulfill this engagement. It is most
important to me and my Co-Defendants that the
trial of this action should either take place at
once or that the action should be dismissed before my departure.

5. The case was set down for trial by the
order of Mr. Justice Joyce in the month of May
last and I verily believe that the Plaintiff Chang
and the said Gustav Detring have been kept fully
informed of its position on the Cause List and
that it was expected that it would be reached for
trial either in the beginning of August or at the
end of October and they have had ample time,
opportunity, notice and warning to come over to
England to attend the trial and I verily believe
that the telegrams which purport to have been
dispatched by them upon the suggestion of their
agent Mr. Kingsley (as shown by his letters to
Mr. Hawksley of the 6th and 9th August last)
promising "to be in London for the trial if the
date is fixed for December or January" were not
sent in good faith and that they do not intend
coming over to attend the trial even if it were
fixed to take place in December or January next.
The said telegrams were sent at a time on the
9th of August when it was expected that the case
would be in the List for trial and for the pur-

pose as I believe of securing further delay.

Sworn at St. Stephen's Chambers.

Telegraph St. in the City of London the 1st November, 1904.

Before me

CHARLES STEELE,
Commissioner of Oaths.

(signed) Herbert Hoover.

Senator Lenroot of Wisconsin, who in 1928 issued a signed statement for publication that he had read all the evidence in the case and that Hoover was only a witness, also must have understood this. As a matter of fact, a certain young gentleman now connected much more closely with Mr. Hoover, approached the London Lawyers of Chang some few years ago with a view to buying the record of evidence in the case. A member of the firm of lawyers told the writer that he was "astounded" at such a request, and asked if they do such things in America.

The statement of claim was presented by Chang's lawyers on June 17, 1903, but not for over four months did Hoover's firm put in a defense. And what did they plead? In paragraph 16 of their defense they pleaded:

"These Defendants deny that the said Herbert C. Hoover and Chevalier De Wouters or either of them executed the said memorandum as agents or agent for the Defendants or any or either of them or that such memorandum was or was understood or intended to be an agreement. If, and in so far as the same contained any representations (which is not admitted) the same were merely statements of intention which the said Herbert C. Hoover and Chevalier honestly believed to exist."

— 183 —

And what did the Company, for which Hoover "took" the mines, plead? Paragraph 8 of their pleadings reads:

"The Defendant Company does not admit that any such memorandum as is referred to in paragraph 12 of the Statement of Claim was ever executed. If any such memorandum was in fact executed, the same was not executed by the said Herbert C. Hoover and Chevalier De Wouters or either of them as the agents or agent of the Defendant Company, but was executed entirely without the knowledge, consent or authority of, and is ultra vires of, the Defendant Company and its Directors."

Could that be beaten for audacity? Both firms absolutely repudiated the Memorandum signed by Hoover, and denied he was their agent! Remember that when these pleadings were filed Hoover was a partner of Bewick Moreing & Company, and not only a director, but the "main cheese" of the *Chinese Engineering & Mining Company, Limited.* Bear in mind these pleadings of his and his associates when you read the evidence he gave in this lawsuit.

Every artifice known to the law was employed to defer the action from coming to trial. Motions for this, motions for that, in efforts to wear out the patience of the Chinaman.

Meanwhile, the firm which had obtained possession of these vast properties, secure under the protection of the British flag, continued working them with "preliminary lawyer" Wilson as "expert" Engineer-in-Chief. In December, 1903, Yuan Shi Kai, the great Viceroy of Chi-li, received secret orders from the Imperial Court to try and recover for China at least the port of Ching Wan Tao, which property had not been included in the transfer executed by Chang, but the title deeds of which had been taken "by force" for the British Empire. However, the British bulldog had its teeth on that bone, and what a sweet one! *"In any naval war, coal is the determining factor, and we have the coal."* An idea of the protection afforded by England to these people can be gained from the fact that during the Russian-Japanese war of 1904 they did not even trouble to insure their steamers against war risks. Three of their vessels—the *Providence, Hsiping* and *Peiping* were captured by the Japanese actually carrying contraband but, instead of being condemned, they were released with apologies. We have seen how in the same year 1904 they were given the monopoly for the recruiting and shipping of the Chinese slaves to South Africa. They could do much as they pleased under the sheltering wing of the British vulture.

What chance had Chang of ever recovering these huge properties for China in an English Court? All he could hope for was a declaration recognizing the rights of the Chinese in the new Company. If he failed in that, his life would be forfeited. Before leaving for England, at the end of 1904, the Empress bestowed on him a Mandarin's button of the third class, so that he could, at least, appear before the British Court as a nobleman. He arrived in London in December 1904, accompanied by a retinue of servants, and took up residence at Morley's Hotel. From the windows there he could look out on Trafalgar Square, where the huge stone lions symbolized British power and the Nelson shaft flung a challenge to the world.

The case came on for trial in January and February, 1905, before Mr. Justice Joyce. It was one of the most famous actions of the time, not only for the vast properties involved, but for the great array of counsel, which included the leading members of the Bar, Rufus Isaacs, afterwards Lord Chief Justice of England, being among those appearing for the Hoover firm, and Mr. Haldane, later on Lord Chancellor, for the new English Company for which Hoover had grabbed the mines. There was more, too, at stake than that. The dignity of a nation, which had been despoiled, and the fate of a Chinese nobleman, who had been ordered to win or to lose his head.

It was the morning of the 17th of January, 1905. "Order in the Court!" bawled the Court officer. There was silence like gloom. The English are great respectors of the majesty of the law. Chang Yen Mao was there, attired in all the glory of the East, in wonderful garments of silk and brocade, ornamented with jewels, and wearing a black skull cap, in which was set a pearl the size of a pigeon's egg, in itself worth a fortune, a gift from the Empress in his younger days. He was then about fifty, over six feet in height, a mountain of a man, and as keenly intelligent as remarkable in physique. He overshadowed everyone else in the Court by his commanding presence and the magnificence of his attire. The Judge himself felt that this personage could not be treated as any common plaintiff, and provided Chang with an armchair near the Bench to show that he respected this man of authority from a strange land. Day after day the Court was crowded, the public being mostly interested in the personage of Chang and his fabulous garments. Few seemed to realize that here sat a man actually on trial for his life.

Chang was the first witness, speaking in Chinese, and having his evidence translated by the famous Chinese scholar, Sir Walter Hillier. He spoke with great volubility. He told of what a joke Hoover had been when in his employment as an "engineer," of the reasons why he had agreed to putting the great mining property under British protection, and of the negotiations preceding the signing of the deed of transfer, and the memorandum agreement of Hoover of the 19th of February, 1901. He told how Hoover had threatened him on that occasion, that if he did not sign, Hoover would have him broken by the American and British Governments, and, on Chang still refusing to sign, used such a filthy expression to his former employer, the mandarin who had saved his life during the siege of Tientsin by sheltering him, that Sir Walter Hillier did not venture to translate it in Court. Chang, however, wanted the Court to know how vile the insult was, and endeavored to show by gesticulation the nature of Hoover's expletive, to the great astonishment and amusement of the public. What an impression Chang's evidence made on the Court is shown by the Judge's summing up on March 1, 1905:

> "It has not been shown that His Excellency Chang has been guilty of any breach of faith or of any impropriety at all, which is more than can be said for some of the other parties concerned."

Detring then gave evidence, largely confirming Chang, and telling how Moreing came over at the end of 1901 with his bribe of more than 50,000 shares, and how he, Detring, had deposited it in the Bank and made a declaration before the British Consul of the circumstances under which it was given. He also told the story of his negotiations with Hoover, of how he had given Hoover the Deed of Trust and made the condition that Hoover should not form part of any new company that was formed, of how Hoover had had the Deed of Trust changed, and of Hoover's letter of February 9, 1901, in which he assured Detring that the control of the Company would be in the China Board and that Chang would be Director General for life.

Then the defense opened up. Mr. Haldane K. C. at once attempted to influence the Court by showing that the British Government was involved. This is what he said:

> "The Court had not to deal with any ordinary case but one of far-reaching diplomatic consequences."

To the honor of British Justice, as we shall see, Judge Joyce was not impressed by this threat. He was there to maintain the great British tradition of justice in the Law Courts, which has enabled England to maintain her prestige throughout the world, the meanest of her subjects knowing that they will always get fair play before an English Court of Justice. When it was apparent that Judge Joyce was not a man to be intimidated even by the Foreign Office, Mr. Levett, one of the counsel for Chang, asked leave to amend the statement of claim by alleging that Mr. Detring was induced to agree to the alterations in the agreement by the misrepresentations of Moreing and Hoover. He also desired to add that the plaintiff Chang was further induced to execute the indenture of transfer by the misrepresentations of Moreing and Hoover. We now quote from the *Financial Times* of February 10, 1905:

> "Mr. Hughes objected to the proposed amendments and said he should want to see the particulars of the misrepresentations alleged.
>
> Mr. Haldane, for the Defendant Company, also objected.

His Lordship—Mr. Levitt did not say the misrepresentations were fraudulent.

Mr. Levett: I did mean fraudulent misrepresentation.

His Lordship said that when he gave judgment it would be time enough for him to say whether he allowed the amendment or not. The case would probably go to the Court of Appeal, and though somewhat late in the day, it was right that Mr. Levett should make the application. Mr. Levett knew his business, but he doubted the wisdom of saying 'fraudulent misrepresentation.'

Mr. Levett: I will bear my own burden. I rely on what was said in the letter of the 9th November from Moreing to Detring and that of the 9th February, 1901, from Hoover to Detring. I say these letters were wickedly untrue."

Hoover was the first witness for the defense. He made a very poor impression on the stand. His apologists in this case, too numerous to mention, all stoutly affirm that by his straightforward testimony he helped to elucidate the case. But the facts do not bear them out.

The only sound point in his whole evidence was when he admitted that in the matter of raising $2,500,000 debentures, the China Board had not been consulted. And remember Hoover was on his oath in a Court of Law.

The evidence for the defense of J. Bromley Eames, the lawyer whom Hoover had employed to draw up the Deed of Trust, was also very interesting. In the course of his testimony he swore:

"On the ratification by Moreing and the formation of the Company, Hoover became trustee for the new Company. When Hoover asked him to make alterations, he certainly was not told of the ratification, nor did he think that the Company was formed."

When asked: "If you had known that the Company had been incorporated and that Hoover was trustee for it, would you have consented to make the alterations without the Company being represented?"

Eames replied: "I do not think I should."

Q. "Did you understand the Company was going to issue 1,000,000 shares without receiving a penny?"

A. "No."

The solicitor's position was that Hoover had even flummoxed his own lawyer.

The fact of his being trustee for the new company made any alterations in the Deed of Trust illegal, and all the subsequent proceedings fraudulent.

The hearings were not concluded until February 11th, 1905, and in the course of them was brought out the whole story of the "taking" of the mines (as the Judge called it), and of how the 625,000 shares were divided among the gang, everyone getting his share, down to Mr. Bussy of the *Westminster Gazette* and Mr. Madge of the *Globe* who had agitated for the grabbing of Ching Wan Tao, and to Mr. Eames the lawyer who had drawn up the Deed of Trust for Hoover, and afterwards made the alterations in it, that were in reality illegal. The Judge was shocked. But his was not a Criminal Court but a Court of Equity and all he had to pass on was the claim before him. Here is his judgment where he gave Chang what he claimed, but left it open to him to sue at any time the defendant Hoover on the grounds of fraudulent misrepresentation.

In the High Court of Justice
(Chancery Division)
Mr. Justice Joyce.
Wednesday, the 1st day of March, 1905.
Between His Excellency CHANG YEN MAO and The
CHINESE ENGINEERING AND MINING COMPANY of TIENTSIN,
Plaintiffs.

and

CHARLES ALGERNON MOREING, BEWICK MOREING AND COM-
PANY, and THE CHINESE ENGINEERING AND MINING COM-
PANY, LIMITED,

Defendants.

THIS ACTION coming on for trial on the 17th,
18th, 19th, 24th, 25th, 26th, and 31st days of
January and the 1st, 2nd, 3rd, 7th, 8th, 9th, 10th
and 11th days of February 1905, before this Court
in the presence of Counsel for the Plaintiffs and
for the Defendants and upon reading the pleadings in this action and the certificate of the funds
and upon hearing the evidence of the several
persons named in the schedule A hereto on their
examination orally before this Court on the days
mentioned in the second column and upon production to them of the several exhibits specified
in the third column of such schedule and upon
reading the correspondence and other documents
specified in the schedule B hereto and upon hearing what was alleged by Counsel for the Plaintiffs
and for the Defendants.

This Court did order that this action should
stand for judgment and the same standing in the
paper for judgment this day accordingly in the
presence of Counsel for the Plaintiffs and for the
Defendants.

THIS COURT DOTH DECLARE that the memorandum dated the 19th February, 1901, in the pleadings mentioned is binding as against the Defendants and that the Defendant Company was not and is not entitled to take or retain possession or control of the property comprised in the indenture of transfer dated the 19th February, 1901, also mentioned in the pleadings or the benefits thereof without complying with and performing the provisions of and obligations contained in the said memorandum.

AND THIS COURT DOTH ORDER that the Defendants the *Chinese Engineering and Mining Company, Limited,* do pay to the Plaintiffs their costs of this action to be taxed by the Taxing Master Bouchier Francis Hawksley, the solicitors for the Plaintiffs personally undertaking in the event of the judgment being reversed on appeal to abide by any order the Court may make as to their refunding to the Defendants, the *Chinese Engineering and Mining Company, Limited,* the said costs.

But this judgment is to be without prejudice to any action or other proceedings that may be brought or taken by or on behalf of the Defendants, the *Chinese Engineering and Mining Company, Limited,* or against any of the Defendants by any person in reference to the promotion or formation of the Defendant Company or the issue of any shares or debentures of the Defendant Company or any of the transactions of the Defendant Company or its directors, and is also to be without prejudice to any action or other proceedings that may be brought or taken by the Plaintiffs or either of them upon the ground of any alleged misrepresentation, whether fraudulent or otherwise, contained in the letter of the 9th November, 1900, from the Defendant Charles Algernon Moreing to Gustav Detring or the letter of the 9th February, 1901, from Herbert Charles Hoover to Gustav Detring, copies whereof are contained in the said bundle of correspondence.

And it is ordered that any question of damage that may arise in respect of any default or delay in the performance of the obligations and provisions contained in the said memorandum of the 19th February, 1901, he reserved.

And it is ordered that the funds in Court be dealt with as directed by the Payment Schedules I and II hereto.

And any of the parties are to be at liberty to apply as they may be advised.

Chang was vindicated. He returned to China and was restored to his honors and titles.

This did not mean, however, that the judgment won in the British Court had done more than vindicate Chang's honor. The Hoover Moreing Davis Turner gang in charge of the *Chinese Engineering & Mining Company, Limited* were not the ones to disgorge anything. But the Chinese are patient. Yuan Shi Kai, Viceroy of Chi-li, brought over a British mining engineer and commenced mining operations at Lanchow and Kailan in the vicinity of the Kaiping mines, gradually building up a formidable competition to the *Chinese Engineering & Mining Company, Limited,* and eventually the latter Company had to come to terms and amalgamate with the Kailan Company in 1912. The importance attached to this event by the British Government is evidenced by the fact that it was the subject of a special

Treaty with China. and it was then, and only then, that Chang Yen Mao was indemnified for the loss of his position in the old Chinese Company from which Hoover had "taken" the Kaiping mines. The new English Company had to disgorge 1,000,000 Taels (about $700,-000) as compensation for Chang, and a further 900,000 Taels for other liabilities that Hoover's Company had conveniently overlooked. On the formation of the *Chinese Engineering & Mining Co., Ltd.,* in 1900 Hoover had broken his promise to Detring that he would not form part of that Company, but the Chinese have long memories and, in 1912, when the amalgamation was put through with the Lanchow Mining Company, Chang Yen Mao saw to it that the new company should get along without the peculiar services of Hu-Hua, otherwise Herbert Hoover, Esquire. Hoover was thrown out.

CHAPTER THE ELEVENTH

The Zinc ("Stink") Corporation

IN the invisible world that surrounds us, there is nothing so real as a smell. We cannot avoid it, we cannot forget it, and, dear reader, if you were a shareholder of the Zinc Corporation in the year 1907, you would never be likely to forget that malodorous company. The recovery of zinc is, of course, associated with the most repugnant of nasal stimuli. But it is the moral stench that is here referred to.

Before Hoover had fairly got his pumps going on his *Deep Leads of Victoria,* in his endeavor to extract gold from the underground rivers, or rather, to pump it from the pockets of the investors, he had a new major scheme on hand. Just across the border from Victoria, there were in the Broken Hill district of New South Wales great silver and lead mines, and on the surface were enormous heaps of slag or tailings discarded by the mines, but containing considerable quantities of lead, zinc and even silver. Hoover thought that these Australians, who discarded this slag, did not know enough to come in out of the rain. Or else, and more probably, he considered that the prospects of recovering the ores from the slag was something that would appeal to the speculator.

In July 1905, after the hearing of the Chang case, he left via the United States for New Zealand to inspect the *Talisman* mine, of which his firm were managers and he a director. From New Zealand he came over to Victoria and with Govett and Lionel Robinson, the stockjobber we read about in the *Boulder Deep* scandal,

secured, under the name of the Hill Syndicate, options
to purchase about two million tons of these tailings at
a price of about a dollar per ton. And then, on October
1905, he floated a company in Victoria with a capital
of $1,750,000 of which $1,200,000 was subscribed by the
public, $400,000 of shares being allotted to the pro-
moters for the "benefit" of their contracts for the tailings. This was the little bit of fat which the men who
strike these happy ideas for making millions reserve
for themselves without any base cash consideration.
Now they had to have a mine to go with the tailings.
In November 1905, they registered the *Broken Hill
South Blocks* with a capital of a million dollars, a half
share in this mine having been obligingly bought by
Govett with funds of the *Lake View Consols*. Both of
these companies were registered in Victoria, so that
the promoters might make use of the notorious Waiver
clause, which had been declared illegal in England,
and the effect of which was to enable the directors to
do what they very well liked with the assets of a company. They then decided on a smelting plant to go
with the mine and the tailings and complete the outfit, and they accordingly, in December 1905, registered
the Australian Smelting Company, with a capital of
$1,750,000 and $500,000 debentures. This project was
highly endorsed by Hoover and in it we find Hoover for
the first time associated with Richard Tilden Smith, the
man who helped Hoover to "put over" the *Burma Mines,*
and later in 1921, when Hoover was Secretary of Commerce, whipped Hoover to a standstill in the fight
for control of that vast property. Smith was in himself a "one man gang." Here is a reference to Smith
from the great English journal *The Economist* of April
7th, 1906:

"Another curious development of the financing syndicate which has been in evidence this week is the Share Guarantee Trust, which has taken an active part in the reconstruction of Rhodesia, Limited. At the statutory meeting of the new company on Wednesday a shareholder expressed doubt as to whether the trust had any real existence, whereupon 'Mr. Tilden Smith stated that within the last 18 months the Share Guarantee Trust had dealt with the rearrangement and construction of companies having a capital of £8,500,000, and had raised upwards of £2,000,000 during the same period.' This recital of the magnitude of the trust's operations was no doubt impressive, but an examination of the records at Somerset House reveals the fact that the issued capital of the concern comprises 40,007 £1 shares, 40,000 of which stand in the name of Mr. Richard Tilden Smith, who is the sole director. It is rather remarkable, after Mr. Smith's description of the operations of the Trust, to find the following paragraph in the report of the Paringa Mines, which was recently issued:—

"The balance sheet shows that of £3,095 due on account of 30,950 shares issued, only £1,543 has been received, leaving £1,551, with interest thereon, still due, and that these 30,950 shares have been forfeited. 30,754 of these shares were held by the New Century Trust, Limited, of which one of this company's directors (Mr. R. Tilden Smith) was managing director, and applications for payments having been ineffectual, the board has much to its regret, been obliged to take legal proceedings to recover the amount due."

"The ways of company promoting are indeed wonderful, and the facts we have cited above show how desirable it is that investors, when they see the intervention of a syndicate invoked in a prospectus, should investigate the position of that syndicate before involving themselves in the enterprise."

The Zinc Corporation now proceeded to erect a plant on the grounds of the British *Broken Hill* mine, whose tailings they had contracted for, and Hoover, naively imagining that the concentration of zinc was something like shelling peas, personally engaged a smelter, A. L. Queneau of the New Jersey Smelting & Refining Company, to go out and smelt the peas. When Queneau arrived, he found that the peas were not shelled and that it was one hell of a job to shell them. As a matter of fact, these tailings consisted of combinations of zinc, lead and silver with the "gangue" or stone, and the problem of separating the metals was one of the greatest of that period. The great silver mines in the Broken Hill district had been experimenting with this very problem for some time, and there were several processes in the field, as Hoover could have found out by enquiring, all based on the "flotation" principle. This wonderful idea of mineral "flotation" which has added so much to the wealth of nations was the invention of a Chicago woman school teacher, the principle being that mineral sulphides finely crushed are held in suspension by the bubbles given off in an acid bath, thus forming a froth or scum containing the mineral which floats on the surface, and can thus be removed. Of the processes then being tried out in *Broken Hill* there were four principal ones, the *Potter, De Bavay, Elmore* and *Cattermole.* Hoover had the in-

vestors' money to experiment with and, after trying
everything from magnetic separators to vacuum cleaners,
let Queneau have a shot at the Potter process, used on
the neighbouring *Broken Hill Proprietary* mine. Queneau did pretty well, and, on October 19th, 1906, the Zinc
Corporation issued a statement from its Secretary
David Anderson, the former accountant of Whitaker
Wright, telling the shareholders of the wonderful results obtained by Queneau and showing that he was
able to recover in the concentrates 81% of the zinc, 55%
of the lead and 55% of the silver. These concentrates
are concentrated forms of the ore or tailings, rich enough
in mineral in their concentrated form to undergo the
operation of smelting, when the pure metal is obtained.
Good boy, Queneau. The shares jumped in value.

This afforded another opportunity of extracting some
cash from the shareholders and, at the end of October,
the Zinc Corporation issued the following circular:

> "In view of the extremely satisfactory results
> of the treatment on a working scale of the Com-
> pany's tailings, it is proposed to increase its
> Capital to £500,000."

The shareholders were accordingly "jacked up" for
a further $1,000,000 by the issue of 150,000 new shares
at a premium of 25%. This provided more money for
"experimenting" with.

There were two other processes, however, being used
on nearby mines. These were the Elmore and the Cattermole and when it was found out that they were giving
better results than those obtained by Queneau and at
a lower cost, this put another complexion on the situation. Hoover's elder brother Theodore, who had gotten
tired of typesetting had also obtained a diploma from
Stanford for his knowledge of elementary geology and

had set up as a mining engineer. In 1906, he had been wandering all around Mexico, looking either for a mine or a job but without success, when brother Herbert "wangled" him into the position of general manager of *Minerals Separation, Limited,* the firm which owned the Cattermole "flotation' process. Just as Herbert was an "engineering" expert, so Theodore was now miraculously converted into a "flotation" expert. But he made up for his want of knowledge of the subject by being in a position to inform Herbert of the highly successful results being obtained by both the Elmore and Cattermole processes, which were practically similar. Hoover and Govett did not hesitate in making a decision. With this information, were they to make a fortune in those millions of tons of tailings for the more than two thousand investors who had put up their savings to finance the experimental stages of the company? Don't imagine anything of the kind. These small investors were not accustomed to wealth and must not be exposed to temptation. There must be no profits for them. The insiders decided to grab the company for themselves. They started selling Zinc Corporation shares.

The word was passed around that the Potter process was a failure. It was not a failure in the *Broken Hill Proprietary* mine. But it was known that everything was in a kind of a mess at the Zinc Corporation plant, where they were even pumping sulphuric acid liquor through ordinary cast iron centrifugal pumps, supplied by the great expert, who apparently did not know that acid attacked iron. The trouble had to be blamed on someone. They fired Queneau in March 1907, saying that he was a failure. Queneau flatly denied this. But alarm began to spread and the shares which had risen in February to twelve and a half dollars each fell in March to seven. Then the Chief Engineer Faulls was dismissed. The shares dropped further. Shareholders, who enquired at the company's offices as to the cause of the break in the shares, were given no information whatever. By July they had broken the value of the Zinc Corporation shares to twenty-five cents, a drop of 98% in value in five months. London stockbrokers, realizing the dirty work that was being done, promptly dubbed the company the *Stink Corporation*. Ugly rumours began to spread about Hoover and Govett wrecking the company they were directors of, for the purpose of gaining complete control, and it was thought at one time that there would be a Government prosecution. But, as we have seen in the *Boulder Deep* and *Perseverance* and *Golden Horseshoe* scandals, these "gentlemen" were immune. The *Bulletin* of Sydney, the great newspaper of New South Wales, where the plant was located, has described the situation in verse. The "Bull" referred to is John Bull the British investor.

ZINCS

Now speak Sorrow!
  All the shares—
And tomorrow
  All the bears
Can beg or borrow —
  Go to Bull!
  He is full!
  Full of Zincs!
  Full of Zincs!
That's why he drinks;
  Hence his sorrow.
Bought them up to fifty
  bob;

(Now, if you're inclined to
  rob,
You may net just one and
  six)
  Sad tomorrow!
Fifty bob to nearly nix-
Zincs!
Stinks!
Now the office goes to
Bull!!
He is full!
Full of Zincs—
Though the awful fact he
blinks

Taking in despair to drinks;
Hear Bull's boodle as it clinks
While Bull sadly pays for Zincs
Sellers playing lofty jinks.
  Each his profit loudly chinks,
Made of Zincs—
Name that stinks
Worse than many kitchen sinks,
Bad as minks!
  Zinks!!

The *Rialto,* a London Stock Exchange sheet, had some very sarcastic comments on this market wrecking. On July 10, 1907, it wrote:

> "Zinc Corporation have abandoned all old processes as unsatisfactory. Have bought 2 vacuum cleaners and start them tomorrow morning. Perhaps they will extract something. You can sell my shares at best price."

A week later:

> "Hail Columbia Hoover has arrived back from his long trip to Australia, so we ought soon to know something about the Zinc Corporation and Broken Hill ventures. Wake up, Hoover. We are all broke."

It was on July 17th, 1907, that the *Rialto* let loose its bitterest jibe:

> "Hail Columbia is naturally very vexed at the report in circulation to the effect that he has made a large sum of money by bearing Zinc Corporation shares. It is really scandalous that such rumours should be spread, particularly in a case such as this, as Hail Columbia loathes speculation and, even if he did not, the terms of his partnership in Bewick Moreing and Company would prevent him from speculating."

To appreciate the irony of that paragraph, one must

remember that the writer of it was perfectly familiar with the *Great Fingall* speculation and forgeries, the *Golden Horseshoe, Boulder Deep, Perseverance* and other "ramps" of Hoover, and was just "rubbing it in." An idea of the reputation of the Hoover, Govett, Robinson crowd can be gained from a paragraph that must have slipped in unnoticed in the *Mining Magazine* a publication founded by Hoover and the Rickards, in the form of a newsletter from Melbourne regarding the Broken Hill South Blocks amalgamation with the Zinc Corporation:

> "So far the ups and downs of its shares in the market have indicated a manipulative power by some crowd that no one on this side of the equator wishes to meet in the dark."

On July 30, 1907, a meeting of the Zinc Corporation was held in London, and Mr. Govett showed the shareholders what a desperate plight they were in. A new plant would be required, which they would have to buy from the Elmore people, as the Cattermole process which they had tried out did not seem to be adapted to their grade of tailings. They had already had to borrow $150,000. The first portion of the new plant would cost $250,000, and there would be other large payments to meet. New capital would be needed, but he loved the shareholders too much to suggest a reconstruction, and make a call on them for more money. He thought the best plan would be to issue some new shares. But, on account of the desperate situation of the company, these new shares would have to be given special privileges as an inducement for subscribers to come in. He accordingly suggested the issuing of 182,-000 Preference shares of one pound ($5) each, these preference shares being entitled to the first 100%

earned, and to a 20% cumulative preference dividend thereafter, and then sharing equally with the ordinary shares in any further dividend earned. These new preference shares would also have three votes to each one vote held by the ordinary shares. Finally, the shareholders were told that Hoover's firm (Bewick Moreing & Co.) and Lionel Robinson had "magnanimously" offered to guarantee 100,000 of these preference shares. Of course, the insiders, knowing that all was now plain sailing, grabbed the preference shares, which gave them not only the profits, but the control of the company through the votes. They then knew positively that the tailings could be worked at a considerable profit, and that there were millions to be earned. But not for the original investors in the company. These were to be left, as Govett expressed it, with just a thread of hope.

The original shareholders had been ruthlessly frozen out of their interest, and the "insiders" now had absolute control of the corporation. Realizing too late the trick that had been put over on them, two of the shareholders, Victor Lawson and Grant, started a collection of shillings and sixpences among the other unfortunate shareholders, who were mostly poor people, with a view to instituting proceedings for the prosecution of Hoover and Govett. But the collectors were bamboozled, and the wreckers escaped scot free.

Hoover and Govett now went boldly to the front, assured of success. They installed an Elmore plant of sixteen units capable of treating five hundred tons of zinc tailings a day, and contracted for the sale of the output of zinc concentrates to the firm of Aron Hirsch & Son of Halberstadt, Germany, until 1919. They had now no need for the smelting works at Port Kembla, and the Australian Smelting Company was closed down without any notice before it had ever started work, at a loss to the share and debenture holders of over a million dollars and to the Victorian Government of a hundred thousand dollars, which had been spent in jetties and wharves for the company. Like Arabs, they folded up their tents at Port Kembla, and silently crept away. It was their usual method.

The newly equipped company at once began to show good earnings, and to avoid having to pay too much of the profits in dividends on the ordinary shares, the value of these was reduced in 1909 from five to four dollars and, when the amalgamation with the *Broken Hill South Blocks* mine was put through in 1911 at an enormous profit for the "insiders," the nominal value of the ordinary shares was further reduced to two and a half dollars. If it could be helped, these "ordinary" holders should not get any dividend at all. Then, when profits became larger, Hoover and Govett, the managing directors, decided not to demoralize the shareholders by giving them too much of the profits, but to make the corporation "an ordinary investment trust with ordinary powers of investment and of underwriting issues which are exercised by the successful investment trusts."

This meant simply that Hoover and Govett intended to do with the shareholders' money of the *Zinc Corporation* what they had already been doing with that of the *Lake View Consols,* lending each other money for market operations and investing the rest of the company's profits in ventures, in most of which they were themselves interested, and which, if "plums," became their personal property, but, if "culls," became the property of the corporation. We find that in 1912, the *Zinc Corporation* had already lent out $585,000 to God knows who, for God knows what, as they did not give the names of the borrowers. By 1914 their "investments" on behalf of the *Zinc Corporation* had reached the great total of $1,600,000, which should have gone to the shareholders in dividends. A list of the investments on that date shows that the majority of them were worthless, consisting mainly of depreciated or valueless railroad stock of A. M. Grenfell, the banker gambler, with whom Hoover was then associated in other shady enterprises, or of shares or debentures in some of Hoover's wildcat schemes, such as the *Barrier South, British Sulphur, Eastern Trading* and *Granville Mining,* connected with the great Klondyke swindle, and *Inter-Californian Trust* and *Western Ocean Syndicate,* connected with Hoover's attempts to grab the independent oil lands of California for England.

In July 1911, Hoover and Govett brought off a great "coup" with the amalgamation of the *South Blocks* mine with the *Zinc Corporation,* and they accordingly registered a new company under the same name in England, but containing the notorious Discovery Clause, which we have seen used in the *Chinese Engineering & Mining Company,* and which had the effect of preventing shareholders from seeing the books of their own companies. They must be blindfolded, too. The new company now abandoned the Elmore flotation process for the Cattermole, which they had formerly condemned. However, brother Theodore Hoover was manager of the *Minerals Separation Company,* which owned the Cattermole patent, and an order for a new outfit of machinery would do him no harm. Theodore had at this time taken into his employment another Stanford man, a classmate of his named J. M. Hyde, who suddenly turned up at Butte, Montana, in 1913 with a "flotation" plant of his own, which he sold to the *Butte & Superior Mining Company.* Of course, Hyde learned all about this enormously valuable process while in the employment of the *Minerals Separation Company* under Theodore Hoover. But how he got the materials from London to set up the flotation plant in Butte has always remained much of a mystery. It is too long a story for us to go into. But brother Theodore was separated from the Minerals Separation company. They knew.

The Great War broke out in August 1914, and brought fortune to the Zinc Corporation. Zinc was needed for the shells and lead for bullets to kill the Germans we are now so anxious to save. Within one month of the outbreak of War, Hoover and Govett were around, hat in hand, at the Board of Trade in London, to make a deal with the British Government. They had a contract with Aron Hirsch in Germany running until 1919. This contract provided that in case of any occurrence preventing deliveries, the contract should be suspended for that length of time, but that was not Hoover and Govett's idea of keeping the contract. They succeeded in getting the Board of Trade to break it and then they entered into a deal with the British Government through a company they helped to form, called the *Zinc Producers Association Proprietary,* by which the British Government not only gave them a grant to increase their plant and took all their output during the war, but also for nine years after the official termination of the war at the price of a hundred and fifteen dollars a ton. This arrangement only expired in June 1930, and during all these years Hoover's associates have been drawing an enormous subvention from the British Government.

It is true that Hoover resigned as director of the

Zinc Corporation in 1916. But he did the same in the Burma Corporation in 1918, and yet he retained his interest in that company. It is reasonable to suppose that he also retained his holdings in the Zinc Corporation. But it is impossible to tell how extensive they were, as he has always been in the habit of holding all his stocks and shares in the names of nominees, banks, or associates. Moreing also had something to say as to his leaving the directorate of the *Zinc Corporation.* From the time Hoover had been forced out of Bewick Moreing & Company in the beginning of 1908, although obliged to employ the services of his old firm in the mines he now controlled, he evinced great hostility. Moreing had given him another hair shirt. In combination with Govett, Hoover had gradually gained control of the Boards of many of the gold mining companies in West Australia—the *Lancefield,* the *Lake View & Star,* the *Oroya Links, Yuanmi, Great Fingall* and *Sons of Gwalia*—and was gradually elbowing out Moreing's firm from the management.

Moreing's five year contract for the management of the Zinc Corporation ran out in 1916, and Hoover gave him notice of dismissal. Moreing, however, was a fighter, and was not the kind of man to give in. He quietly started collecting proxies from Australian shareholders for the annual general meeting of June 26, 1916. These proxies he had sent to F. C. Auld, a Scotch lawyer who was chairman of the *Talisman,* a New Zealand mine managed by the Moreing firm. This is the same Auld who had replaced Hoover on the Board of the Talisman, when Hoover was removed in 1907. Circulars were then printed and issued to the shareholders, showing them how their properties had been wasted by the Hoover company, who were de-

nounced in the most unmistakable language. One
of these circulars was issued in the name of F. C. Auld
and another in the name of A. Leonard, an accountant.
They were signed by persons of great prominence, who
were friends of Moreing, such as W. Graham, chairman of the *Financial Times*, E. M. Rodocanachi, the
banker; E. Rowbotham, the shipowner; M. Spurweg;
and Sir Edward Samuel, Baronet. These circulars
pointed out how the shareholders' money was being lent
out for market purposes, and invested in securities of
doubtful or no value, in which Hoover was interested.
They also showed how the *Sunny Corner* mine, a worked
out property, abandoned fourteen years before, had been
bought for a large sum from a syndicate, of which
Hoover's brother was chairman. Moreing forced the
hand of the Board and had his contract renewed for a
further five years, and Hoover stepped out as director
of the company. Such terrible accusations had been
made in the above circulars about the Hoovers that
something had to be done to save their face. They issued
no fewer than five different writs for libel against Auld,
and Auld's lawyer Crane, Nevill, Rowbotham, Spurweg
and Rodocanachi. Then, when the excitement subsided,
they withdrew the writs and paid the costs. They
well knew they dared not go into Court.

Ever since that time the history of the *Zinc Corporation* has been one of smooth sailing and large dividends,
thanks to the war "boom" and the subsequent subvention from the British Government. From an engineering standpoint, too, the management of Bewick Moreing & Co. improved out of sight after the removal of
Hoover from the corporation.

CHAPTER THE TWELFTH

AND IN NICARAGUA—

THE stench from the *Zinc Corporation* and the *Deep Leads of Victoria* scandals was too much for the Institute of Mining and Metallurgy in London, of which Moreing had been one of the founders. In the year 1907, Hoover, Moreing and four others of the firm resigned. This was a great blow to Moreing, who was so proud of the institute that he had once made the statement that if you wanted to see if a mining engineer is really "eminent," you must first look and see if his name is among the members of the institute. It was beginning to be seen that the fictitious reputation of the great "expert" Hoover was a false alarm. Moreing had seen that for himself on a visit to Australia in 1906. Already on April 18, 1907, the Sydney *Bulletin* was writing:

"Bewick Moreing's star isn't as bright as it was in London, and the financial houses are beginning to throw out hints that they are about ready to beat their joss. This side, the firm never has had the reputation that claquers made for it on the other side, where it seems to be taken for granted that it manages everything worth managing—forgetting small things like the B. H. Prop., Mt. Morgans, Mt. Lyell, Great Cobar, Wallaroo and Moonta, Suphide Corporation and Briseis. The fact is that London investors and speculators have fooled themselves over this business, the firm's alleged domination of Australian

mining is a myth; the failure of Bewick Moreing's
enterprises will leave the mining on which
Australia has built its reputation practically un-
affected. All this, however, won't save Bewick
Moreing. One has only to point, a London paper
says, to the continued delays in connection with
the Deep Lead group, the present temporary
trouble with the Zinc Corporation's expensive
process, the mistakes that have occurred at the
Lancefield, and the other instances where processes to treat refractory ores have been in course
of erection under Bewick Moreing auspices for
some time past without finality of expense or
success. If that feeling spreads the firm will be
in for a bad time, for most of its alleged success
so far has depended upon the willingness of the
London crowd to keep on backing the firm with
unlimited cash."

Things came to a crisis between Moreing and Hoover
at the beginning of 1908. Hoover had to "get out,"
giving up the partnership with Moreing which he had
earned as part of his reward for the "taking" of the
Kaiping mines. He was now a free agent. But he still
retained his interest in the Bewick Moreing properties.
His first concern on leaving Moreing was to take Anderson, his brain box, with him. He took offices in the
same building as Moreing, but on the London Wall side,
where his brother Theodore was also located. It was
now good-bye to Australia. He would never visit it
again. The world was now his territory. He had been
in the habit of going down to Australia every year, this
humanitarian by habit, as Hard describes him. And
what do you think, for? To visit the graves of the
scores of men killed in his mines and the hundreds

that died from miners' complaint every year, and to
relieve the unfortunates maimed for life while laboring
for him, and left with no resource but crutches and the
beggars' dish? We have no means of knowing that this
was not so. It is simply not in any of the available
evidence.

Hoover was now a free agent. But he did not have
to go alone. A man of his peculiar talent, a miracle
man who could glance at a hole in the ground and see
a mirage of millions, was in much demand. He had
already been facing both ways, getting around Moreing to some extent by his close association with the
stockjobber Govett, and with the tailor Doolette and the
Anglo-Continental gang, Davis and Turner. Then, too,
when he came to New York in the Summer of 1906, he
rented an office in his own name at 111 Broadway.
This was the time when he spent a couple of weeks up
at Massena, looking over the St. Lawrence River Power
company plant. He was no longer Moreing's doctor
of sick mining companies, or anything else to Moreing. Most of the mines he had been connected with
had already "passed out," but there were a couple of
healthy ones that no end of bad physicking seemed able
to kill, although dying a lingering death. One was the
Bellevue, where two managers were driven to suicide,
a good rich mine with ore worth twenty dollars to the
ton. It had at one time a market value of $1,750,000
and, during five years under Hoover's control, had produced over $2,000,000 worth of gold, but this was all
lost, as well as the capital, owing to ruinously high
costs and faulty management. Another was the *Lancefield,* which J. H. Curle, in his book, included among
the great gold mines of the world. It was one enormous

chute of ore. It had been worked by a small local
company and had always paid large dividends until it
came into Hoover's hands. At the meeting of December
1903, of the *London & West Australian Exploration
Company*, Moreing had said:

> "Mr. Hoover, my partner, who is now in West
> Australia, has found the property for us and he
> wires me it will be the most profitable business
> we have undertaken since the *Sons of Gwalia*.
> The property is the *Lancefield* mine in the Mount
> Margaret district."

It certainly was profitable for the "insiders," who
bought it at a net cost to them of about $150,000 and
floated it on the London market with a capital of $1,000,-
000, the difference representing their profits. The shares
were grabbed up by the public, for Hoover had estimated
the profits at about $2,000,000, not including what was
contained in a large heap of tailings. This estimate
was made, of course, to gull the public, for Hoover
evidently did not believe it, as we find him selling out
on March 1, 1905, the shares he had received as his
part of the bargain. The profit was in the flotation of
the company, and Hoover received his share. The shareholders were quickly disabused. At the very first meeting of the company, they were callously told that their
capital was all spent, and that if they did not put up
$300,000 more, their shares would be worth no more
than "cigarette paper," Over $1,200,000 was invested
in this great mine, which produced millions of dollars
worth of gold, but never one red cent for the investors
who lost everything. This was due to the ruinous working costs and failure of the method of treatment introduced by Hoover. Indeed it was found later on,
when too late, that under the treatment installed by

Hoover the gold was being volatilized with the chlorides from the salt water and, as Moreing afterwards described it: "The gold went up the chimney." After the *Lancefield* mine was abandoned, it was taken possession of by creditors, who sold it to local miners. We learn from the *Bulletin* of Sydney:

"Frank Moss, George Ridgway and 2 or 3 other cute Westralian mining men, who got hold of the Lancefield last year, seem to be succeeding where Hoover, Govett and Bewick Moreing & Company failed."

There were other fairly good mines, too: the *Vivien, Great Tower Hill,* the *Lake Way,* on all of which Hoover had reported favorably, evidently with the intention of tempting investors, for these mines were never given a fair chance. All the money put into them and all the gold produced was lost, at least for the shareholders.

When Hoover separated from Moreing at the beginning of 1908, he had given up his job as medico and mortician to the Bewick Moreing managed mines. From now on, he converted himself into a kind of mining midwife, who brought new companies to light with astonishing rapidity.

He first of all picked up with his old pal, Govett, who took him to his bosom and made him a director of the *Lake View Consols,* and they immediately began using the funds of this company to finance the *Burma Mines* venture, in which they were both interested. Davis and Turner, the Anglo-Continental gang, which had played such a part in planning the Kaiping mines taking in China, also put him on the Board of their company. Then there was his old friend, Doolette. Let us tell you something about this gentleman. He was a tailor from Adelaide, about sixty-five years old at this

time, who had taken a great liking to Hoover as a
kindred soul. He was an oily tongued fellow who had
gotten into the mining game early and had been connected with the flotation of some forty mining companies in Australia, nearly all of which went the way
of all flesh. In 1903 already, we find him throwing com-
pliments to Hoover at a banquet in London, and in
the photograph reproduced herewith you can see Doolette and Hoover, with his high collar, seated at the
same table, under the shelter of the Union Jack, at the
banquet of the Council of West Australian mineowners
in London, in 1906. The table decorations prove that
there were no drys in those days, at least not in "dear
ole Lunnon." In 1908, they were both directors of the
famous *Oroya Brownhill* mine, of which Hoover had
been made managing director, and of the *Oroya Black
Range* mine, which had been floated in 1906 on one of
the wildcat reports of Hoover, who had an option on
the leases, which were sold to the new company for
$250,000 cash and $500,000 in shares out of a total
capital of $1,000,000. This property had been described
by Hoover as possibly another *Great Fingall,* and probably the longest lode in West Australia. Well it was
not so hot, but the shareholders who invested on the
strength of these wild statements of Hoover lost some
$625,000, only two-thirds of their capital. There must
have been some slip-up to let them get away like that.
Hoover was also a director in Doolette's *Great Fitzroy
Gold and Copper* mines which, like the Lancefield and
Bellevue, might have been a success but for bad management and too much "expert." The shareholders were
shaken down for about $3,000,000.

In 1908 both the great old mines, the *Oroya Brownhill* and the *Lake View Consols* were still "going

strong." At the annual meeting of the *Oroya Brownhill* in 1907, Doolette, the chairman, said that they expected to be able to keep up a production of 30,000 tons of ore a month "for years to come." Things changed when Hoover became managing director. At the next meeting, on April 7, 1908, Doolette told the shareholders that Nature had played a scurvy trick on them, and that the ore had given out and that, consequently, dividends would have to be reduced to a low basis. The mine was played out. The falsity of these statements is proved by the official returns of the Chamber of Mines of West Australia, which shows that in 1912 alone $500,000 worth of gold was produced from this mine that was supposed to have given out. Hoover, Doolette and Govette were, however, playing a deep game. The *Oroya Brownhill* had in 1908 cash assets of about $1,-750,000. It was suggested that this be distributed among the shareholders. Nothing doing. The directors had a better use for that cash. At the annual meeting of June 7, 1909, Doolette told the shareholders that "it would be little short of madness to distribute any part of our cash reserves at the present moment." He told them that they had decided, instead, to invest the money in new mines for the company, that they were using the services of the great expert Hoover for that purpose, and that he had already bought one great mine for them at a marked down figure, $250,000, located in the highlands of Nicaragua, where the revolutions come from. This is what the "boys" had decided to do, to "wangle" the cash out of the pockets of the shareholders into their own.

In December 1909, under the name of *Oroya Links,* they formed a combine of the *Golden Links* and the *Kalgoorlie Amalgamated* with the mine and 50 stamp battery and $75,000 cash of the supposedly broken down *Oroya Brownhill*, giving the *Oroya Brownhill* shareholders only 500,000 shares of $1.25 each as against 650,000 given to the other two companies, which were practically derelicts. This is what is called an "inside job." Then, on March 18, 1910, they floated the above-mentioned Nicaragua mine under the name of *La Leonesa* with a capital of $1,000,000, and advanced it over $250,000 for working capital. They were getting rid of that $1,750,-000 cash reserve pretty fast. Wonder who was getting the money!

Then on the same date, March 18, 1910, they floated the *Oroya Exploration Company* to take over the share holdings of the *Oroya Brownhill*, and options on mines, as well as $500,000 in cash. Then the following month, April, they liquidated the *Oroya Brownhill* distributing $168,750 cash among the shareholders, which is all the cash these shareholders got out of the $1,750,000. The rest was being "invested" for them. The $500,000 taken over with the *Oroya Exploration* did not last long. Before a year had elapsed, in February, 1911, we find Hoover appealing to the shareholders to put up another $500,000. And yet he had in the meantime put over the deal of the *Mountain Queen, Limited,* which he floated with a capital of $625,000 and sold to it the *Mountain Queen* leases for $135,000 cash and on the strength of his report that this mine had 58,500 tons of ore reserves of value of over $500,000 above the 200 ft. level alone. This meant ore worth $8.60 per ounce, but the ore in the *Mountain Queen* never ran over $5.60 an ounce, which was quite unpayable in West Australia. This was not bad enough. But in July, 1912, Hoover sold the *Mountain Queen* company the so-called Transvaal leases for $20,000 in cash and $225,000 in shares.

These Transvaal leases were worked out properties that
never after yielded more than fifteen ounces of gold.
You can readily imagine that all the capital of the
Mountain Queen Company was lost also.

Regarding the *Oroya Exploration* meeting of February, 1911, above referred to, here is a description of it
from the leading New South Wales paper, the *Bulletin*:

"At the *Oroya Exploration* meeting in London
lately, held with the object of inducing shareholders to put up £100,000 more cash to develop
five mines; because the market was not favorable
for floating them at once, chairman H. C. Hoover
was in great form. The *Youanme* mine in W. A.
covered 4,000 ft. along the proved ore-body. At
the 80 ft. level (down to which a wild cat might
fall from the windlass without hurting its spine),
the reef was 1,156 ft. long, 5 ft. 6 in. wide, and
worth 50s. a ton. This body for every 100 ft. in
depth would yield a profit of £60,000. At the
170 ft. level, the shoot was 480 ft. long and worth
50s., showing a profit of £40,000. They wanted
to open out at 300 ft., and if the ore body did not
lose its character (sounds like the lapse of a
servant girl) the mine was worth over £300,000!
(Prolonged applause). The *Meekatharra* was another phenomenal property. Above the 160 ft.
level (the wild cat might crack his spine or break
his legs falling this far) there were 47,000 tons
of ore, which would give a profit of £42,000; and
every 100 ft. of extension in depth would mean
another £30,000. If the 250 ft. level were as good
as the 160 ft., the profit above that depth would
be £72,000! (Applause). Hoover then transported his shareholders to the *Babilonia* and *Los*

Angeles mines in Mexico, where the revolution is coming from. The *Babilonia* was worth £45,000, and the *Los Angeles* £20,000 per 100 ft. of depth. Another wave of the hand, and the Oroya illusionist took his spellbound hearers to the Maikop oil-field in Russia, where—. But, anyhow, the total profit (on paper) was £252,000, and with an expenditure of £25,000 another £120,000 could easily be earned, or £372,000 in all. After all this there was only one dissentient, deaf man, and the shareholders uproariously agreed to subscribe for 200,000 new shares at 10s., making the capital of the Oroya Exploration Co. £250,000. Nobody thought of asking what the directors meant to do with the balance of £75,000 of new capital. Possibly it will be deposited with the Birkbeck Bank."

The Birkbeck Bank referred to was one that had just failed in London, and the inference is that the money was just as safe there as with the Hoover gang. In the above speech, Hoover said that the *Youanme* mine would be worth $1,500,000 profit if the lode continued down to 300 feet. The lode went down hundreds of feet further, but nobody ever saw that profit, at least no shareholder of the new company that was formed to exploit it in April, 1911, ever did. The *Youanme* mine was a good one. But it was all "me" and no "you." In 6 years it produced nearly $16,000,000 worth of gold. But this money also must have gone "up the chimney," for it was all lost, as well as $1,500,000 of the investors' money.

The *Meekatharra* mine referred to was worked by Hoover's *Oroya Exploration Company* itself. He said this had a profit in sight of $210,000, and would show an additional profit of $150,000 for every additional one hundred feet in depth. This was about as sincere as his other statements. The ore was there, but instead of being worth ten dollars to the ton it was worth only eight, and could not be worked at a profit, at least not by Hoover. The *Babilonia* mine mentioned was in Nicaragua. What Hoover actually said at the above-mentioned meeting was that there was a profit proved on ore in sight of $225,000, and a probable profit of $300,000 for every hundred feet in depth. In November, 1911, he said that $350,000 worth of ore was actually blocked out at the mine. A company was floated under the name of *Bablionia Mines, Limited,* to exploit this wonderful mine on June 9th, 1911, with a capital of $700,000, afterwards increased to $1,000,000. All this money was lost, every cent of it. Hoover, however, had made his share. He had sold the mine to his own company for $200,000, a nice little sum in pre-war days. The rest of the $1,000,000 disappeared, although practically no work appears to have been done on account of revolutions. To give an idea of the real value of this mine thus foisted on the British public, it has been under option for the past three years together with all the plant supposed to have been erected there, for the mean sum of $35,000.

Just as Hoover and Doolette had done with the assets of the *Oroya Brownhill* mine, forming a multiplicity of companies, of all of which they were directors, receiving good fat salaries, as is the custom in England, so Hoover and Govett proceeded to do simultaneously the very same way, with the *Lake View Consols.* The procedure adopted was identical. Word was passed around that the great *Lake View* mine had given out. Then two derelict mines, the *Hannan's Star* and the

Boulder Deep Levels were amalgamated to form the *Hannan's Star Consolidated* with a capital of $500,000, which the "insiders" held. Then this *Hannan's Star Consolidated* was put in on even terms in a combine with the *Lake View Consols* mines, battery, treatment plants, etc., etc. It was another "inside" job. The *Hannan's Star*, however, had before amalgamation a certain amount of cash, and also other assets in the form of a saloon at *Ravensthorpe* and an interest in the *Sybu Syndicate* exploring for tin in Nigeria, so these assets were taken by Hoover and Doolette and formed into a separate company called *Star Explorations*. They needed that cash. They had use for that saloon. And they certainly wanted very badly to find tin in Nigeria.

Although the great *Lake View Consols* was still left with tailings and other assets worth $1,750,000, these jugglers reduced its capital from $1,750,000 to $875,000, and then amalgamated it with Hoover's *Oroya Exploration Company*, which needed still more capital for its peculiar mining operations, under the name of the *Lake View* and *Oroya Exploration Company*. Hoover inducing the shareholders to combine by holding out prospects of 30% dividends at least. More bunco steering! At the same time he had the *Oroya Black Range* swallowed up by the *Youanme* on the pretext that the *Black Range* mine was worked out, which was also untrue, as this mine afterwards produced large quantities of gold. In all this "wangling" of companies, it was Hoover that did the "wangling," and, as can be seen from the grand reports and promises handed out, he was the master bunco steerer. Referring to the *Youanme* and *Oroya Black Range* combine, the Sydney *Bulletin* of November 30, 1911, had the following to say:

"As in the case of the *Lake View* and *Oroya*

Exploration combine, Hail Columbia Hoover, as-
sisted by F. A. Govett and G. P. Doolette was
the moving spirit behind the scenes."

The same paper commented further on this amalgamation, as follows:

"It ought to further impress on the minds of
investors that nowadays, when they invest in
(say) the Great Bluebottle Ltd., believing that
this Great Bluebottle is a big mine, they are
liable presently to find that the Board in London
has pooled the profits from the Bluebottle with
the funds of some concern whose ostensible object
in life is to dryblow iceburgs for brass."

The *Lake View Consols* and *Oroya Brownhill* had
disappeared as mining propositions, and in their place
was left a kind of investment trust of the "not you but
me" kind. Almost immediately after, we find the port-
folio of this *Lake View & Oroya Exploration Company*
full of shares and debentures in all kinds of wildcat
ventures sponsored by Herbert Hoover, such as in the
Russian Maikop oilfields and the Granville mining deal
in the Klondyke.

All was now serene. Much money had been made
by the "insiders." The rich assets of the *Oroya Brownhill* and *Lake View* mines had been taken care of.
Simultaneously Doolette's *Bullfinch* in Meekatharra was
warbling merrily away, luring millions out of the
pockets of investors who trusted in this unholy three.

What was the method of operation of these promoters? Let us read the report from the great English
financial paper the *Statist* of the *Oroya Brownhill* meeting of June 7, 1909, Chairman Doolette speaking:

"In view of the urgency of our obtaining other
profitable business for the Company, and in view

of the extreme difficulty of finding anything likely to answer to the severe tests we intended to apply before seriously entertaining any project, we decided to secure the services of our good friend Mr. Hoover. He was, fortunately, free to help us. We therefore appointed him our general manager for this branch of our business. He has gone into the particulars of possibly 600 or 700 different propositions, of all degrees of merit, and the directors have perused and considered the reports on 60 properties in the Malay States, 65 in Western Australia, 93 in the Eastern States of Australia, 22 in Burmah and 125 in other countries of the world. Out of the number of properties submitted to us, the only one taken up, as you know, is the *La Leonesa* mine in the Highlands of Nicaragua, Central America. Mr. Hoover succeeded in getting the vendors to agree to a great reduction in the purchase price, with the result that we are now possessed of a property of much larger dimensions than anything we have previously held for the sum of £50,000 a price well below the estimated profit of the ore in sight namely £60,393."

After reading the above, one can form an idea of what a miracle man Hoover really was. With all this floating and wrecking and amalgamating of gold mines, without yet mentioning his oil companies or adventures in Burma, we find him within a year examining 600 or 700 mining propositions in various parts of the world and reporting on 350 of them, and yet during that time he had time to visit New York, and take a trip to Korea in the Far East, and also publish that remarkable mining treatise, the *Principles of Mining*. Nonsense! Hoover did not have to examine 700 mine propositions to select the one he himself had for sale, the *La Leonesa.* And as for the *Principles of Mining* it should be sufficient to say that it shows the master hand of a practised writer.

You can see from Doolette's speech to the enthusiastic shareholders of the old *Oroya Brownhill* that Hoover made a great bargain in securing the *La Leonesa* mine for the sum of $250,000. To exploit the mine, the *Oroya Leonesa, Limited,* was formed on March 18, 1910, with a capital of $1,250,000 and $253,125 was advanced by the *Oroya Brownhill* to the new company for working expenses. A further sum of $175,000 in debentures was issued in May 1912. The company was twice reconstructed within a few years and further calls of $140,000 made on the unfortunate shareholders, who neither ever got a penny of their investment back or ever saw any of that £60,353 supposed to be in sight at the start of operations. All was lost, as usual.

The explanation is very simple. The whole business, like the sale of the Transvaal and other Australian mines to the *Oroya Brownhill* was a coup. Hoover was "relieving" the shareholders of the company of which he was managing director and trustee. Here is the story of the *La Leonesa* mine as supplied by the Public Registrar of Property of Nicaragua in a report to his Government in March, 1930: (Translation from Spanish)

Matagalpha, March 19, 1930.
To the Minister of Government and Justice.
Managua.

As it has not been possible to find the original entry as to who was the owner of the *La Leon-*

esa mine in the year 1908, I am furnishing you the following data from other records. A certificate was issued and registered by the State Bureau of this County on March 13th, 1906, showing that Mr. Jose del Carmen Ruiz, as legal representative of Mr. Herbert Clark Emery (sic), applied for the concession of the mining site called "Guabule" in April 1903 as an extension of the other sites established for treating the metals of the *La Leonesa* mine and other gold mines, and that he obtained this concession, but, on finding, after an examination of the ground, that it was not large enough to produce a sufficient head of water for the said mining enterprise belonging to his principal, he applied for two lots of ground adjoining the grounds of the "Guabule" site, which were granted him by said State Bureau for the mining site that Mr. Herbert Clark Emery (sic) was trying to establish. On December 18, 1908, Mr. William August Wheeler, as representative of Mr. Herbert Clark Emery (sic), sold the extention of the Guabule site to Mr. Jose del Carmen Ruiz who, in turn, on the 19th of the same month and year above mentioned, sold the said extension of the Guabule mining site to the company called *La Leonesa Mining Company,* located in the City of Chelsea, County of Suffolk, State of Massachusetts, United States of America, the sale of the same being accepted by Mr. William August Wheeler, as representative of the *La Leonesa Mining Company,* all of which goes to show that in 1908 the owner of the *La Leonesa* mine was this company, of which Mr. Herbert Clark Emery (sic) undoubtedly formed part.

Afterwards, on January 16th, 1909, Mr. William August Wheeler, as legal representative of the abovementioned *La Leonesa Mining Company* of the City of Chelsea, in the name of that company sold the La Leonesa mining property to Mr. Charles Simon Peter Herzig, together with all its appurtenances.

On September 27th, 1910, Mr. James Semmens Allen, as legal representative of Mr. Charles Simon Herzig, sold the said *La\ Leonesa* mining property to the *Oroya Leonesa, Limited,* of London, England, for FIFTY THOUSAND POUNDS STERLING, which the said Oroya Leonesa, Limited, paid to the Oroya Brownhill Company, Limited, and which payment Mr. Herzig acknowledeged as correct, the Oroya Brownhill Company, Limited, having supplied him with the said amount to make the purchase for it, this sale having been accepted on behalf of the Oroya Leonesa company, Limited, by its representative, Mr. John White Hercklin.

On June 26th, 1914, Mr. John McPhail, as representative of the Oroya Leonesa, Limited, and of George Goldthorp Hay, liquidator of the same company in London, sold to the Central American Mines, Limited, of London, the La Leonesa mining property, the sale being accepted by its representative, Mr. Charles E. Bunker.

And, on the first of October 1918, Mr. Henry A. Caley, as representative of the Central American Mines, Limited, of London, and of George Goldthorp Hay, liquidator of that company, sold the abovementioned *La Leonesa* mining property to the Leonesa Mines, Limited, represented by

Mr. Frederick L. Thomas.

And, there having been no other transfer of the *La Leonesa* mine, this means to say that at present it belongs to said Leonesa Mines, Limited, for although it appears that this company has made some sales in the year 1921 through its general attorney, Mr. Albert Travis, residing at the mine called La Babilonia, located at La Libertad, County of Chontales, these sales have only been of superficial rights of the soil and did not include the mineral rights belonging to La Leonesa mine.

Thus, in the above terms, and without indicating who were the managers, for this does not appear in the respective entries, I beg to furnish you the report you requested from me in your telegram of the 17th inst.

Respectfully,

(signed) G. Pasquier,
Public Registrar.

(Here is a seal reading:
Public Registrar of Property,
Matagalpha, Republic of Nicaragua,
Central America.)

We produce a photostat copy of a Statistical Report of the Republic of Nicaragua for the year 1908, showing the *La Leonesa* mining claims registered in the names of La Leonesa Mining Co. William August Wheeler and Herbert Clark Emery (sic). By a strange coincidence, this document disappeared from the New York Public Library, the very next day after the photostat was obtained.

The first line of the report of the Public Registrar of Property of the Republic of Nicaragua is very illuminating:

"As it has not been possible to find the original entry as to who was the owner of the *La Leonesa* mine in the year 1908."

What became of this record?

And since we are asking questions, it might be in order to inquire whether we are keeping our precious youngsters in Nicaragua to fight bandits, or to protect bandits?

In connection with Nicaragua, it may interest the American mining men who have heaped honors on Hoover to know that it was he who, fishing in muddy waters after the downfall of President Zelaya, obtained for his English *Oroya Exploration Company* the notorious Irias concession, which gave that English company the exclusive prospecting rights for ten years and mining rights for a subsequent fifty years over twenty square kilometers of the richest gold lands in Nicaragua, to the exclusion of all American prospectors. Needless to say, one of the first acts of Diaz, when installed with the help of the United States, was to abrogate this concession, so manifestly unfair to America.

CHAPTER THE THIRTEENTH

TIN TRUMPETING IN NIGERIA

SIR GEORGE LEWIS, the celebrated English lawyer, who had represented Hoover's firm in the Chinese case and many other tangles, retired from practice in 1910. Some time previously he had written the following:

"It seems to me that fraud has been and is on the steady increase, both in volume and in scope. As the law tightens its grip, so the dishonest rascal exercises greater ingenuity in his methods, and the result in the end is the same—the surplus money of many fools slides into the pockets of one wily and unscrupulous individual. There is an old Yankee saw which says that a man who steals a nickel is a thief, but the man who steals a million dollars is a genius. Many of the huge fortunes which have been amassed by mushroom 'financiers' and promoters during the past decade have been built up on foundations of trickery, deceit and fraud, and if we examine the methods employed we find them little different from those of the racecourse thimble rigger."

Sir George Lewis knew what he was writing about.

When housewife Hoover was cutting down the old suits of clothes of the grandpas *Oroya Brownhill* and *Lake View,* and converting them into a patchwork quilt, incidentally emptying the pockets of thousands in the process, he was a very, very busy person in other directions. Early in 1910, he had crossed London Wall (it is a street, not a wall) to his new large offices at No. 1 London Wall Buildings (phone 3700, Wall) alongside the long nosed South African mining magnates, who were soon to become his associates in the oil business. Oh, yes, he was very much engaged at this same time in oil and in tin. This was for the purpose of hooking in the small fish, for shares in such companies were generally of small denominations, so as to give the poorest class of investors a chance to bite. Besides, the public were getting a bit tired of being flimflammed in his gold mining companies. How about tin for a change?

If you look at a map of North West Africa, you will see a very large country called Nigeria, traversed by the great river Niger and extending up from the Gulf of Guinea to the interior. It is the place where negroes came from. It is a British colony, and extensive concessions were held here by a development company known as the Niger Company. In 1906, the Niger Company had discovered and begun to exploit alluvial tin properties, and the tin they exported was found to be of very good quality. Now the word "tin" sounds good to an Englishman, who colloquially uses it as synonymous with "money." How about gettting the suckers in on tin?

The *Anglo-Continental Syndicate,* so prominent in the planning of the *Oriental Syndicate* in the Chinese deal, was reconstructed in December, 1909, under the name of *Anglo-Continental Mines,* the directors being the three musketeers Hoover, Davis and Turner, and Johann Schaar, publisher of a mining market tipster sheet. A great combination. You have already read something of Davis and Turner, the squeegee twins, in connection with the Kaiping mines case. At the period referred to, Davis had a record of having been a director of a hundred and twenty-six companies, several of which were reconstructed and only six surviving and paying dividends without reconstruction. His reputation is well summed up in the *Rialto* of May 22, 1907:

"Edmund Davis is making many journeys to Italy in connection with a nitrogen extraction process. Edmund was always a successful extractor, and now that the pockets of the public are empty, he is trying the air. We cannot help feeling sorry for the air."

They had decided to exploit the tin game. The first thing to do was to hire an "expert." We have seen that Hoover knew the public liked to be buncoed, for, in addition to himself, he had foisted a number of other mining "experts" on them, such as the preliminary lawyers Wilson and Dennis, already mentioned. This time, he picked out as "expert" a young man named John Thomson, who had, like Hoover, neglected to study mining engineering in his youth and could not tell tin ore from tinned sardines. Early in 1910, John Thomson left a good home to go out to the table land of Nigeria, where it is very dry and there is no prohibition, to look for tin. Now, it takes quite an expert to locate tinstone, or "cassiterite" as the geologists call it, and Thomson saw no tin. He must have got his signals mixed up, for he had to come back twice to London within a year to get his final instructions as to when and where he was to find that tin. However, that did not prevent the Anglo gang from floating in February, 1910, the Northern Nigeria (Bauchi) Tin Mines with a capital of $1,000,000, the shares of which they manipulated to a premium of over 50%. Out of this $1,000,000 capital, the Anglo crowd took $200,000 cash and $500,000 in shares. And what did they give the new company in exchange? Just the prospecting rights for one year over some sixty-two square miles marked red on the map of Nigeria, which anyone could obtain on payment of a fee of a few dollars!! Hoover put in charge of this "property" his old pal Jack Means of Stanford, who had been with him in Australia and China. It was some fifteeen months after the formatien of this company before it ever held a single claim! Meanwhile the "insiders" had taken in one million dollars from the public.

In February, 1911, a year after their first tin flotation, the Anglo gang floated the *Gurum River* (*Nigeria*) *Tin Mines* with a capital of $625,000 to acquire three leases they had not then got, having at that time only one lease, which had been issued only a few days previously and where, as a matter of fact, there was no tin ever found. For this valuable "property" they took in payment $500,000 in shares, which they sold out to the public at a premium. All these pickings helped.

We have seen that when Hoover formed the *Hannan's Star Consolidated,* he stuck to the cash and the *Ravensthorpe* saloon and the interest in the *Sybu Syndicate,* which had also sent an expedition to Nigeria to find tin, and that he had converted these assets into a new company called *Star Explorations.* In this business he was associated with tailor Doolette and, to place himself in a position where he was not tied to either crowd, he stepped out as director of both the *Anglo-Continental* and the *Star Explorations,* and formed a third alliance to exploit Nigerian tin. This was with Govett, and, in May, 1910, they formed the *Kano Syndicate,* which applied for prospecting licenses in Nigeria. Govett, being a stockholder, had to be careful about floating a company that had no property or leases whatever. So they made a deal with the *Tin Areas of Nigeria,* a company run by what was known as the Smithfield Market crowd, nearly all the shares being held by butchers in that market. The Smithfield butchers joined hands with

Hoover and Govett, putting in one of their leases in the formation of a new company, called *Kano (Nigeria) Tin Areas,* which was floated in May, 1911, with a capital of $1,000,000, Govett underwriting $200,000 of the issue for a commission of 20%. For the one claim of one square mile put in by the Smithfield butchers, and a one year prospecting license on forty square miles marked red on the map of Nigeria, the new company had to pay these gentry $580,000. It looked cheap. The prospectus issued stated that they had proved reserves worth gross $1,620,000, but this was like a lot of the proved reserves that had so often been reported in West Australia, Victoria, Nicaragua and elsewhere. They simply did not exist. There was no tin there at all. The people who bought shares on the strength of this prospectus were being tricked, as usual. They lost all their money. Then, when the "properties" were found to be worthless, instead of announcing it in a business-like way, other properties were quietly substituted in the interests of the "insiders" who still held blocks of shares to unload.

Interest in Nigerian tin was being gradually worked up by a campaign of "puffery" in the press. The London *Evening Times* wrote in February, 1912:

> "Insidious paragraphs have been appearing in papers, pointing out that as alluvial tin is exported, there must be big lodes somewhere and if these tin lodes can be found vast profits will result to the lucky finders. This is the veriest rubbish and the paragraphs were only inserted in order to enable the Edmund Davis group to boost up and unload Anglo-Continentals."

Then, when the time was thought ripe, the promoters stepped on the gas. Thomson must have had a few extra cases of whisky sent out to him for Christmas 1911 (yes, that is what white men drink in Nigeria), for his reports began to come in as required. In December, a report came in from him, that he had discovered a tin outcrop in the Jemaa district where he was prospecting for the Anglo. Then, further reports converted this outcrop into a lode, assaying as high as 25% tin. The *Anglo-Continental* meeting was held on February 23, 1912, and, as these extraordinary coincidences miraculously happened with these people, a cable arrived from Thomson just in time for the meeting, stating that he had traced the lode for a distance of 5 miles and that it was in places a hundred feet wide. Turner, who presided at the meeting, said he would not attempt to figure this out for the shareholders. They could do that for themselves. Wethered, one of the gang, suggested that the meeting should adjourn to give them time to go to the Stock Exchange! The ball had been started rolling.

Now, any investor who took a pencil and started figuring could see that the above report included millions of tons of ore containing 25% of tin. And if Cornwall mines were paying dividends on a yield of 2% of tin, what a chance for making money with ore containing 25%! This was not enough. On March 15th, the Anglo gang sent out a circular through the mails, stating that they had received a cable from Hoover's expert Thomson to the effect that the lode had been traced for over 8 miles, that for 1 1/2 miles the average width was thirty feet and the average value 20% of tin! The investing public went tin crazy. Clean out the savings from the bank, sell the store, hock the piano, let's buy some of those beautiful tin share certificates. In the cold London Winter drizzle, crowds mobbed around Throgmorton Street as late as 8 o'clock at night, where dealers were still yelling the prices of tin shares and giving all and sundry a chance of coming in and making a fortune. The Anglo-Continental shares, which had stood at $2.75 in the middle of January jumped to nearly $40 in the middle of March. The *Tin and Copper World* of London wrote on March 21st:

> "The excitement, as we all know, was started by the Chairman's speech at the Anglo-Continental meeting. This as far as the public were concerned, but those behind the scenes had been buying Anglo-Continentals for weeks, well knowing that a tremendous effort would be made to push them up. That effort succeeded."

Davis now thought it time to "pull out the pin," and squeeze the "bulls" who were not insiders. A few days later the shares fell in a few minutes from forty to twenty dollars a share, one concern having to pay up a difference of $450,000 in settlement, quite a tidy amount in pre-war days. Now the market had to be jacked up again, and they called in the help of the *Consolidated Goldfields* crowd, which was at that time associated with Hoover in the Granville swindle, and which had been gambling wildly in the Anglo-Continental shares. The Consolidated stepped in and bought 10,000 shares at twenty-five dollars a share for the "call" on ten thousand a month and Turner told the world that he had bought a thousand shares for his aunt, so as to leave her in luxury for the rest of her days. Then, on April 12th, the shareholders received by mail a circular informing them that the following cable had been received from Thomson:

> "Examined lode on the surface and costean

trenches; splendid body of ore, very rich. Judging from surface indications the lode has every appearance of being permanent in depth."

This cable had its effect, and prices rose 25% in one day, notwithstanding the fact that the cable was ridiculous in the extreme, and enough to make any mining man snigger. For how could anyone tell from surface indications if the lode was liable to be permanent in depth? However, the "tin expert" Thomson was no more a mining engineer than the "gold expert" Hoover, one of whose first reports on the *Sons of Gwalia* mine was strangely similar and similarly ridiculous. This was the one he sent over the cable on March 23, 1898, when the *Sons of Gwalia* shares were needing a boost and he not only found one ounce ore to assay seven ounces six dwt., but added that the mine "promised" exceedingly well for the future.

When the tin boom was at its peak in the third week of March, 1912, Hoover's *Star Explorations* company got busy. The *Tin and Copper World* of March 28, 1912, tells us that the Star Explorations company, of which Mr. Hoover is a prominent director, has sent out a circular by mail on the *Sybu Syndicate* telling the world that five hundred tons of tin had been proved on their "property." Now the *Sybu Syndicate* did not own any property at all or even hold a lease. All they had was a one year prospecting license over some sixty square miles of the map of Nigeria. This did not prevent them from floating a company, called the *Dua (Nigeria) Tinfields,* at the height of the boom in April 1912, with a capital of $750,000, of which $500,000 was paid these philanthropists for the wonderful "property" with 500 tons of tin already proved, which they did not own. The records of the Government of Nigeria show that down to the end of 1912, neither the *Sybu Syndicate* nor the *Dua* (*Nigeria*) *Tinfields* ever owned a claim or held a lease. These rascals were simply selling plots marked red on the map of Nigeria, that did not belong to them and on the fraudulent pretense that they contained enormous deposits of valuable tin. Dr. Cook certainly made a terrible mistake by not staying in Europe. With the money the promoters took in, they substituted other leases and thus managed to continue working until all the shareholders' investment was exhausted, meanwhile drawing fat directors' fees, and then close down. The gold in West Australia might have gone "up the chimney." But the tin in Nigeria went "down the chute."

As proof of what rogues these promoters were, one has only to note the fact that W. R. Rumbold, the great tin expert, visited the Jemaa district in March, 1912, and knew what conditions were there. But on his arrival in London in April, to prevent his making his information public, he was at once engaged as Consulting Engineer by the Anglo gang. But his appointment was not announced until June. The tin "bubble" was eventually pricked by the *Financial Times* which sent out an independent expert, C. H. Wray, who cabled on April 20th that there was no tin lode that he could see. Perhaps he drank a different kind of liquor.

At the same period, J. F. Balfour of the West African Mines, a company closely associated with the Anglo-Continental, visited Jemaa and sent in a cable stating that he would be surprised to find 1½% tin. This cable was received in London on April 25th, but was not communicated to the shareholders until May 21st. Information was held back until the suckers were bled white. Balfour sent a second cable on May 30th, stating that he estimated the percentage of tin in Jemaa at ½% only. This cable was held back from shareholders for a week and meantime the insiders sold out and the bottom fell out of the market. As a matter of fact, there was nothing there at all, for Rumbold, who had returned to Nigeria, reported in October that Jemaa was "hopeless even as a prospect."

During this most extraordinary tin boom, many mushroom companies sprung to light, with which Hoover, Govett, Doolette and the Anglo gang were connected, even as far away as in Burma. The loss to the British public was enormous, reaching a total of probably one hundred million dollars. There had not been, according to the *Tin and Copper World,* a worse scandal in the City of London in thirty years. The press began to demand a Government inquiry and the exposure of the guilty parties, the *Financial Times* stating that the prominent standing of many of those directly and indirectly connected with the Anglo-Continental was all the more reason for an inquiry. The *Pall Mall Gazette* asked: "Is this another scandal to be buried, and inquiry to be balked?" It was, just like the West Australian scandals.

Where did all the money go? Herbert Hoover, himself, in a long letter written on this very subject on May 7, 1912, to the *Mining Magazine* explained what happened to money thus lost and practically defends the stealing of it. He takes as an example a company with a capital of a million pounds which is a total loss, and of which, say, a hundred thousand pounds is spent in development, equipment and management, five thousand pounds in directors' fees, registration and secretary's expenses and fifteen thousand pounds in the cost of living of the promoters and their satellites, and shows that

the balance of eight hundred and eighty thousand pounds
lost just goes into the pockets of the insiders, and then
he goes on to say:

"From an economic point of view, this £880,000
of capital in the hands of the Insiders is often
invested to more reproductive purposes than if it
had remained in the hands of the Idiots who
parted with it."

Hoover was speaking as an Insider, who had had
both hands in the bag.

CHAPTER THE FOURTEENTH

Oil, Slush and Hush-Hush

TRUTH is said to lie at the bottom of a well. But somehow it always comes out on top—just like oil. This is a story of oil. With the invention of the Diesel crude oil engine and its application to mercantile and war vessels, a tremendous demand for mineral oil developed during the latter part of 1909, and the English investing public caught the oil craze. Hoover did not wait for the poor fish to escape. He hired another "expert," this time a dredging engineer, whom he had met in Tientsin in 1901, and miraculously converted him into an oil expert overnight. This man, Lindon W. Bates, afterwards for a time manager in New York for Hoover's Belgian Relief Commission, was the expert to delude the shareholders and Hoover the promoter, to get them. From Hoover's office at No. 1 London Wall Buildings, these thirty-five dollar companies marched out, one after the other, not tin soldiers this time, but oilomatics.

Someone had discovered oil in the Maikop field in South Russia. That was good enough for Hoover. Just as in Nigeria, without any preliminary trial drillings, he just picked out plots from the map, rented them from the Russian landowners and proceeded to exploit them, disregarding the fact that there was no legal mining title from the Russian Government whatever. Companies were formed, the directorates, as usual, containing the names of some guinea-pig "misaristocrats" such as Prince Saltykoff. Who could fail to invest in a company that had a real live prince for a director? Here is a list of some of them:

		Floated	Liquidated	
Maikop	Neftiania Synd.	April 22, 1910	June 16, 1910	$ 175,000
"	Shirvansky Oil Co.	May 6, 1910	Nov. 3, 1911	750,000
"	Apsheron Oil Co.	June 28, 1910	Sept. 27, 1912	2,250,000
"	& Gen. Pet. Trust	Feb. 22, 1910	Sept. 27, 1912	1,502,500
"	Oil & Pet. Prod.	Mar. 24, 1910	Dec. 5, 1912	2,125,000
"	Areas Oil Co.	April 20, 1910	Sept. 27, 1912	3,000,000
"	Valley Oil Co.	April 5, 1910	Value in 1914	Nil
"	Mutual Oil Tran. Co.	May 11, 1910	April 12, 1912	1,312,500
"	Hadijensky Synd.	June 27, 1910	Sept. 27, 1912	150,000
"	New Producers Co.	Feb. 20, 1912	Mar. 17, 1915	1,500,000
Amal.	Maikop Oilfields	April 18, 1911	Nov. 26, 1914	1,500,000

No magician ever took rabbits out of a hat or made them disappear, as quickly as these Maikop companies. First of all came the pompous sounding *Maikop & General Petroleum Trust,* in February, 1910, with a capital of $1,502,500, the $2,500 representing 10,000 twenty-five cent shares which the promoters thoughtfully reserved for themselves and which, on the off chance of finding oil, were to get one third of all the profits after the shareholders received 10%! Then the Trust within a few weeks floated four new companies with a combined capital of $9,375,000, the promoters taking in exchange $397,000 in cash and $4,900,000 in shares for these "valuable properties," to which they had no regular mining title. Indeed, it was only in September, 1911, when the Russian Government saw that the whole boom was a "washout" that it legalized the titles. Then in the same month of April, 1910, they formed the *Neftiania Syndicate,* which in May floated the *Maikop Shirvansky,* which, a few months later, was gobbled up by the *Maikop Apsheron.* Then followed amalgamation jugglings, with fresh issues of partly paid shares to actually draw the last penny out of the suckers who invested, even stooping so low as to take one penny (2c) calls in one of these companies. It was without avail that leading newspapers, such as the *Morning Leader,* the *Pall Mall Gazette* and *Truth* warned the public against these *Maikop* promotions. Even the Standard Oil Company issued a circular warning in October, 1910. But it was useless. The "idiots" wanted oil shares and Hoover's engravers turned out the prettiest share certificates in London.

What work was done with all the capital subscribed to develop these "valuable properties?" Practically none. In September, 1910, a London *Times* correspondent wrote that the results were very poor. A writer in the *Novoe Vremya* of St. Petersburg said that very little work was being done. And the special correspondent of the *Petroleum World,* who visited the *Maikop* field in February, 1911, found that there was practically no work done by the above Hoover companies. Just a few tanks and derricks had been erected (evidently for the photographers), and a few hand-dug wells, which, by the way, was contrary to the Russian law, which prohibited hand-dug wells on acount of the danger the men ran of being suffocated by fumes.

Only on one plot was oil found, and that was on plot 490 of the *Maikop Oil & Petroleum Producers,* where they found a few pailfuls, which these adventurers, in their reports, magnified into a gusher or "fountain," as they called it, giving it the grandiloquent name of *Coronation Well.* The report submitted to shareholders of the *Trust* at its meeting in August, 1911, told of the great "fountain" and of a contract having been entered into for the sale of 1,200,000 barrels a year for ten years. This was, of course, the usual bunco. And what did they do with this company with the wonderful *Coronation Well?* They just formed a new company, the *Maikop New Producers,* with a capital of $1,500,000 in 600,000 shares of $2.50 each, giving the old shareholders 73,000 $2.50 shares in the new company out of 600,000, the promoters apparently keeping the balance of 527,000 shares for themselves. It seems incredible, but these shareholders were poor people of the class who believe in miracles. Then the new company told them that all they got was holes in the ground full of water!

Then Hoover and his associates, in October, 1912, turned most of these companies over to the Tweedy crowd, which floated the *Maikop Combine,* with a capital of $3,750,000, jacking up the shareholders in the old companies for more cash by giving them partly paid shares in the new company. The accounts of this "Combine" to January 13, 1914, show that the Combine had a stock of oil of the value of $145!

The *Oil News* of March 29, 1913, contains a letter from a shareholder in one of Hoover's companies, who received one $2.50 share in the Combine ($1.25 paid) in exchange for each of the $5 shares he held in the old company, and then, after paying an 84c call in the month of January, fond that his new shares were quoted in March at 12c bid! The British public sank over $60,000,000 in all in the Maikop field and the pockets of the promoters. All the old gangs were down there in Maikop with Hoover and his "oil expert" Bates. There were Davis and Turner, Doolette, Govett, and even Moreing.

Once he had gotten all the "fat," not oil, out of the Maikop field, Hoover closed his bag of tricks and moved again. This was Trinidad, in South America, where he was operating at the very same time. It is said that oil and water do not mix, but oil and whisky evidently do, for we find at this time Hiram Walker, the whisky manufacturer of Walkerville, Ontario, exploring for oil in Trinidad. Hoover, too, with his old friends, Davis and Turner, was in that field with their *Trinidad Oil Exploration Syndicate.* With Bates as a catalyst, they combined with Hiram Walker to form the *General Petroleum Properties* of Trinidad, which sallied out from Hoover's office in March, 1910. The capital was $1,500,-000, of which $1,250,000 was issued, the share of the "fat" for the insiders being $1,000,000 in shares and $137,500 in cash. They also arranged that Bates, who had desk room in Hoover's office should receive $2,500 a year as managing director and $3,500 a year for providing office space in Hoover's office. The shares were sold and, as you can see, the money went into the pockets of the promoters, the result being that on August 31, 1912, the company had a cash balance of only $935! It had, however, something as valuable as cash, and that was oil within 12 miles of seaboard. Yes, oil had been found at fairly shallow depths, but were the more than 600 shareholders asked to put up more money, as they would have been only too delighted to do? Bless your heart, no! These gentlemen did not do business that way. They closed down the wells and suspended operations for want of capital and then set about selling out the shareholders.

This was not the only oil company Hoover floated in Trinidad. Within twelve months from May, 1910, there issued forth from his office at No. 1 London Wall Buildings the *B. W. I. Syndicate,* the *Trinidad Cedros Oil Co.,* the *Russper Syndicate,* the *Trinidad Mayaro Oil Co.,* the *Trinidad Forest Reserve Oil Co.,* the *Trinidad Morne Enfer Oilfields* and the *La Lune (Trinidad) Oil Blocks,* with a combined capital of over $4,000,000, of which well more than half was "fat" for the promoters. Not one of these companies held a single lease, nothing but prospecting licenses. It was Nigeria business all over again.

Hoover's *B. W. I.* and *Russper* syndicates took control

of four of the above "prospects" and turned them over together with the *General Petroleum Properties of Trinidad* to a South African crowd, the *Central Mining & Investment Company*, which was practically identical with the *Consolidated Goldfields* mob that was in with the *Anglo-Continental* gang in the Nigerian tin swindles, and with Hoover and Beatty in the Granville Mining "ramp." They floated a new company, the *Trinidad Leaseholds*, with a capital of $2,750,000, of which the *General Petroleum Properties* shareholders with their rich oil lands only received $625,000 in shares, whilst Hoover's *Russper Syndicate*, which held nothing but prospecting licenses on land where never a drill had gone down received $225,000, and the *Central Mining & Investment Company* received $725,000 in shares. For what? This is rich. "In exchange for the surrender to the Government of the concessions and licenses." Now, what did they surrender? The leases of the *General Petroleum Properties of Trinidad* and the prospecting licenses of the *Russper Syndicate*, and in exchange they received from the Trinidad Government a lease over the whole territory covered by these leases and licenses for fifty years, renewable for thirty years. What a surrender! There was, however, a string attached. The Trinidad Government specified that the new company must at all times remain a British concern and never be directly or indirectly controlled by foreigners or a foreign company. Americans, keep off!

In the formation of the *General Petroleum Properties of Trinidad,* whose shareholders had been thus sold out, care had been taken to insert in the Bylaws the Discovery Clause, to prevent shareholders from seeing the books and accounts of the company. After the dirty deal with the cosmopolitan South African crowd had been put through, for fear that something might ever come to light, a special resolution was passed that the books of the company be destroyed!

Peru, too, had been simultaneously invaded by the three musketeers—Hoover, Davis and Turner. There was a company there called the *London and Pacific*, which had, as far back as 1889, secured the oil rights over a large tract in Peru. They had had some trouble in getting work started on account of the backward condition of Peru at the time. At the end of 1908, the "set up" dredger Bates obtained from them the prospecting rights with option to take a lease over four square miles of their lands. Hoover and Govett, in the usual way already described, took the money to finance the prospecting from the *Lake View Consols* they were managing directors of, and, when the boom in oil set in in 1910, decided to float still another company. In April, 1910, the *Lagunitos Oil Company* trotted out of Hoover's office with a paid up capital of $35 and a nominal capital of $1,250,000, the promoters taking $125,000 in cash and $625,000 in fully paid shares. For what? For Bates' prospecting rights which he had transferred to the Anglo-Continental gang—Davis, Hoover and Turner —for $25,000 in shares in the new company. The new company was very fortunate right from the start. High grade oil was struck at shallow depths in almost every well they drilled and, at the end of 1912, they had some 58 wells sunk, large storage and delivery tanks erected and a three mile light railway constructed to connect with the London & Pacific Petroleum Company, which had contracted to buy their oil at a fairly high price. Their regular production was now about 10,000 barrels a month. Everything was now ready to go ahead full steam. And what did Hoover and his friends do?

Just as they did with the Zinc Corporation and the Burma Mines. They froze out the shareholders to gain complete control. They put out the old story—no money for development, desperate situation, etc. The five dollar *Lagunitos* shares were sold down to 60 cents. Of the 250,000 *Lagunitos* shares, only 200,000 had been issued, and instead of offering the remaining 50,000 to the shareholders or making a call on them for fresh capital, which they would have been only too glad to furnish where so much rich oil had been found, 30,000 of these shares were taken and converted into *Preference* shares and, exactly as Hoover and Govett had done with the *Zinc Corporation,* these preference shares were given 100% of the profits, and then a further 20% cumulative preference dividend and then a further equal share in the profits. Of course, the insiders took up these preference shares themselves, which they had had "guaranteed" by Hoover's *Lake View & Oroya Exploration Company,* whose funds were always conveniently available for all Hoover's speculations. They were not through yet. Dredger Bates had prospecting rights on another four square miles from the *London & Pacific.* This concession, however, was valueless on account of the high royalties provided, and, as a matter of fact, it was afterwards abandoned. This did not prevent the "sale" of it by Bates to the *Lagunitos* company in November, 1913, for $10,000 cash and $150,000 in *Preference* shares. This necessitated the creation of more preference shares and accordingly the capital of the company was increased by $350,000 in preference and $150,000 in ordinary shares. Of course, Bates was only a dummy in this transaction, the shares he was supposed to receive being allotted to a bank manager nominee. As a matter of fact, of the 74,900 *Preference* shares allotted in the last week of December, 1913, we find 40,289 in the name of "Govett and Lloyd" (presumably for the *Lake View & Oroya Exploration Company*, of which Govett was joint managing director with Hoover, and Lloyd the secretary) and 24,696 in the name of Berkely, the bank nominee. Then with the preference shares "in the bag," the insiders sold out to the *London & Pacific*, which in turn sold out to a branch of the *Standard Oil Company*, the *Preference* shares being bought for $10 each, and the ordinary for $2.50.

It is a very remarkable fact that in the accounts of the *Lake View & Oroya Exploration Company*, made up to June 30, 1914, no shares whatever of the *Lagunitos Oil Company* are included in its assets, although "Govett and Lloyd" still held on that date and sold on July 21, 1914, 62,045 ordinary and 49,874 preference shares of the *Lagunitos Oil Company*, which had apparently now become "plums" and as such were reserved for the "insiders." Why were these shares held in the name of "Govett and Lloyd" and not in the name of the *Lake View & Oroya Exploration Co.*, which put up the money? How much cash did the shareholders of the *Lake View & Oroya Exploration Co.* receive for these shares? Ask Hoover and Govett, the managing directors. They know. The shareholders apparently never learned.

Hoover's oil interests were not confined to Russia, Trinidad and Peru. We also find him connected with oil in Newfoundland and Rumania and Mexico. Everywhere he had his hands in oil and everywhere it left a stain. Now let us come back to the good old U. S. A.

Hoover had been very busy in 1912, as usual. Besides a string of financial syndicates he had formed to exploit this, that and everything, he had on his hands the expiring gold mines in West Australia, the non-existent tin lodes in Nigeria, the mud holes in South Russia, the highlands of Nicaragua, not forgetting the hundreds of millions of cubic yards of gold bearing gravel in the Klondyke that he forgot to register title to. Then there were the lead and zinc mines in New South Wales and Burma, iron ore in Norway, copper in Siberia, gold dredging in the Argentine. Here he was, chasing back and forth between his home in London and New York and the Californian oilfields, and in between times translating from mediaeval Latin (don't all laugh at once!) that monumental work on mining in the Middle Ages *De Re Metallica.*

Yes, he was beginning to discover California, and actually rented a house in San Francisco in the Fall of 1912. The English newspapers were beginning to hear of California. Here was a country which had enormous mineral oil resources and which, with the opening of the Panama Canal, would become, as Hoover expressed it in a letter to the London *Times,* "practically a province of Europe" (wonder how the Californians like that!). The British Government was then searching anxiously for a source of supply of oil for its warships. Leave it to the miracle man Hoover. He would find it for the great Empire that had treated him so well. California was the place and, with the opening of the Panama Canal, oil could be shipped from California to England over a route which Winston Churchill described in the House of Commons as one "we can easily and effectively control."

To find this source of oil supply for England, Hoover set out to explore and exploit California. In 1912, in association with Beatty who was already connected with him in the *Klondyke Granville Mining Camp,* he formed the *Inter-California Trust,* and succeeded in obtaining control of the *Continental Oil Company* owning land in the Midway and Coalinga fields in California, and 5,500 acres in Eastern Mexico. He sold the *Continental* in November, 1912, to the new *General Petroleum Company,* which was already a huge $50,000,000 concern, and was made a director of that company. The *General Petroleum* had just exercised an option to purchase the controlling interest in the still greater *Union Oil Company.* Here was a combination that would make the *Standard Oil Co. of California* sit up and take notice. At the same time, Mark Requa of the *Nevada Consolidated Copper Company,* who had converted himself into an oil expert, set about bringing the independent producers together into the *Independent Oil Producers Agency* and a combination of these with the *General Petroleum* and *Union Oil* was looked forward to, even hoping to bring in the Doheny interests. In furtherance of this plan, Hoover set about forming in March, 1913, the *Empire Mutual Oil Company,* with a capital of $40,000,-000 to bring together the independents in the Santa Maria and Midway fields. But nothing came of this. He is also said to have been one of the crowd that let W. P. Hammon down so badly in the *Coalinga Oilfields Company.* Now the year 1913 was one of over-production in the California oilfields. The *General Petroleum* had been expanding too rapidly, and there was no ready market for the huge quantites of oil coming in from independents, which it had to take under contract. This resulted in a shortage of ready cash, and in April, 1913, the *General Petroleum* had to issue $3,000,000 in gold notes, putting up $6,000,000 bonds as security. Later in the year conditions only became worse and the company needed fresh financing. Who could save them? Who, but Hoover?

To finance the *General Petroleum Company*, the *Western Ocean Syndicate* was formed in London, in November, 1913, by Hoover, the banker-gambler Grenfell, Tilden Smith and Andrew Weir, a shipowner and large shareholder and director of the *General Petroleum*, whose brother William was an accountant at No. 1 London Wall Buildings. The articles of association of the syndicate stated that the purpose for which it was formed was to get control of the *General Petroleum Company* and the *Union Oil Company of California*. That was their game. They told Eugene de Sabla, president of the *General Petroleum*, who went over to London on this business, that they would finance the *General Petroleum* to the extent of $3,000,000. On the strength of this, Hoover, Weir and Smith left for California in December and actually took over the *General Petroleum Company* together with its option to buy the *Union Oil Company*, appointing a new board of directors and moving the *General Petroleum* office from San Francisco to Los Angeles.

This was in February, 1914. When Hoover returned to England by the *Lusitania* in the middle of March, he found that one of his partners in this game, Grenfell, had crashed for millions.

In the reliable *Oil Paint & Drug Reporter* of May 18, 1914, (confirmed in other English and American journals), we read the following news item:

"*California Oil for British Ships*: It is becoming more and more apparent that the British interests which have recently secured the *General Petroleum* and the *Union Oil* companies, thereby coming into control of 90,000 barrels a day of the State's output, are very close to the British Government and are figuring on supplying the English navy with its fuel oil. It has been learned that the *Western Ocean Syndicate,* the name of the concern in whose interests the California oil properties were acquired, is owned and controlled by men of prominence closely associated with the English Government, and it is said the Syndicate has already entered into a contract to furnish the English Navy with fuel oil for its new type of oil burning battleships."

Now who were these men of the *Western Ocean Syndicate,* who were closely associated with the English Government? This syndicate consisted of thirteen members, there being on the one side Hoover and six of his men—A. M. Grenfell, the gambler, of the Canadian Agency, who failed in 1914 for millions; F. A. Govett, Hoover's stockbroker associate in most all his ventures; Tilden Smith of the notorious *Share Guarantee Trust,* who backed the *Australian Smelting* swindle and the *Burma Mines,* and three of the Hoover-Govett companies, and on the other side were Andrew Weir and his associates, the *East Asiatic Company* and the *Landsmans Bank* of Copenhagen. Weir imagined that he controlled the syndicate, but he did not know the crowd he was up against and it was only when it came to a showdown on May 1, 1914, that he found Hoover was in control by taking up shares in the syndicate in the names of dummies.

How did Hoover's *Western Ocean Syndicate* finance the *General Petroleum?* In March, 1914, the syndicate registered the *General Petroleum Company, Limited, of London,* with a nominal capital of $16,250,000 and an actual paid up capital of $35!! The agreement made by the syndicate with the *General Petroleum* called for an exchange of shares and preferred stock of the English company for shares and bonds of the Californian company, which was to deposit in the name of the English company 51% of its common stock and $8,000,000 of its bonds by January 7, 1914, in consideration of which the English company would guarantee the interest on the Californian bonds to the extent of $1,500,000, and to the extent of $3,000,000 if the Californians deposited $9,500,000 of their bonds. Just get the significance of this. There were $19,000,000 of bonds outstanding and if $9,500,000 were put up with the English company, these, with the bonds held by his *Inter-Californian Trust*, would enable Hoover to wreck the company at any time by giving him the majority. The Californians. imagining that the English company had a paid up capital of $16,250,000, did deposit in the name of the *Western Ocean Syndicate's English General Petroleum Company, Ltd.*, $8,119,900 in bonds and $29,615,800 in common stock, receiving in exchange 1,664,580 preference and 1,448,474 ordinary shares in the $35 English company, which were worth nothing! What did Herbert Hoover's precious firm do? They moved the bonds from California to Canada under the British flag and pledged them for $3,000,000, lending the Californians the first half year's interest on their bonds (in other words, lending them some of their own money). Even then, the money was not lent outright. The California company was obliged to draw 60 and 90 day drafts on London, which were discounted there and, as these drafts matured, new drafts had to be drawn, thus keeping the California company in constant jeopardy. When the second half year's interest on the bonds fell due on May 1, 1914, Andrew Weir, a responsible business man who is now Lord Inverforth, wanted to pay it, but he found Hoover was now boss of the *Western Ocean Syndicate*. Hoover

refused to pay, alleging that he had not deposited his
bonds to secure the payment of interest to bondholders
who had not put up their bonds. He just wanted that
$9,500,000 put up, so as to give him a majority of the
bonds. This caused a break between Weir and Hoover,
and Weir refused to make the payments on the option
for the control of the *Union Oil* which he had personally
guaranteed. Weir thereupon made a separate deal with
the *Union Oil Company* but, on the authority of Charles
Remington, the well-known financial writer of the San
Francisco *Chronicle*, Hoover hi-jacked him for a one-
sixth interest in the new deal in favor of the *Western
Ocean Syndicate*. It was a long time before the Californians realized that they had been absolutely "buncoed,"
and it was not until May, 1915, that Victor Etienne,
Jr., a Vice President of the *General Petroleum*, filed
a suit, alleging fraud, in the Superior Court in San
Francisco and applying for an injunction against these
English "financiers" against making use of the bonds,
which had only been deposited "in trust." The injunction was granted by Judge Crowthers and this resulted
in arrangements being made for the restoration of the
bonds. It was certainly a terrific joke on the Californians. Meanwhile, however, as there had been default
on four installments of the interest on the bonds, the
General Petroleum Company was forced to go on the
auction block and undergo reconstruction. The *Western Ocean Syndicate's* $35 *General Petroleum Co.* of
London still held in its name 8,600,000 of the bonds
and put up a desperate fight to obtain control of the
great company. The New York bondholders, however,
who held $6,000,000 bonds in escrow, threw in their lot
with the Californians, and Hoover's English gang was
licked. In June, 1916, the *General Petroleum Company*

of California was reconstructed, and $25,000,000 of Common Stock was absolutely wiped out, and $12,000,000 of bonds converted into common stock without guarantee of interest payments, as they had enjoyed before. This was a tremendous loss to the Californian investors in this great company which, since its amalgamation with the *Standard Oil Company of New York,* is now a $450,000,000 corporation, and meant to them not only the loss of their capital but of the many, many millions they would have since received in dividends if they had had an honest deal from the *Western Ocean Syndicate.* And yet they never knew exactly who "did them dirt."

And this was in California in July of 1916, when Hoover was on his way to Belgium to accompany the German Foreign Office representative in Belgium, Von der Lancken, to Berlin to arrange about food supplies with von Sauberzweig, the Chief Quartermaster of the German Army and former Military Governor of Brussels, who had obligingly signed the death warrant for the food "spy" Edith Cavell less than nine months before.

At that very same time, July, 1916, Mark Requa, Hoover's "man Friday," who had rendered Hoover such excellent services two years before in the endeavor to establish a naval oil reserve for England in California, and who, as chairman of the *Nevada Petroleum Company,* had been associated with Doheny for six years, was drawing up a report on the *Elks Hill* reserve informing the U. S. Naval authorities of the "drainage" on the reserve and recommending that they lease it. It "pained" him terribly to see the Navy losing its oil by "drainage" when they could lose it some other way.

When Hoover was sent over from England in April, 1917, to take control of American food supplies for the Allies, he may have known little about food, except the peas, beans and rice, mouldy flour and rotten bacon and lard he was buying, shipping and selling to Belgium. But we must admit that, with his experience, he certainly should have known something about oil. As Food Administrator, he also had charge of the oil fuel of the United States, and whom did he put in control of it? None other than his "man Friday" Requa. In June, 1917, almost immediately after his return from England, where he had rushed over to put through those receiverships for the *Granville Mining Company,* he appointed Requa his assistant and, in January, 1918, named him General Director of the Oil Division of the U. S. Fuel Administration. And whom did Requa appoint to take charge of the Western oil lands including *Elks Hill?* None other than T. A. O'Donnell, Doheny's partner. We have it on the authority of Albert B. Fall, then Secretary of the Interior, that as soon as Requa took over the Oil Division, he personally went to the Secretary of the Navy and handed him a copy of his report of July, 1916, urging the leasing of the *Elks Hill* reserve.

Meanwhile, Harry Sinclair saw the advisability of having with him a man so close to the "Dictator" in Washington, and one so openly in favor of leasing the naval oil reserves. In June, 1919, he made Requa Vice-President of the *Sinclair Consolidated Oil Company,* from which Requa resigned in time before the little deal was put through in the Harding cabinet in June, 1921, transferring the naval oil reserves to Secretary of the Interior Fall. At that time, it puzzled the American public why this was done. But it has since been pretty clearly shown that it was because Fall needed the money. What is a little favor among friends, even if they are Cabinet Ministers? You know the gang that sat around that table, administering the affairs of the greatest nation in the world—Daughterty, Fall, Hoover, Denby and, once or twice, Theodore Roosevelt, Jr., in place of Denby —when the dirty deal was put through to the prejudice of the national defence. Hoover, the friend of Requa, the oil expert of California, Mexico, Peru, Trinidad, Rumania and Russia, sat there and twiddled his thumbs. He knew, but he was quiet and still—as Oil.

We all know the rotten and disgraceful story of the leasing of the *Elks Hill* and *Teapot Dome* naval oil reserves, accompanied as it was by all kinds of slush, bribery, lying and chicanery, and of how Teddy Roosevelt, Jr., heroically stormed *Teapot Dome* with the U. S. Marines and, at the point of the bayonet, drove out the workers of the *Mutual Oil Company,* which had invested their money there, so as to make room for Harry Sinclair's *Mammoth Oil Company.* There are few, however, who know that prior to the bayonet charge and to his appointment as Assistant Secretary of the Navy, Teddy Jr., had been a director of the *Sinclair Oil & Refining Company.* He was working not for the United States of America but for Harry Sinclair, his former master and the present master of his brother Archie, who was then a highly paid employee of Sinclair.

It was a sordid act, played by a sorry gang, without honor, without principle, this story of Oil, Slush and Hush-Hush.

CHAPTER THE FIFTEENTH

TIGERS IN THE JUNGLE

ONE of the prevaricating propagandists of Hoover tells us in his remarkable volume how the adventurous Hoover, in his search for wealth, was crawling through a tunnel in the jungle of Burma, knife between his teeth, when he came across the tracks of a tiger—and retreated. Hoover did not have to do that. He could sit in his London club, sip his whisky and soda, and revolve the geographical globe to Burma or any other part he was interested in. Hoover never was in the jungle of Burma. The only jungle he knew was the London Stock Exchange, and the only animals —the "bulls," the "bears" and the "goats."

Let us see how Hoover's companies operated in the flotation of his string of companies, of which we have mentioned a few. The first step was to secure a mining lease, or an option on one, or a prospecting license or only the hope of getting one, or just a spot on the map, and put it in the name of a "syndicate." Then a company was floated, almost invariably with a paid up capital of $35, representing the value of seven shares, the minimum required by law, and with a nominal capital of the amount the promoters thought the market could absorb. To the new company the anonymous "syndicate" would sell the "valuable" property or rights or concession, or whatever they called it, for any amount up to the total of the nominal capital of the new company, this representing the promoters' "fat." A prospectus was seldom or never issued, for, according to English law, directors are jointly and severally liable for the accuracy of the whole contents of a prospectus, and a summary of the by-laws must also be printed in that document. Thus, to avoid disclosing to the public the clauses inimical to their interests, such as the Discovery Clause, which prevented them from seeing the books and papers of their own company, and the one authorizing the directors to buy shares in other companies and speculate with the shareholders' money, these companies were launched without a prospectus, and the shares were not offered direct to the public. Instead, the shares were "introduced" on the Stock Market, often at an enormous premium, through a firm of brokers, to whom blocks of shares were optioned at rising prices. These stockbrokers would hand out printed slips giving brief particulars, but unsigned, so that no one could be held legally responsible for their contents, and would then put through a few "wash sales" to "make a market." The public, foolishly relying on paid puffs in the press, and thinking that the price thus established was the value of the shares, would come in and buy. The insiders would then sell out as soon as possible the shares they received in the promotion of the company, pocket the proceeds, and then let the venture take pot luck. If it failed, as generally happened, they kept it alive as long as possible by reconstructions or amalgamations, so as to continue enjoying the fat directors' salaries. If successful, they generally sold out the shareholders to some combine for what profit they themselves could make, or else froze out the shareholders altogether and made themselves masters of the property. It was Robbery with a capital R. But not openly and in daylight. Secretly, and by stealth. It was burglary behind a mask, and that mask was the "syndicate." These syndicates or promoting companies were intangible beings, whose entity was but a legal fiction. As the *Mining Journal* of London wrote:

"It is true that in order to create this entity 7 individuals must exist, but having found those 7 it by no means follows that you have found the mind, the body and the substance which directs, controls and creates the operation which brings about the illusion. He is impalpable, he is the promoter. No less impalpable is his picture and his allurements. He has no prospectus, he has no reports, he has nothing to check. The entity arranges for the creation of the market. * * * The practice is in fact a criminal practice. Conspiracy is the foundation and soul of it."

The accounts of these companies were, of course, audited. But the auditors were appointed from year to year and were accordingly at the mercy of the directors. For, to hold their job, they had to shut or wink their eyes when required. The shareholders, too, had an opportunity of having their say at the annual meetings. But a fat chance they got of opening their mouths. The usual procedure at these company meetings was to hold them at noon. Then the Chairman would get up and make a speech for an hour on the great 'prospects" or, if Hoover was in the chair, feed them on illusions and promises of vast wealth. One o'clock. The Chairman would pull out his watch. It was just time for lunch. The shareholders, talked half asleep by this time, would immediately see visions of roast beef and green cheese and beer. Thereupon the Chairman would put the resolution, which would be immediately seconded, a vote of thanks passed and everyone was out in the street in five minutes. The shareholder who had the criticism to make seldom got a chance unless he had lots of grit and a powerful voice. There was a "claque" to howl him down and even toughs were sometimes employed to give him the "bum's rush" if he became obstreperous. Yes, your racketeers and hi-jackers had little on these tough baby London mining promoters.

Of course there were laws to protect the public. But laws are generally meant to apply against the "small fry," and, as we have seen more than once, we are dealing here with people who, for certain Chinese reasons, were "above the law" in England. The False Statements (Companies) Act of 1904 provided:

> "If any person, being a director, manager, secretary, or other officer of any company or being the auditor of any company, whether an officer or not, wilfully circulates, publishes or makes or prepares for circulation or publication, or concurs in so circulating, publishing, making or preparing any written statement of account relating to the financial affairs or property of the company which he knows to be false in any material particular, he shall be liable on conviction on indictment to imprisonment for a term not exceeding two years, or, in the discretion of the Court, to a fine not exceeding five hundred pounds."

Section 84 of the Larceny Act stipulated:

> "Whosoever being a director, manager or public officer of any body corporate or public company, shall make, circulate, or publish, or concur in making, circulating or publishing, any written statement or account which he shall know to be false in any material particular, with intent to deceive or defraud any member, shareholder or

creditor of such body corporate or public company, or with intent to induce any person to
become a shareholder or partner therein, or to
entrust or advance any property to such body
corporate or public company or to enter into any
security for the benefit thereof shall be guilty of
a misdemeanor. On conviction for the offence
mentioned, a person may be ordered to be kept
in penal servitude for any term not exceeding
seven years."

We do not need to quote the act on perjury, for
everyone knows that this offence is a felony. But it is
advisable to bear the above in mind when reading the
jungle tale of the Burma Mines. According to Hoover's
"liographers," he just kind of stumbled across these
mines while he "wandered about in the jungle, killing
tigers and killing time." But this is just one more of
the illusions from the Hoover phantasmagoria.

The Burma mines, the richest lead-zinc-silver-copper
mines in the world's history, are located at a place
called Bawdwin in Tawngpeng, one of the northern Shan
States of Burma, in a mountainous region 140 miles north
of Mandalay. They were known to the Chinese as Lao
Yin Chang or Old Silver Mines and were first worked
by the Chinese of Yunnan in 1412, and for centuries
gave employment to thousands of workers, who treated
the ore for the silver it contained in little beehive
furnaces, first drawing off the lead and then heating
further until the silver came. In 1855 the Panthay
rebellion broke out, and the Mohammedan fanatics de-
vastated the country, killing off the inhabitants, and
the mines were abandoned. In 1890 A. C. Martin of
Rangoon, an engineer in charge of the *Mandalay Canal
Works,* happened to notice that some of the pilgrims

to the great religious payadi in Mandalay wore silver
ornaments, which was not customary in Burma, and
on enquiring where they came from was told that they
were natives of Tawnpeng. This whetted Martin's
curiosity and he made a trip there, and located the
old Bawdwin mines on a high hill, 4,000 feet up, where
there was only one single banyon tree left pointing the
road to China, and never a trace of jungle or sign of
a tiger. Indeed, there was no vegetation whatever. The
country was as bare, bleak and barren as a Scotchman's
family estate. There Martin saw huge heaps of slag
which the Chinese had left behind after extracting the
silver, and miles of tunnels and underground workings
showing how the Chinese had extracted the ore. On
a subsequent visit, Martin took a few mule loads of the
slag back with him to Rangoon and showed it to Mr.
A. Sarkies of the Rangoon Hotel, whom he interested.
The result was the formation of a company called the
Great Eastern Mining Company, in 1902, with a capital of $250,000, the directors including Martin,
Sarkies and M. F. Kindersley, a former official of the
Indian Government, who obtained the mining concession for Sarkies. They sent out a smelter to Mandalay,
and commenced building a light railway 51 miles long
from Manpwe Junction on the Burma Railroad to Bawdwin. But their capital was not sufficient, and they
started looking for further funds. It was under these
circumstances that they got in touch with Hoover's firm,
Bewick Moreing & Company, who had the property
examined and then, with Govett and Tilden Smith of
the *Share Guarantee Trust,* and later of the Western
Ocean Syndicate, decided to take over the venture—
provided it cost them nothing. Burma, yes, that was a
name that would appeal to shareholders. Why, that

was where the rubies came from. Of course, the proposition was really a big gamble consisting as it did of about 150,000 tons of lead slag in the mountains of far away Burma, hundreds of miles from a shipping port and without railroad connection, and just the possibility of finding a mine underneath. These gentlemen were not, however, putting up any money of their own. No, indeed. In 1906, there issued from Bewick Moreing's office, and sponsored by Hoover, Govett and Tilden Smith, the Burma Mines with a paid up capital of $35 and a nominal capital of $1,300,000 in $5 shares, and $750,000 in 6% debentures, the Great Eastern Mining Company receiving $250,000 of the debentures and 114,700 of the new shares, the promoters keeping 145,-300 for themselves and thus having control of the company right from the start. The debentures were mostly foisted off on companies controlled by the Hoover firm and Govett, such as the *London & Western Australian Exploration Company* and the *Lake View Consols*, the funds of which were always conveniently available.

In the financing of the *Burma Mines*, Hoover made extensive use of the method described by *Truth* as the "debenture flap-trap." The issue of debentures not only depreciates the value of the shares but, as the debentures can be paid out of the capital instead of the profits, they are a constant menace and club over the heads of the shareholders. Besides, they afford a fine opportunity for insiders to earn big commissions by acting as brokers or underwriters for the companies they are directors of. Hoover, you may be sure, did not hesitate to take advantage of this. In March 1908, we find the *Burma Mines* registering an issue of $200,000 debentures for a bonus of $300,000 (150%!)—Govett and Hoover, two of the directors, being the mortgagees! Of course,

directors of a company should not act as brokers in their own interest as against the interest of their company, but the business code of Hoover and Govett was quite different. They did not regard themselves as trustees for the shareholders but, as Govett once callously admitted, as privileged speculators.

When the first issue of $750,000 debentures was made in 1906 it was estimated that it would require $350,000 to complete the railway and smeltery. And yet the accounts for 1908 show that $1,105,915 (nearly 3½ times as much) was supposed to have been spent on those items and the company apparently short of funds. Yet the smeltery had been erected at Mandalay, where the birds sing all day, and the railroads run to within a few miles of Bawdwin, so that everything was ready to start operations.

On January 17th, 1909, the first train load of slag came down the line to the Mandalay smelter. Work had begun. The business looked good. It was now time to start some share juggling with a view to getting rid of the original investing shareholders, and putting the entire company into the hands of the insiders. With this object there began a series of share wanglings such as was seldom or never been seen. In April, 1908, the Hoover firm took 45,000 of the original $5 shares and converted them into 450,000 50c. shares, giving the new shares 95% of the profits. This did not produce the desired result. Accordingly, in February 1909, they created 463,686 preference shares of 75c. each, giving these new shares 95% of the profits. This, too, fell short of the mark and, in June 1909, they created a further 478,090 "A" preference shares giving this last issue 95% of the assets and profits and not only that but 5 votes for every 1 vote held by the other classes of shareholders. This did the trick. The manipulation had reduced the interest in the company of every $8,000 of the original share to just $1! Of the 288,090 new "A" preference shares issued, practically 90% were held by Smith, Hoover, Govett and the *Lake View Consols,* of which Hoover and Govett were managing directors, and they still held 190,000 shares "in the bag" for future eventualities. Don't imagine that they paid for these shares. They simply got rid of their old free original $5 shares in time and converted the proceeds into the new $1 "A" preference shares, which now appeared on the books as "50c paid."

In 1909, the first year of operation, the *Burma Mines* did pretty well. The accounts show that 11,850 tons of the rich Bawdwin slag and 485 tons of ore were treated, yielding 5,030 tons of lead and 27,500 ounces of silver, value $286,110. This looked pretty good for a start, for the slag only cost about 75 cents a ton to break down or sluice, and the lead contents ran as high as 50%. How much profit did they make? None, at least their books showed none, because the gang that was running these mines did not want the public to know the true state of affairs. The balance sheet for 1909 actually showed a loss of $616,005! Yet, you will say, the auditors must have passed on this balance sheet. But bear in mind that all these operations were carried on in far away Burma, and the Burma books (the whole business in fact) were never seen by the auditors, who certified this on each succeeding balance sheet. One can imagine what these balance sheets were worth!

The facts were that in 1909 the railroad had been completed right up to the slag heaps. Drill holes had been put down under the slag heaps, and proof found of one of the richest mines in the world. They had discovered Aladdin's cave. They were sitting on the top of the world. They were not satisfied to hold 90% of the shares. They wanted them all, and for nothing or next to nothing. How did they accomplish this? In November 1909, they took in as a director J. M. Fells, an expert accountant and former associate of the notorious crook Whitaker Wright, and he showed them a trick or two. The smeltery and railroad had just been completed in their entirety, and yet they wrote off nearly one third (about $500,000) of the total cost of this brand new equipment. Then they wrote off the little sum of over $600,000, supposed to be the expenses of formation and organization of the company which they had walked right into free of charge! And thus they managed to leave the accounts for 1909 showing a loss of $616,000! It looked bad. But in the report which Hoover and Govett had sent out to the *Lake View Consols* shareholders in the Fall of 1909 they let slip the information that the *Burma Mines* were soon expected to be self supporting and that good profits would be obtained in the early months of 1910.

Hoover, Govett and Smith now knew that there was a great mine under those slag heaps of a richness hitherto unknown in silver-lead-zinc mines. They held nearly all the "A" preference shares. Now they must get rid of all the other classes of shareholders. To accomplish this the company decided to break the value of the property. This balance sheet drawn up on December 31, 1909, had reduced the value of the railroad and smeltery from $1,500,000 to $900,000. But it still left the value of the mine property at the original nominal value of $1,300,000, although the insiders now knew that it was worth indefinitely more. On the 1909 balance sheet the value of the property with other assets stood at $2,250,000. With the knowledge that the mine had been proven, and in spite of this balance sheet which had just been compiled before their eyes, they resolved to reduce the capital and wipe out the old shareholders completely. This, however, could not be done except by decision of a Judge of the High Court based on sworn affidavits.

On February 4, 1910, Herbert Hoover made a sworn affidavit before Justice Neville of the Chancery Division of the High Court, and on February 23, 1910, another one correcting the figures in the first one, in which he recited that he had been a director of the company since its incorporation and accordingly was aware of the status of the company and that of the paid up capital of $1,778,750 at least $1,610,100 had been lost or was unrepresented by available assets and that the deficiency of $1,610,100 must be regarded as a permanent deficiency and ought to be written off and cancelled. He was reducing to $168,650 the value of that Golconda, which, a few years later, he was advertising as being worth hundreds of millions of dollars. In his affidavit, Hoover cunningly introduced the name of Lord Herschell, son of the great Lord Chancellor, who had taken some shares from his brother-in-law Kindersley, and the Judge, probably taking it for granted that a Herschell would not be mixed up in any questionable business, approved the reduction of capital.

After filing this affidavit, Hoover's company proceeded to clean the slate. The debit balance of $616,000 was written off, as well as $875,000 from the value of the property, and a further $119,000 from the railroad and the capital reduced to $503,252 in 503,252 shares of $1. And what did they do to the old shareholders? The outstanding $205,260 preference shares of 75c were reduced to $23,902, new $1 shares, the $130,-000 of 50c ordinary shares to $1,195 and the $1,300,000 $5 shares of the original shareholders to $151!! Of course, the "A" preference shares held by Hoover and his crowd were left intact. They now practically had the mine in their pockets.

Wonderful new discoveries were made in 1910. In March of that year the Shan, Burmese and Meingtha lodes were all proved, showing an enormous wealth of ore. The smelter was moved from Mandalay to Namtu, near the mines, in order to be able to handle quickly the increased quantities. And what encouragement was given to the debenture holders? None. No interest was paid on the debentures. The accounts were made to show losses year after year, and false balance sheets presented, none of which were certified correct by the auditors, as required by law.

What was the game? To increase their shareholdings in exchange for fake loans and to secure the original debenture holders, so that they might pick up at a bargain their debentures, which had the privilege of being exchanged into shares. Thus it was that at the *Lake View & Oroya* meeting in 1911, when everything was going swimmingly, Govett confessed that about the *Burma Mines* he was a "bit dubious." In May, 1913, the great Chinaman lode was discovered, a solid core of enormous extent containing practically 60% metal—lead, zinc and silver. This meant fabulous wealth, untold riches. And what did Hoover do? At the annual meeting of the *Burma Mines* in July 1913, he spoke of having had to borrow money from the Inter-Continental Trust (one of Hoover's own syndicates), mentioned the great metallurgical difficulties (the old Australian blind) and said that the *Burma Mines* would require

$1,000,000 to $1,500,000 for re-financing. They were, he said, with their "back to the wall." At that very same time they were arranging through the Inter-Continental Trust the flotation of the *Burma Corporation* to take over the *Burma Mines,* and preparing statements for the press to tell the world of the enormous riches of the *Burma Mines,* promising profits of $5,000,- 000 to $6,750,000 per 100 feet in depth!!

The *Burma Corporation* (Curb traders know this bird), promoted by Hoover's *Inter-Continental Trust,* staggered out from Hoover's office in October 1913, to finance the *Burma Mines* with a paid up capital of $35 and a nominal capital of $3,750,000 (soon after increased to $5,000,000) in $5 shares, the majority of which were allotted to the *Inter-Continental Trust* and then sold to the public on the ballyhoo campaign started in the press. Through the *Inter-Continental Trust,* the *Burma Corporation* acquired nearly all the debentures and 99¾% of the shares of the *Burma Mines* and thus became the holding company. The directors of the two companies were practically identical and were to all intents and purposes the same outfit. And yet we have this curious anomaly. In December 1915, the paid up capital of the *Burma Mines* was some $268,000 and its books showed a loss of $277,545 and the *Burma Corporation* (which was supposed to hold nothing but *Burma Mines* shares and debentures) had at that date a paid up capital (shares sold to the public or held by insiders) of $4,566,745 of a market value of over $9,000,000!

What is the explanation? It is very simple. The whole business was a swindle and fraud right from the beginning. The Burma Mines were a paying proposition from the start. But these gentlemen fixed the books to make it appear that they were working at a huge loss, so as to freeze out the other share and debenture holders and get sole control of the property. Then, when they thought the time ripe, they prepared for a killing by forming the Burma Corporation as a holding company with a capital of nearly 30 times as great as the paid-up capital of the *Burma Mines* and marketing these shares of the *Burma Corporation* at a premium with the aid of ballyhoo in the press. They succeeded. In 1913 the *Burma Mines* shares had not a quotation and in 1914 the *Burma Corporation,* with nearly 30 times the capital, sold up to 65% premium!

Then the unexpected happened. War broke out in 1914. A 40% excess profits duty (in 1917 increased to 80%) was levied by the British Government on companies. The *Burma Mines* would have to pay this duty on any profits made in excess of 6%, and this would, of course, prevent the *Burma Corporation* as holding company from earning anything. But there is always a way out of these little difficulties. An agreement was made, purporting to be executed and conveniently dated May 29th, 1914 (prior to the war), according to which the Burma Mines (Hoover, Govett and Tilden Smith) would pay 75% of their profits to the *Burma Corporation* (Hoover, Govett and Tilden Smith) for managing the *Burma Mines.* Can you beat it? It is a remarkable fact that this precious agreement was not filed with the Registrar of Joint Stock Companies and was first heard of towards the end of 1915. The *Burma Corporation,* in turn, pretended to lend back this 75% of the profits to the *Burma Mines* for expansion.

The *Burma Mines* company, of course, make use of the Discovery Clause. And, although shareholders or debenture holders might be astounded to find the yearly accounts showing that it was costing as much as $67.50

a ton (year 1913) to produce lead from slag with a 50%
content, they dare not venture to ask to see the account
books of their own company. No, this would never do.

It would take a volume to analyze the accounts of
the *Burma Mines* and no doubt it would not be very
interesting reading. But let us take something that
everyone can understand. In the first nine years of
operation from 1909 to 1917 inclusive, when the slag
heaps were finally exhausted, we find the following
from the reports of the Indian Government and from
the *Burma Mines* own accounts:

Year	Ore (tons)	Slag (tons)	Lead (tons)	Silver (oz.)	Sold for
1909	485	11,850	5,030	27,500	$ 286,110
1910	975	29,533	12,896	49,680	804,590
1911	3,218	31,954	13,185	103,850	906,485
1912	2,950	22,563	8,531	93,476	781,380
1913	3,939	16,360	5,858	125,209	695,275
1914	8,769	24,901	10,548	236,446	1,209,635
1915	4,094	32,534	13,522	284,875	1,617,850
1916	8,839	4,771	13,790	759,012	2,624,650
1917	54,616	6,282	16,962	1,580,537	3,981,135
	87,885	180,748	100,322	3,260,585	$12,907,110
Bullion in transit 1917					284,185
					$13,191,295

This slag and ore realized, less treatment and shipping costs, as much as $49 a ton, based on their own
returns of what they received, and these are somewhat
open to doubt. For we find that in the very first year
they gave the receipts for bullion as $286,110, whereas
the Indian Government gives the amount realized as
$340,500. That the ore was so enormously rich can be
seen from the statement of Govett at the meeting of the
Burma Corporation in December 1914, when he said:

> "The ore has a value of £11 ($55) to £18 ($90)
> per ton. We can place it in the metallurgical
> establishment of Europe at a cost not exceeding
> £3 ($15) per ton."

Now, what did it cost to treat this rich lead slag and ore? The *Burma Mines* report for December 31, 1910, shows that the cost of treatment, inclusive of general expenses, at the Mandalay smelter was Rupees 9.7 ($2.75) per ton. The report for December 31, 1911, shows that the cost of treatment at the smelter when removed to Namtu in the mine district was practically the same. The cost of breaking down or sluicing the slag was under 75 cents a ton and the cost of mining the first ore was only $1 a ton, as it was taken from open workings, and the serf labor employed earned only 20 cents a day. When we take into account that after the outbreak of War, nearly all the production of lead and silver was sold locally in India, it is hard to see how the cost of extraction, treatment, transport, shipping, etc., could have reached $8 a ton, which would leave a profit for these 9 years of over $11,000,000. That these profits were earned, there is no doubt. Already in December 1915, at the meeting of the *Burma Corporation,* Tilden Smith said that over $10,000,000 had been spent on the equipment and development of the mine, and it was later confirmed by Sir T. Wynne in 1920 that this $10,000,000 was supposed to have come out of the earnings. Now, let us see what development was done. Down to the end of 1917 the total development was only some 20,000 feet, which, at the rates of wages paid, would not cost over $400,000. And what about the equipment? The *Burma Mines* accounts for December 31, 1917, show the value of the buildings, plant, machinery and equipment as only $173,040! Of course they spent something on their 2 ft. railroad and on their plant every year, and wrote off still more for depreciation. But they must have had a railroad wreck every week or blown the smelter roof off every day to account for the balance of the ten millions! Maybe humanitarian Hoover ordered it spent for the benefit of indigent Chinamen! Wrong again. While Hoover was in Berlin in the first week of August 1916 discussing the question of food supplies with the Von Sauberzweig, Chief Quartermaster of the German Army (and don't forget that in August 1916 Germany was on its last legs, absolutely starving), the dread Plague stalked through the valley of Namtu in Burma, closing down the mines and leaving the unfortunate Chinese serfs, for serfs they were, to die of hunger.

Now let us see how these people kept their accounts. In the year 1917, a total of 60,898 tons of lead ore and slag was treated for a yield of 16,962 tons of lead and 1,580,557 ounces of silver. On the basis of previous actual costs of $2.75 per ton (inclusive of general expenses), the cost of treatment and general expenses for this quantity of slag and ore would amount to $167,470. What do the *Burma Mines* accounts for 1917 show?

Treatment	$1,494,302
Operating expenditure	335,371
General expenses	66,299
Experimental expenses	44,475
General expenses (London)	32,121
Bad debts, depreciation	272,840
Salaries and wages	93,782 etc.

in all, over $3,000,000 charged against the 60,898 tons of ore and slag, an average of $50 a ton! One hundred and seventy-eight dollars per ton of lead produced!! This still left a profit in the 1917 accounts of $960,-722, which was subject to an excess profits duty of 80%. Seven hundred twenty thousand five hundred and forty-two dollars of this was placed to the credit of the *Burma Corporation* (the left hand to the right) for managing the mines! After this deduction there still remained a profit of $240,130 subject to the excess profits duty on the excess of 6%. But the Hoover crowd appealed to the British tax authorities, alleging that the *Burma Mines* was a branch of the *Burma Corporation,* and, as such, only liable for tax on the excess of 12½%, thus escaping paying duty altogether.

Now let us look at the remarkable Balance Sheet of the *Burma Mines* for 1917. It shows:

Cash	$1,242,200		
Bullion in transit	284,185	Creditors	$1,000,125
War bonds	307,875	Loans from banks	984,300
Debtors	582,445		
Stores	1,313,721		

If they had all that cash, what did they need to borrow money for? Then there appeared the amount of $2,467,490 as owing to the *Burma Corporation* which, as explained, was just experimental bookkeeping. The auditors, of course, did not dare to certify these accounts.

In the *Burma Mines* company, Tilden Smith had always held a majority of the shares. But with the formation of the *Burma Corporation,* Hoover's *Lake View & Oroya Exploration Company* received 100,00 *Burma Corporation* shares in exchange for the debentures and shares held in the *Burma Mines,* and Hoover, of course, controlled these shares. Then, when Tilden Smith was over in California in the beginning of May 1914, with Andrew Weir, negotiating for the California oil properties, Hoover played the Artful Dodger in real earnest. A new board of directors was appointed, consisting of Hoover, his brother and Govett on one side and Tilden Smith with two of his friends on the other, with two engineers. Hoover, however, saw to it that these engineer directors, one of whom was an associate of his and was afterwards let in on the Belgian Relief, were on his side and he consequently controlled the board of directors, five to three. He then formed his *Bawdwin Syndicate,* to which he had allotted over 100,000 more shares and gave an option on an additional 200,000. Hoover thus double-crossed Smith as he did at the same time in the Western Ocean Syndicate and gained control of the *Burma Corporation.* How far he may have been aided in this by C. S. Magennis, Tilden Smith's director is not known, but 1898, and was subsequently employed in Hoover's firm for years before Hoover wangled him into the position of accountant with Smith. Hoover now was the lord of the *Burma Corporation,* and in 1915 even took in as director Sir Arthur Lawley who, as Lieutenant Governor of the Transvaal, had awarded the Chinese slave business in 1904 to Hoover's *Chinese Engineering & Mining Company.* Smith, however, was not the kind of man to lie down. He was a lone fighter and had been hit hard by the outbreak of the war. But he was one of the bulldog breed and from then on he put up a silent bitter, continuous fight to regain control of the *Burma Corporation* in the jungle of the London Stock Exchange.

In 1918, still greater progress had been made by the *Burma Mines,* and its books were again padded to show an even greater sum owing to the *Burma Corporation.* The stock, in spite of no dividends, was being bought at ever advancing prices and at the end of 1918 the five dollar shares reached almost twenty-five dollars. To avoid tax complications with the British Government, the Hoover crowd decided to convert the concern into an Indian company and, in December 1919, registered the *Burma Corporation of India* in Rangoon with a capital of 180,000,000 rupees (about $80,000,000) in 18,000,000 shares of 10 rupees each, exchanging fourteen fully paid shares in the new company for each

share of the *Burma Mines*. They accompanied the issue
by a most extensive advertising campaign showing that
the *Burma Mines,* which had never paid a dividend, and
was apparently always in debt, was earning profits at
the rate of $3,000,000 a year, and had proved ore re-
serves valued conservatively at over $500,000,000!!
The English *Burma Corporation's* $5 shares soared to
nearly $70 each! This was certainly a wonderful coup.
Many millions for Hoover.

The last act, however, had yet to be played. The
English *Burma Corporation* had assets in cash and investments of nearly $8,000,000. Were they distributed to
the shareholders? Bless your simplicity, no. The *Burma
Mines* company still had 241,936 shares unissued. This
afforded an opportunity for some more fancy financial
juggling. The *Burma Corporation* made a contract with
the *Burma Mines* on October 16th, 1919, purporting to
sell to the *Burma Mines* all its cash, stocks, shares and
securities (except those in the *Burma Mines*) to the
Burma Mines in exchange for the 241,936 unissued
shares. Now, of whom did the *Burma Mines* company
consist at that time? Just Hoover, Smith and their
satellites. They would divide up that melon of $8,000,-
000 or thereabouts. And what became of the 241,936
shares, which were each exchangeable for 14 shares in
the *Burma Corporation of India?* That was in great
part divided too.

Hoover was very busy just then in other directions
with the U. S. Food and Fuel Dictatorship, European
Relief, etc., where there was bigger money to handle and
even less control. But the *Burma Corporation* business
was a bone with too much meat on it for him to let go,
and he still retained his directorship of that company.
Self-relief first. It was on August 6th, 1920, that the

showdown came. On that date a special meeting of the *Burma Mines* company was held for the purpose of resolving the liquidation of the company, and the distribution of the assets, which included the millions from the *Burma Corporation.* The shareholders of the *Burma Mines* were at that time a handful—Hail Columbia Hoover, Carbine Govett and Silent Smith and their tribesmen. They only mustered forty-one adherents at the meeting. Almost immediately the Chairman put the resolution to liquidate and distribute the assets, naming as liquidator David Anderson, Hoover's company secretary and brainbox. At the meeting, Smith disdained sitting with the Hoover gang of directors, and stood up in the body of the hall and moved as an amendment that Sir Walter Peat be appointed as joint liquidator. Uproar. The gang of wolves saw a spectre at the feast. The amendment was howled down. Smith demanded a poll. The original resolution to leave the liquidation in Anderson's hands was then put and passed by 35 votes to 6. Smith again demanded a poll. He knew; he had the votes in his pocket. For five long years he had striven for this, silently, secretly, stubbornly, sacrificing other interests, always on the trail like a jungle tiger to catch and beat the man who had double-crossed him in California as well as in Burma. The meeting was adjourned for two weeks and then it was seen that Smith held command and he was left to arrange distribution of those assets. It had cost Smith very dear, but he had his day of satisfaction, if one can say such for a man who had just lost his only son in the service of his country. The great mining newspaper, the *Mining Journal* of London in its obituary notice on the death of Tilden Smith in December 1929, wrote as follows:

"In later years a struggle for the control (of the *Burma Mines*) developed, which was only terminated when the Hoover interests were bought out at the end of the War. The real history of those years will probably never be written, but it was a source of keen gratification to Mr. Tilden Smith. * * * It was a struggle which involved great financial exertions as towards the end the extraordinary value of the deposits became widely recognized."

This is the story of the *Burma Mines,* one of the greatest in the world's history. Mistake not. This goose with the golden eggs was not discovered in the Burmese jungle by Hoover, but was delivered to his doorstep as a chick to be reared and the golden eggs it laid were substituted by china ones until the time when the original owners lost all interest in it. Then when its real value came to light it was fought for and won in the jungle of the London Stock Exchange by two-faced humans, more to be dreaded than any jungle tiger.

CHAPTER THE SIXTEENTH

THE MORE MUCK, THE MORE LUCK

A MONTH or two after Hoover was on his way in 1897 to the sunburnt wastes of West Australia as field agent and reporter extraordinary on mines for Moreing, others were preparing for the trek North to the Yukon. The Klondike gold rush was on. From all parts of the world, the gold-greedy foregathered. All the hardships and sufferings, comedy and pathos of this strange exodus have been pictured for us on the screen. Stories and poems have been written of those wild lawless days in the North West. As Kipling wrote: "There aint no law of God or man North of 43." As usual, some few struck it rich. But many left their bones in the snow-covered icy fields of the North. Of the early settlers who made good, one, A. N. C. Treadgold, came from England and another, J. W. Boyle, from Woodstock in Canada. They became magnates in Dawson City.

Most of the gold obtained in the Klondike was by placer mining, digging and washing the gravel in the river valleys, This was exceedingly difficult work, for it necessitated the removal, not only of trees and bushes, but also of a layer of moss and vegetation of some two feet in thickness and then an overburden of frozen, decayed vegetable matter and earth, called "muck" which might be from five to fifty feet in thickness, and was frozen solid to the consistency of sandstone. It was only then that the goldbearing gravel was reached, and it, too, was frozen and had to be thawed out before it could be worked. The oldtimers' placer mining methods consisted in digging a trench down to the gravel and then making a fire with wood to thaw out the gravel sufficiently to be worked. This work could only be done in the Winter on account of the fumes from the smoke not rising into the lighter rarified air in the Summer. As all work was done by hand and labor cost seven dollars a day this process proved to be very expensive, so that only the richest patches could be worked.

After the peak year of 1900, many of these claims were gradually abandoned. In 1902, Treadgold obtained from the Canadian Government a concession of nearly all the abandoned worked out place mining lands, together with the right to take water from the creeks free of charge, and went to England to try and promote a company to exploit them by dredging. While there, he saw Hoover and Moreing, but they were too busy in West Australia just then to go into the proposition. This concession was cancelled later on, owing to the bitter opposition of local miners. A few years later, Treadgold interested the Guggenheims in this dredging proposition and, after exhaustive tests, a new company was formed, the *Yukon Gold Company,* which took claims on practically all the most important abandoned gravels in Bonanza, Eldorado and Hunker creeks, operating 8 dredges and recovering about $3,000,000 worth of gold yearly. The method of working adopted by the *Yukon Gold Company* was the removal of the "muck" in the usual way and then the thawing out of the gravel by steam produced by portable boilers and applied through steel points forced into the gravel. The cost of operating in this way was thirty cents per cubic yard of gravel extracted. Another successful operator as dredger was Boyle, who operated under the name of the *Canadian Klondike Mining Company* in the watershed of the Klondike River, where he held a lease known as "Boyle's Concession" covering the entire flat of the Klondike valley and containing some 250,000,000 cubic yards of gravel. Boyle had a great advantage in working, as the Klondike river flowed through the valley throughout the year and the underground flow and seepage of water formed naturally thawed areas, to which Boyle restricted his operations. The result of these favorable conditions was that Boyle could operate 260 days in the year as against 160 worked by the Yukon Gold, and not only that but he did not have to use steam for thawing out the gravel, but, after removal of the "muck," sluiced the gravel out with water diverted from the creeks and thawed it out naturally with the heat from the sun and air. His working costs were accordingly only about ten cents per cubic yard of gravel, on account of the exceptional conditions in this watershed washed by a great river.

In 1910, Hoover got in touch with A. Chester Beatty, with whom he was connected in the *Continental Oil Company*. Beatty had been employed by the Guggenheim firm, and was familiar with all these Klondike operations, and, of course, so was Treadgold, who had been managing director of the *Yukon Gold Company*. Klondike matters were discussed and the possibility of operating there. Outside of a few private claims, the only lands obtainable were those of the semi-defunct *Dominion Mining Company, Calder Mining Company, Big Creek Mining Company* and *Sulphur Mining Company* in what was called the Indian Watershed and which had already been worked to death, having already produced $24,250,-000 worth of gold. Drillings were made in part of these grounds and it was estimated that they still contained thirty cents worth of gold to the ton of gravel, which would not quite cover operating expenses. Then there was a stretch in the Bonanza Basin held by the *Bonanza*

Basin Gold Dredging Company estimated to contain 100,-
000,000 cubic yards of gravel running only twenty cents
worth of gold to the cubic yard, which would not pay to
work. There was no possibility of forming a successful
company with these claims. Hoover, however, saw things
differently. Why, here they had all the elements for a
"killing." It was the *Madame Berry Deep Lead* all over
again. Just as he had made use of that famous name in
the *Deep Leads of Victoria* coup, here he could take
advantage of the prestige of the *Yukon Gold Company*
and play up the low costs of *Boyle's Canadian Klondike
Mining Company.*

Treadgold was brought down from the Klondike in the
Winter of 1910, and in March, 1911, he met Hoover and
Beatty at 71 Broadway, where they laid the plans for
the new company. Treadgold was to assemble the above
placer mining claim, and Hoover would form a company
to exploit them. Hoover and Beatty at once registered
in Delaware a concern called the *Eastern Trading Company.* The *Mining Magazine* of April, 1911, tells us:

> "A syndicate with a capital of £200,000 ($1,000,-
> 000) has been formed by H. C. Hoover and A. C.
> Beatty, half the amount being placed in New
> York and half in London. The intention is to
> bring out a company later with a view to exploit-
> ing a number of claims situated in Dominion,
> Quartz, Last Chance, Eldorado and other famous
> creeks near Dawson."

The shareholders of this syndicate were Hoover and
Govett (and, of course, the companies they controlled
and whose funds they could gamble with—the *Ivanhoe,
Oroya Exploration* and *Lake View Consols*), Beatty, the
Consolidated Mines Selection Company and the *Gold-
fields American Development Company,* these being two

branches of the *Consolidated Goldfields of South Africa,* which was very prominent in the following year in the tin coup in Nigeria.

Treadgold assembled some 8,000 acres of placer mining claims as the "property" to be taken over by the new company. Now, all the property one could have in a Yukon placer claim was a measly one year lease, renewable from year to year on payment of a fee and on presenting proof that at least $200 had been spent on the claim within the year. Not much property! In August, 1911, the *Granville Mining Company* (what a pretty name!) was floated in London without any prospectus, as usual, and with the usual $35 paid up capital to acquire this "valuable property." Hoover himself named the first Board of Directors, which, of course, included himself and Carbine Govett, and also made himself a manager of the company, together with Beatty and Treadgold. He was the one who had discovered this "melon," and he wanted the cutting of it.

And what was this melon? Oh, boy! The nominal capital of the *Granville Mining Company* was $6,000,000, soon increased to $7,500,000. It was made to appear that Treadgold was receiving $6,000,000 in shares, $500,-000 in 1st mortgage debenture bonds and $345,000 in cash for these semi-defunct placer claims. Hoover's *Eastern Trading Company* received $550,000 in shares for placing $2,200,000 1st mortgage debenture bonds, and Hoover a further $150,000 in shares for some kind of "services rendered" in addition to the block of shares he received from Treadgold. For, of course, the 1,000,000 shares allotted to Treadgold were not for him at all. They were divided up among the boys. Out of the 1,500,000 $5 shares they stuck to 1,310,000, leaving only 190,000 in the company's treasury to provide working capital, if

sold, for the company. It was the same "divvying up"
as had been done in most of Hoover's other companies.
For working expenses the "debenture flaptrap" game was
again used. Yes, sir, this precious company issued
$4,500,000 1st mortgage debenture bonds against this
"valuable property," to a solitary claim of which the
Granville never held title. This was worse than Nigeria.
$1,800,000 worth of these bonds were sold in September,
1911, and what became of this money? Practically every
penny of it was immediately paid over to Hoover's *Eastern Trading Company* on the pretext that it was a refund
for advances made to Treadgold in the Klondike. They
did not dare advertise these bonds for sale, as this would
require the publishing of a prospectus. So they "put
them over" through brokers and on companies they themselves had control of, the patient and long suffering
Lake View being "let in" right at the start for $128,370
of these bonds as well as $146,025 of the shares by man-
aging director Hoover, although they had not even been
admitted to trading by the Stock Exchange for nine
months afterwards.

The insiders now wanted to "make a market" for the
1,310,000 shares they had bagged. But as they had really
nothing to show as assets, not even a claim in their own
name, the Stock Exchange could not give them a "settlement." Neither could they publish a prospectus for a
bond issue. Hoover accordingly had Treadgold, who returned home to the Klondike in September, 1911, bring
back to London with him early in 1912 none other than
Joseph Whiteside Boyle of the *Canadian Klondike Mining
Company.* And then the rarest kind of a deal was made,
or rather, supposed to have been made. Of the claims
held in trust by Treadgold and brought into the *Granville Mining Company* by Treadgold, there were those of

the *Bonanza Basin Gold Dredging Company* covering about 100,000,000 cubic yards of gravel in the Bonanza Basin, close to Boyle's Concession. The value of the gold on this "property" had been estimated at twenty cents per cubic yard, and it was therefore worthless, for experience had shown that it would cost far more to even clean the "muck" off it. These gentlemen, however, purported to make a deal whereby, in exchange for this "valuable property" and a loan of $1,350,000 to Boyle for the purpose of buying new dredges, Boyle agreed to give the *Granville Mining Company* $1,200,000 6% bonds in his *Canadian Klondike Power Company* and also $1,500,-000 6% 1st mortgage bonds and $2,320,000 common stock out of $8,000,000 in his *Canadian Klondike Mining Company*, guaranteeing to the *Granville Mining Company* an assured income of $240,000 a year until 1928.

This supposed agreement, on the face of it, is ridiculous. A remarkable feature about it is that it was not registered, as required by law, with the Registrar of Joint Stock Companies, and Boyle apparently never paid the slightest attention to it. For, the *Granville Mining Company* never received these stocks and bonds in the *Canadian Klondike Mining Company*, nor the supposed guaranteed income of $240,000 a year. It was just a trick to prepare the way for some further juggling.

On the strength of the announcement of the deal with Boyle, a prospectus was issued offering for sale $2,200,-000 more 1st mortgage debenture bonds, which were subscribed. At the same time, July, 1912, the *Granville Mining Company's* shares were "introduced" to the Stock Exchange, accompanied by the usual ballyhoover. What became of the $2,000,000 odd received from the sale of these bonds? $1,350,000 of it was supposed to be paid to *Boyle's Canadian Klondike Mining Company* for those stocks and bonds of his. Boyle apparently got the money, but whom he "divvied up" with is not clear. It is certain, however, that he never gave the *Granville* any bonds or shares. The only effect of the transaction on Boyle was to have him, without any apparent reason, at once change the name of his concern to *Boyle's Concession Limited.*

After paying out the $1,350,000 to Boyle, the *Granville Mining Company* was once more without funds. Treadgold had been sitting for months in the Victoria Hotel in London, doing nothing but signing transfers of shares made out in his name but sold to the investing public for the benefit of the inside gang which pocketed the proceeds. This was too much. It was he who had brought the goose and all these jackals were giving him was the pope's nose. He was a little hard-boiled himself and had not been raising chilblains in the Klondike for fifteen years for nothing. He refused to transfer any claims to the *Granville* and returned to the Klondike in the Summer of 1912, when he gave back to most of the private claim holders the claims they had transferred to him for the purpose of entering the *Granville Company.* Some of these lads knew how to use a gun. He returned to London in the beginning of 1913, accompanied by Boyle, determined to spill the whole rotten hill of beans unless he got his share out of it. The *Granville Company* might be without funds. But its directors were not without resources. On July 1st, 1913, they took the balance of their "valuable property" in the Indian watershed and converted it into a new company, the *North West Corporation,* which issued without a prospectus, as usual, but with the usual $35 paid up capital, and a nominal capital of $7,5000,000 in shares, of which $5,000,000 were given in payment of the "property," no, not to the *Granville*

Mining Company, which was supposed to own it, but to a syndicate they bought it from, consisting of three nominees parading under the name of the North West Syndicate, which had a paid up capital of $85, and which took these 1,000,000 five dollar shares and transferred them to the *Goldfields American Development Company* which, of course, included Hoover. Treadgold was supposed to get $1,000,000 in cash for developing the property. Then, on September 12, 1913, there appeared in most of the papers what seemed to be a prospectus of the *North West Corporation,* but which contained in small letters the wording "for information only," the evident object of this being to bunco the public by giving the impression that it was a genuine prospectus, and that its statements were true.

On the very same day the shares were "introduced" on the Stock Exchange, actually at a premium of 10%! This was followed by the usual ballyhoover, and puffs in the newspapers and, a few days later, a meeting of the *North West Corporation* was held and its report widely advertised in the press. At this meeting, Treadgold, who presided, repeated the precious statements of the prospectus and promised an annual net profit of $1,450,000! Just as with the *Granville,* the cash receipts from the sale of shares and bonds of the *North West Corporation* were paid out as quickly as they came in. Still, this company did manage somehow to pick up an old dredge somewhere, and, two years later, in September, 1915, it waddled up the *Last Chance* creek in the Klondike and waddled back again, for the Yukon winter had set in and there was not even money enough left to pay for fuel. On December 31, 1915 (after two brief years), the *North West Corporation* had $175 in cash and some $70,000 in debts!

The *Granville,* as can well be imagined, was no more fortunate. It was the holding company, holding the mythical stock in Boyle's *Canadian Klondike Mining Company,* and holding the equally mythical stock in the *North West Corporation,* which was in reality held by the *Goldfields American Development Company,* whose agent in New York, Alfred von der Ropp, who also represented the *Granville Mining Company,* occupied offices in the Woolworth Building, where Hoover made his New York headquarters until 1914 when he went into the relief business.

Year after year, at the annual meetings of the *Granville Mining Company,* the shareholders were told of the great earnings of Boyle's *Canadian Klondike Mining Company,* just as if it were their own, and year after year the books of the *Granville Mining Company* were wangled to make it appear that the $240,000 a year was being received from Boyle. They even borrowed money for this purpose, having the gall, in July, 1915, to issue $550,000 Prior Lien bonds pledging the Canadian Klondike stocks and bonds which they had never seen! Oh, yes, they made great efforts to collect these stocks and bonds from Boyle. When he was in England, at the beginning of 1913, they "forgot" to ask him for them. But when the War broke out and Boyle set out at the head of the little warrior band he himself had organized in the Yukon to go and fight the Kaiser, they had a process server out with a writ for him, and, when this poor creature reached the bloody battlefront of the Somme in his search for the bold, bad man, he discovered that Boyle had found the Western front far too cramped for him and was away with his hairy warriors and their shaggy nags to the steppes of Russia, where a man has fighting room anyway. This is the story that was spread. The 1,310,000 shares the insiders held in the *Granville Mining Company* had to be pushed over on to the public. Hoover aided with his *Inter Yukon Syndicate,* which he had formed in 1912 to deal in these shares. Maps were printed and published extensively showing the "properties" of the *Granville Mining Company* adjoining those of the *Yukon Gold.* On March 25th, 1914, they even succeeded in getting the London *Times* to print a whole column boost of the *Granville,* when that company was in a hopeless position. It was the *Deep Leads of Victoria* racket all over again. The accounts of the *Granville Mining Company* for December 31, 1914, showed it had $650 in cash, and over $550,000 in debts!

In their efforts to hide this business of the Canadian Klondike shares and bonds from the shareholders of the *Granville Mining Company,* the Hoover organization even resorted to the following artifice. The *Mining Journal* for 1917 tells us:

> "In August, 1916, the following financial scheme was adopted: If the ordinary shareholders subscribe £52,875 for the *North West Corporation,* the prior lien and 1st mortgage debenture holders agree to fund their interest for two and three years respectively, thus relieving the guaranteed payments to be received from the *Canadian Klondike Company* to be utilized in making advances to the *North West Corporation* as and when received from the *Canadian Klondike Company.*"

The shareholders of the *Granville Mining Company* believed they held 1,000,000 shares in the *North West Corporation,* and that in this way they would be financing their own property. But, as we have seen, these shares were really held by the *Goldfields American Development Co.* It was just another joker. They even went through with the farce. The *Granville Company* bought 39,657 shares in the *North West Corporation* for £39,657 and was credited with £39,657 as commission for buying them!

It did not take Hoover and his firm long to exploit these hundreds of millions of cubic yards of gold bearing gravel. For there was really nothing whatever to work or exploit. Hoover well knew that the proposition was hopeless from the start. He had the figures of many years' experience of the *Yukon Gold Company* before him to show him that it would cost at least thirty cents a cubic foot to dredge this gravel, which was more than the gold contained in it. He also knew that to work 7,000,000 cubic yards a season as advertised, it would take several years of work to clear away the muck. And, if he knew elementary arithmetic, he could have figured that to thaw out this quantity of gravel would require about 300,000,000,000 British thermal units, which, with his proposed method of exposure to the sun and air would require about a hundred years in a climate where there is only two months Summer and an average Summer temperature of only 55 degrees. Some of these "idiots" were, unfortunately, Americans. Read this from Marvyn Scudder's *Manual of Extinct or Obsolete Companies* (1930 edition):

"*Granville Mining Co. Ltd.*—Organized in England in August, 1911, to operate placer gold properties in the Yukon. Capital stock £1,500,000 shares £1 par. Office at 233 Broadway. Receiver appointed in April, 1917, following financial difficulties. On Dec. 24, 1919, 63,286 shares sold at auction for $15 the lot at A. H. Mueller & Sons, New York."

Well, the owner of these $316,430 worth of shares got

the price of a box of cigars for them anyway. Other investors were not so lucky. They were being taught "the great science of extracting the greatest amount of money from some human being."

There is a sequel to this sorry tale. These two companies dragged along in debt until 1917 (the directors meanwhile drawing their salaries), when *Goodell Clayton & Co., Ltd.,* of Leeds, one of the creditors of the *North West Corporation,* brought a suit in the High Court for compulsory winding up of that company. They had not paid, and could not pay, for that old dredge. The trial was to come on for hearing on May 22nd, 1917. Hoover had just returned to New York from London in March when he received the message. Dismay! Here he was being sent over to the United States to take control of America's food and fuel, and spend over $150,000,000 of good American money in the way he knew best, when this nasty fly drops in the soup. Horror of horrors! the whole dirty stink of the *Granville* and the *North West* would come out in the English Courts. Who was the miracle engineer who could close the valve in time? Who, but Hoover? Which was the first steamer for Europe? It was an old Spanish tub, the *Antonio Lopez* sailing on March 14th, 1917. Across to Cadiz, overland to Paris and London. April 1st he was in London. He arrived in time. Friendly receiverships were arranged for the *Granville* on April 27th and for the *North West* on May 4th. The day was saved. Talk about your ride of Sheridan! What was that to this dash of Hoover in an old Spanish tub!

CHAPTER THE SEVENTEENTH

COPPER, SILVER AND GOLD

WHEN Grenfell, the banker-gambler associate of Hoover in the *Western Oceanic Syndicate* and *General Petroleum Company* deals in California (not to mention the *Consolidated Natomas*, the reconstruction of which was another of Hoover's financial strikes, so disastrous for the old stockholders), failed in May, 1914, for $15,000,000, he decried being called a gambler, asserting that he was only carrying out a definite financial policy. Despite the notorious *Great Fingall* and *Zinc Corporation* ramps, Hoover, too, ever and always posed as a man who loathed gambling, although H. W. P. Hornby, an English lawyer associate of his in several little ventures, tells us in an article in the *London Sunday Express* in 1929, that Hoover was always ready at a moment's notice to jump in to the extent of a quarter of a million in any little deal that looked promising. He also succeeded in posing as being perhaps the only honest mining man in London. This impression was almost entirely brought about by a favorable press, for the mining sheets had a relatively small circulation and depended to a great extent for their income on the insertion of "puffs" of the various companies in which he was interested. A notable example of this is the *Mining Magazine,* a publication founded in London in 1909 by T. A. and Edgar Rickard with the aid of Hoover, and which, for years, appeared to be little more than a catalogue of the mining ventures he promoted or was interested in. In spite of invariably favorable references to him in this publication, the editor, T. A. Rickard, one of the most brilliant of geologists, mining engineers and writers, more than once appealed for a fair run for the shareholders and occasionally let his indignation get the better of him and applied some words of biting sarcasm. How close Hoover stood to this publication is evidenced by the fact that in 1914 he appointed its business manager Edgar Rickard as secretary to the *Belgian Relief Commission,* and afterwards had him put in charge of the *Polish and Russian Relief,* giving him the spending of $20,000,000 of good American money. This Englishman Rickard, who does not appear to have ever changed his nationality, was actually named by Secretary of State Lansing as Food Dictator in the absence of Herbert Hoover. As a matter of fact, Hoover's New York address is in the office of Rickard, who has apparently, like many others, profited from the connection. For, after giving his services free of charge for six years in the "relief" business, we find him to be now president of several corporations, including a few exploiting patents issued by the Patent Office while it was under charge of Hoover, notably the Hazeltine patent under which millions are being "collected" in royalties from radio manufacturers.

Now of the many ventures engaged in by Grenfell and controlled by him, one was the *Camp Bird* gold mine in Colorado, which owned the *Santa Gertrudis* silver mine in Mexico, and had a large interest in the *Messina* copper mine in the Transvaal. Grenfell was chairman of all three companies, and was the whole "works," the other directors just being nominees. To pay for his speculations, Grenfell had been nibbling the assets of these companies and, when he saw the crash coming in May, 1914, arranged for his associate, the Mr. Hoover of the *Western Ocean Syndicate* and *Central American Goldfields Syndicate,* to be appointed temporary chairman of these companies after his own forced resignation. This was to give himself time to straighten out things in the right way.

At this very moment, May 28th, 1914, there sauntered out from Hoover's office at No. 1 London Wall Buildings, the above-named *Central American Goldfields Syndicate* with an option of five mines in its pocket, mines found by Hoover in Nicaragua—the so-called Bonanza group in the Pis-Pis district. These mines were for sale at the price of $1,125,000, and the big idea of Hoover and Grenfell was to float a company with a capital of $5,000,000, of which the *Camp Bird* company would contribute $1,500,000, and then sell the mines to this new company for $1,500,000 in cash and $650,000 in shares, thus clearing up for themselves a little profit of $1,000,000. This proposition, however, was jeered by the press, for it was known that these mines were some twenty miles from the coast by canoe, with no rail connection and great difficulty in finding labor, besides having a history as regards title. They accordingly decided to take an option and bond instead and have *Camp Bird* put up the money. *Camp Bird,* with Hoover as managing director, did put up $300,000 or so in Hoover's *Central American Goldfields Syndicate* on this option. Then it was found that the title to the property was defective, and the proposition was abandoned. But the money had been lost, at least to *Camp Bird* shareholders.

During the first year that Hoover was managing director of these companies, they did none too well in the Stock Market. Despite better prices for silver and copper, the *Camp View* shares within this period fell from two and a half dollars to a dollar and a quarter, the *Santa Gertrudis* from three dollars to a dollar and seventy-five cents, and the *Messina* from five and a half to two and a half dollars. What accounted for this? It was the old game, as practiced with the *Lake View Consols* and *Great Boulder Perseverance,* in Australia. Break the market to come in at the low point. The *Messina* was an extremely rich copper mine, with ore running as high as 10% copper. The ore reserves, when Hoover took control had been estimated at 252,000 tons of eight to nine per cent. copper, and this figure had been checked by Frecheville, an engineer and director of the company. This did not suit Hoover, and the following summer he sent out one of his own engineers, Kuehn (now Keene), who found that the ore reserves were only 130,000 tons of six to seven per cent. copper. Less than half! This report, combined with the fact that the report somehow got about that it was costing over ten cents per pound to produce copper from this practically free fluxing extremely rich ore, eventually broke the market in Messina shares to a dollar ninety cents. Quite a drop from five and a half dollars! Just as with other mines in which this trick had been pulled off, there was no legitimate reason for reducing the ore estimates. The ore was there, for millions of tons of it have since been produced from this rich copper mine which is one of the most important. It was just a trick to break the market.

Before going bankrupt, Grenfell, Hoover's gambling associate of the *Western Ocean Syndicate,* had "taken" the whole new issue of bonds of the *Messina* company ($915,000) for his little stock speculations. Hoover, however, saw that the mine was a good thing and decided to do the refinancing himself. Under the name of the *Inter-Guaranty Syndicate,* in which he had as partner P. L. May the stockbroker, he advanced funds as working capital to the *Messina* in return for calls on shares. He was acting as broker for profit on his own terms and under an alias to the mines of which he was managing director! This was nothing new. He had at this very same time other financial syndicates in the field, notably the *Inter-Russian* and the *Inter-Siberian,* for financing dealing in shares of companies of which he was a director in Russia and Siberia.

CHAPTER THE EIGHTEENTH

THE STATES AND THE SOVIETS

WHATEVER we may think of Soviet Russia, the fact remains that it exists, and it is a monumental fact. We have only to look at the map and see that huge expanse of territory to visualize what an important part it must play in the world's history. It is our duty to be friendly with its people and fair to them, for even if they are not strong patronizers of tonsorial parlors, many a stout heart beats beneath a cotton blouse and many a keen and noble mind under a hirsute thatch. As for the form of government they have chosen, it is obviously their own exclusive business.

Hoover knew Russia. Not the resurrecting Russia of the Soviets, but the decadent Russia of the Czars. Had he not sat on a board of directors with Prince Saltykoff, one of those "misaristocrats" who were perpetuating a system of human bondage and misery? That was in the *Maikop* oil business, which had suffered such an early demise. There were other things to exploit in Russia besides mudholes. There was lead, zinc, coal, silver, gold and copper. In 1906, a company had been formed under the name of the *Anglo-Siberian Company* to try and obtain concessions. This company was promoted by Leslie Urquhart, an engineer of long experience in Russia. Among the shareholders we find our old friend Govett, the old stand-by the *Lake View Consols,* as well as Edgar Storey, the colliery proprietor of Liverpool who had sued Hoover in 1903 for defaulting on payment of the gambling transaction in the *Great Fingall* shares. Another company floated in 1907 for the same purpose under the name *Perm Corporation* succeeded in making a deal with a Russian company operating in the Urals. The *Anglo-Siberian* swallowed the *Perm Corporation* in approved style and took over the deal. The *Kyshtim Corporation* was then floated in October, 1908, with a capital of $5,000,000 as holding company for the *Kyshtim Mining Works,* which held mineral and timber concessions over two thousand square miles in the Southern Urals. The great bulk of the shares were grabbed by the promoters in the usual way, and the working capital was provided by an issue of $3,125,000 1st mortgage bonds. This company at first earned its income from the sale of timber and iron. In 1911, there was an important discovery of copper ore on the property and it was decided to give up the iron business and go in for copper mining and smelting.

Here is where Hoover came in. With A. C. Beatty, with whom he was then associated in the *Eastern Trading Company* preparing the Granville coup, Hoover financed the construction of a smeltery at Karabash for the *Kyshtim Corporation,* and was made a director. The production of copper in Russia was greatly facilitated by a bounty of 33% from the Russian Government, and the enterprise gave good returns from the start. Here began Hoover's association with Leslie Urquhart, which has lasted ever since. Urquhart was not slow as a financier. But there were tricks he had not yet learned which Hoover was a past master at.

In April 1912, Urquhart's *Anglo-Siberian Company* made an arrangement with two Russian banks by which all mining prospects submitted to these banks should be handled by a new company to be formed and accordingly in April, 1912, the *Russo-Asiatic Corporation* was floated with Urquhart and Hoover in command. The capital was $1,500,000 and this new corporation, with the aid of Hoover's *Inter-Russian Syndicate,* at once promoted the *Tanalyk Corporation* to take over a large low grade copper mining proposition in the South Urals.

The high price of copper in 1912 and the bonus of 33% from the Russian Government enabled the *Kyshtim Corporation* to show good profits and a dividend of 22½% was declared. This, combined with the issuing of reports, widely advertised in the mining press, of millions of tons of ore "estimated" from the boreholes augmented by further "probable" ore reserves, forced the five dollar *Kyshtim* shares to eighteen and a half dollars in 1912. This gave a lead to the shares of the *Russo-Asiatic Corporation,* which rose to sixteen dollars and a quarter in 1913 and in 1914 to forty-seven and a half dollars, on the announcement of the taking over of the Russian companies holding the Nerchinsk lead mining concession in Eastern Siberia, the Elkibastus coal fields to the East of the Urals and the Ridder and Kirgiz concession for the mining of silver lead zinc ore in the Altai mountains near Mongolia. To assist in the flotation of companies to work these concessions, Hoover formed his *Inter-Siberian Syndicate* in June, 1914, and was not so busy with the Belgian relief business that he did not have time to launch the *Irtysh Corporation* at the end of November, 1914, with a paid up capital of thirty-five dollars, and a nominal capital of $10,000,000, the "insiders" taking $5,500,000 of these shares and $165,000 in cash, as their part of the spoils. An intensive advertising campaign for these Siberian companies was kept up in the mining journals, generally accompanied by maps of the "properties," athough they were only concessions in the names of the Russian companies, and estimates of millions of tons of "probable" ore. Although not paying dividends, they managed to keep the shares of these companies at enormous premiums and, of course, the "insiders" made millions from the sale of their free shares.

Just as with the *Burma Mines* and *Burma Corporation,* these companies were not allowed to show any profits during the War period. To dodge the income tax collector, the financiers decided to split up the assets of the Russian and Siberian companies between two new holding companies, and in 1917 they accordingly formed in Canada the *Russo-Canadian Development Company* as a holding company for the shares of the original native Russian companies which had been held by the *Russo-Asiatic Corporation,* and another holding company, the *Russo-Asiatic Consolidated,* to take over the cash and other assets outside the stockholdings in the native Russian companies. However, the British tax authorities forbade the liquidation of the *Russo-Asiatic Corporation* until it paid its taxes.

The year 1918 put a different complexion on the situation. In that year the Soviet authorities abrogated the concessions and confiscated the mines. As a result of this circumstance and the energetic action with the British Tax Office of tough baby Webster, secretary of the *Russo-Asiatic Corporation,* this company was permitted to liquidate without paying income tax in 1919, and, in October of that year, the *Russo-Asiatic Consolidated* was formed to take over $5,625,000 in cash and other assets of these companies. The new *Russo-Asiatic Consolidated* had a nominal capital of $60,000,000 in 12,000,000 shares of five dollars each, 8,461,587 being distributed among the old shareholders in the *Irtysh, Kyshtim, Tanalyk* and *Russo-Canadian* companies, the Canadian company receiving over $8,500,000 worth of them, but for what consideration is not quite clear.

The new *Russo-Asiatic Consolidated,* then, from Hoover's office at No. 1 London Wall Buildings, filed a claim with the British Government against the wicked Soviets for $280,000,000 as compensation for the loss of their "properties," "probable" ore and "probable" profit. Of course, these Hoover-Urquhart companies had no direct title to these mining concessions. They were just holding companies for the Russians who had received the concessions, and the amount of actual cash invested by them in their development was insignificant in comparison with the profits they had made out of them by juggling the shares. Yet, they pressed this exorbitant claim, relying on the power of Hoover, who had by then become quite a figure in American politics. This circumstance was taken advantage of to keep the shares "see-sawing" on the Stock Exchange for years by the spreading of reports that arrangements would be made with the Soviets through the influence of Hoover. This continued until 1927.

Meanwhile, to keep the business before the public as a mining proposition, Urquhart acquired, in 1920, a majority holding in the old *Villemagne* (what a pretty name) lead zinc mines in South France, just to help out the French, we suppose, at the expense of the shareholders. For these mines are never likely to pay a dividend.

Then, in 1924, Urquhart and his band turned to other fields. They took up the *Mount Isa* lead zinc silver mines in Queensland, Australia, and a gold mining proposition in the New Guinea island in the Pacific. To read the wonderful press notices and circulars continuously and persistently put out about these two ventures, one would believe that *Mount Isa* was going to produce enough lead to some day sink the universe, and the New Guinea

Goldfields, enough precious metal to provide two pailfuls for every human being. Instead of producing, however, they began absorbing cash far worse than the *Deep Leads of Victoria* or the *Granville* gravel beds. Where to turn for more? Why not take the cash assets of the *Russo-Asiatic Consolidated?* No sooner said than done. In June, 1927, $2,750,000 of its cash was applied to the purchase of shares in the *Mount Isa* lead mine, which are now quoted at exactly one quarter of that amount.

Simultaneously, they reconstructed the *Russo-Asiatic Consolidated,* reducing the nominal capital to $22,500,000 in 36,000,000 shares of sixty cents each, the old "idiot" shareholders receiving in exchange for their 8,462,907 five dollar shares out of 12,000,000 in the old company, only 8,462,907 sixty cents shares out of 36,000,000 in the new company. This left the insiders with over 27,500,000 shares "in the bag" to play with. They sold over 8,000,-000 of them to the public in 1927 and "invested" a great part of the cash in some other dud mining properties.

In 1928, Hoover was elected to the most powerful position in the world. Tough baby secretary Webster of the *Russo-Asiatic Consolidated* immediately called the Russians on the carpet. A meeting was arranged with Soviet representatives in Berlin in January, 1929. Webster used the big stick. As Hoover had done in 1901 in China with Chang, Webster could once more threaten to use the American Government to break the Soviets. Strange to say, these Russians were not impressed. Their arguments were based not on fear, but on reason. These English financiers had no direct title to the concessions they claimed, their demands were ridiculously exorbitant and, not having taken advantage of previous offers made by the Soviets, the latter were now actually working the properties themselves with the aid of dozens of competent up-to-date qualified American mining engineers.

Webster returned to London empty-handed. Did he tell this to the shareholders? Not on your life. This is what he and his associates did. They made believe that the Soviets were giving way and, without exactly saying so, issued a circular in February, 1929, which conveyed this impression. Here is an extract from it:

> "In view of certain proposals made by foreign groups to acquire part of the reserve share capital in connection with the expansion of the company's activities, the board decided that before coming to any arrangement an opportunity be given to shareholders to subscribe for part of the reserve shares at a price lower than that contemplated in the negotiations. Shareholders have therefore been offered shares at 3/6 (80c) in the proportion of one for each five shares held."

On the strength of this brazen circular over 3,500,000 shares were foisted on the British public at a premium of nearly 50%. What did they do with the money? Just as soon as they got it, they reconstructed the *Russo-Asiatic Consolidated* all over again in June, 1929, leaving the new company with nothing but its claim on the Soviets, and $250,000 in cash to help pay directors' fees for a few years to come. All the rest of the assets valued at over $10,000,000, of which nearly $5,000,000 was cash were simply "taken" and transferred to a new holding company called the *Mining Trust,* which had been formed to take over control of the *Mount Isa* lead mines, which had never produced any lead, and the New Guinea *Goldfields,* from which the gold, said to be on the way by airplane, is long past due. In the *Mining Trust* the shareholders of the *Russo-Asiatic Consolidated,* in return for their $10,000,000 of cash and other assets,

there is no need for anyone to bring accusations. The facts speak for themselves.

An army, according to Napoleon, marches on its stomach. Food is more necessary for the winning of a war than munitions. Historians investigating reasons for the outbreak of the World War in August, 1914, have overlooked the fact that Germany had just had a bumper grain crop and was assured of food supplies for a twelve months' campaign. Germany had a population of sixty-seven million to feed and, in normal times had to import one-fifth of its food supplies. It could not go to war without assured food reserves. These it had in August, 1914. Moreover, it is now known that the German General Staff had, in case of war with France, always considered the necessity of an invasion of France through Belgium. The reasons for this were simple. It was the most direct route to Paris and to the Channel ports. And Belgium, besides being a highly industrialized country, was also an extremely rich agricultural land, sixty per cent. of its soil being cultivated intensively, so that it produced far more food than it actually required for home consumption. The German General Staff had provided for all contingencies in case of war, and even had food experts residing in Belgium for as long as five years prior to the outbreak of war, drawing up a detailed schedule for the provisioning of the inhabitants, which the Germans would be obliged to feed in accordance with the Hague Convention. The rationing of provisions for Belgium was organized in Germany long before the war began.

A leading German newspaper, *Norddeutsche Allgemeine Zeitung* of March 4, 1915, page 1, writing on this subject, tells us:

"Justice, however, demands that publicity

should be given to the preeminent part taken by the German authorities in Belgium in the solution of this problem. The initiative came from them and it was only due to their continuous relations with the American Relief Committee that the provisioning question was solved."

The purpose of the relief is explained in this further quotation from the same newspaper:

"The German Government was therefore glad to help in obtaining provisions from neutral countries for the needy inhabitants in order to save German home supplies, and insure its own troops against going short."

That is what the Belgian relief was organized for— to keep Germany in food.

How did Hoover come to be connected with the relief of Belgium, a country he had apparently never visited and the only citizens of which he appears to have been acquainted with, being half a dozen former slave-drivers of the Belgian Congo? In the first days of August, 1914, Hoover became known to Ambassador Page by presiding over a committee called the American Relief Committee in London for the repatriation of American tourists stranded in Europe at the outbreak of war, because of difficulty in cashing checks, etc. Hoover's propagandists have told us how at great personal expense, he sent back to the States a hundred thousand stranded Americans. This is, of course, the veriest tommyrot. The money was advanced by Americans like Hemphill to people who could identify themselves as people of means. It was a case of "Help the rich, let the poor beg."

As a matter of fact, according to Hoover himself, there were only a few thousand actually stranded, and their passage money was advanced against promissory notes, and then only when it was known that there was a shipment of gold on the way from the U. S. A. Did Hoover contribute any of his own money? There is a story told in connection with this business of Hoover parting with one dollar to an American lady who was absolutely broke, and refused to leave his office unless she got something. Perhaps he did give that dollar.

On the outbreak of war there was an almost immediate dislocation of industry in Brussels. A local committee was formed on August 28, 1914, for the relief of those suddenly thrown out of work without resources, and of the refugees who had fled before the invaders. It was the same situation as we have here for the relief of the unemployed in times of peace, and could well be taken care of by the local Belgians. This committee sent an American, Millard K. Shaler, to London to purchase food supplies for these necessitous people in Brussels. The German invaders also provided food for these needy folk, who were not very numerous. For Belgium is the land of savings bank books, and not a family but had one! And there was plenty of food for sale at the usual prices.

While Shaler was in London, the situation at the front had undergone a change. The repulse of the Germans at the Marne and their hold up at the Yser had proved to them that the war was not going to be the walk-over they had expected, and that the campaign was likely to be a rather protracted one. This would result not only in the German Army in Belgium being obliged to live off the land, but in the shipping of a large part of the Belgian produce to Germany itself. The Germans therefore decided to enforce the plan they had devised for the rationing of Belgian civilians. The success of this plan depended on Belgium being able to obtain food supplies from America. This necessitated the creation of the illusion that Belgium was starving and that the whole business was a tremendous American work of charity. In this way, the Belgians would be satisfied with any quantity of food they received, no matter how rubbishy, and England could not well veto the supplying of it without losing the sympathy of America and other neutral countries and incurring the danger of Belgium making a separate peace with Germany, and thus leaving the way open to the sea coast and the Channel ports.

As a matter of fact, this illusion of the Belgian Relief being a great American charitable enterprise was insistently and continuously spread not only in Belgium but throughout the world and came to be generally believed. The German authorities realized the advisability of having the distribution of these food supplies made by Belgians who knew the country and the people. Arrangements were therefore made with Emile Francqui, director of the Societe Generale, a large Belgian bank, who was also a member of the Brussels Relief Committee. Francqui was to obtain the consent of the British Government to the importation of monthly rations of wheat, fats, beans, peas, etc., according to the German program, and the Germans themselves would ration the home produce such as milk, meat, sugar, potatoes, etc. Francqui was to arrange to have the Belgian Government put up the money for the purchase of the imported foodstuffs, and in return the Germans would give Francqui's bank the exclusive privilege of issuing bank notes in Belgium in such a way as to insure against any possibility of loss on the sale of the food imported. In other words, Germany guaranteed to make it a profitable business.

Francqui thereupon opened offices in his bank, the *Societe Generale*, called a meeting of provincial delegates, explained the plan, changed the name of the Brussels *Central Relief Committee* to *National Relief and Food Committee*, and had all executive powers placed in his own hands exclusively. It became a one man show. His bank associate, Jadot, then went, armed with a German passport, to interview the Belgian Government, which had moved to Havre in France, and Jadot arranged that the Belgian Government put up five million dollars a month, in return for which the National Committee would pay the Government expenses in Belgium, in its absence, out of the proceeds of the sale of the food supplies. The German authorities, of course, consented to this arrangement. It was part of their plan.

Meanwhile, to overcome the objections of the British, Francqui, on October 16th, 1914, obtained from the German Governor General von der Goltz, a letter guaranteeing that foodstuffs of all kinds imported by the Committee for feeding the civilian population would be exclusively reserved for the needs of the Belgians and would be exempt from requisition on the part of the Germans. With this letter in hand, Francqui left Brussels on October 17th, equipped with German passports, for London, accompanied by Baron Lambert and Hugh Gibson, secretary of the American Legation. He showed Prime Minister Asquith the German guarantee, and, with the backing of Ambassador Page, received permission

> "to import all goods from neutral countries destined for the Belgian civil population on condition that they be conveyed to the Belgian frontier under the protection of the Spanish and American ambassadors, and from the frontier to places

of distribution under the protection of the Spanish
and American Ministers in Brussels."

With this permit, the entering wedge, in hand,
Francqui made arrangements with the Belgian Government to advance him five hundred thousand dollars out
of the British Relief Fund that had been placed at the
disposal of the Belgian Government by Great Britain.
The British Government gave him another five hundred
thousand dollars and, with a further amount of six
hundred thousand dollars obtained from Belgian banks
in London, he paid for the foodstuffs purchased by Shaler
in London. The relief of Belgium had begun.

Now, who was this Emile Francqui, so interested in
relieving the needy? None other than our old acquaint-
ance, the former Congo slave driver who had stood by
to help Hoover in the "taking" of the Kaiping coal mines
in China in 1901, and who, for ten years, had been a
director with Hoover on the board of that company,
including the period in 1904 when the two hundred
thousand Chinese slaves were sold to South African
horrors. A real humanitarian!

And who were the other members of his National
Relief Committee? Hoover's old pal, DeWouters, of the
Chinese deal, several other Belgian Congo slave drivers,
and a number of gentlemen who were prominently interested in Germany, such as Solvay, who had six factories
in Germany, four in Austria and one in Hungary; Louis
Franck, who needlessly surrendered Antwerp over the
head of the Mayor and the Belgian military authorities,
and whose son-in-law was a German officer; Baron De
Coppee and Baron De Merode, both connected with Van
der Lancken in the German attempt of 1917 to negotiate
a separate peace with France; and Bunge, the grain
merchant, a naturalized Belgian, from whose Argentine

firm Hoover purchased such tremendous quantities of grain, and who was such a patriot that he dismissed one of his employees who had joined the Belgian Army, and even ran a pro-German paper *De Toekomst* in Holland. Even Hulse, the American member, had the closest financial connections with Germany.

On October 19th, the day after his arrival in London, Francqui looked up his old friend Hoover. They were old pals. Francqui knew little English, and Hoover no French. But did these people have to even exchange words to reach a satisfactory and mutually profitable understanding of the business on hand? The prospect was a new and marvelous one for Hoover. Had he not been exploiting the greed for gain of investors in mining companies for over a decade? But here was a source of wealth he had never dreamed of—a mine deeper and richer than any ever explored by pick and shovel—the heart of the world!

A few days later, on October 22nd, a committee was formed by Francqui and Hoover in London under the name of the *Spanish American Committee,* which name was soon afterwards changed to that of *Commission for Relief in Belgium.* The members were mostly Americans, the Chairman being Hoover and the Vice-Chairman Heinemann, an international financier of American nationality and close German connections. The object of forming the *Commission for Relief in Belgium* was to provide a neutral commission that would not only serve to collect funds by appealing to charity, but would also attend to the buying, shipping and banking for the *Belgian National Committee.* For this job, Francqui needed a bird of his own feather, and he accordingly selected the humanitarian who valued a Chinaman's life at thirty dollars and a white man's as being worth less than timber. Just as had been done for Francqui in the *National Committee*, the executive powers in the *Commission for Relief in Belgium* were vested in Hoover exclusively. What a combination! Hoover doing the collecting, buying, shipping and banking, and Francqui the selling (yes, selling) and neither of them having any responsibility to anyone whatever!

Let us read Francqui's National Committeee reports, part 1, vol. 1, pages 33-34:

"The National Committee and its sub organizations were not subject to control of the Belgian Public Administration and neither was it accountable to the Public as public authorities are. The National Committee existed by itself according to the will of its founders and those who had given it their support. It did not emanate from the public will. That is why it was sovereign in the decisions it made: they had to be carried out without anyone having the power to discuss them or modify them. The exceptional conditions in which it functioned, the diverse and often confidential reasons that dictated its decisions excluded besides all control of its actions by the Public, to which it was often impossible to make known the real reasons."

You see, it was just a private little affair. Neither the State nor the Public had any right to interfere. Hoover did the buying (and someone else supplied the money for that) and Francqui did the selling. Did we say selling? Listen to this from page 39 of the same report:

"From its commencement, the Food Division had been organized and conducted on a commercial basis. From the mass of consumers who still

— 314 —

had resources it took as a commercial profit a kind of charity tax to help the needy. But soon, through prudence, and so as not to give the German authorities an opportunity of interfering in the management of the National Committee, this Department found itself obliged to give up taking this profit and left this task to the Commission for Relief in Belgium. This Commission raised its sale prices to the National Committee by an amount equivalent to the profit that had formerly been taken by it."

How simple! Hoover raised the prices to Francqui so that the Belgians would think they were getting the goods at a fair price, when they were being billed by Hoover at the highest prices of the day irrespective of the price paid for them. The word Hoover uses in his accounts to cover all such differences is *benevolence.* There is probably a more appropriate word for it.

By the arrangement made with the Belgian Government whereby, in return for a subvention of five million dollars a month, Francqui undertook to take care of Belgian Government employees. The *National Committee* (that is, Francqui) became a State within the State. Three-fourths of the Government employees stayed at their posts under the German administration and drew their salaries from the Germans. A great many of the rest found employment in the National Committee and received their pay in food tickets, so that with the five million dollars worth of food coming along every month Francqui had tremendous power. The Germans, relying on these imports, were buying up or requisitioning all the food in sight, and leaving the inhabitants dependent, especially for bread, on Francqui who could starve out any parish or individual who opposed him. The German Governor had to interfere. On June 26, 1915, he wrote to the Ministers of Spain and the United States:

> "The Committee must not interfere with personal liberty or freedom of trade. No verbal or written threats against an individual or parish will be allowed nor the stopping supplies of foodstuffs nor demanding excessive prices nor refusing assistance. Police powers are not permitted, but any infractions should be reported to the German authorities."

What did Francqui do? Give way and surrender his autocratic power? Oh, dear, no! He knew he held the German food situation in his hand. He threatened to quit. The German Governor General climbed down and, in a letter of July 29, 1915, gave the National Committee (that is, Francqui) complete liberty of action.

Francqui, the iron man of Belgium, could now do practically what he liked with regard to the distribution and sale of food. He supplied what he liked and charged what he liked. His methods were not above criticism. "Leagues of Public Defense" were formed against his Committee, but he called into play Article 276 of the Belgian Penal Code giving protection against insult or injury to agents of authority in the discharge of their duty. And he prosecuted, too.

The operations of the *National Committee* covered all Belgium, except the war zone, and, from January, 1915, with the permission and connivance of the German authorities, also the North of France.

Now let us see the method of operation of Francqui's National Committee. It appointed committees in each province, with sub-committees in the smaller centers. Each province had to establish credit for a determined amount in Francqui's bank, the *Societe Generale,* and keep an agent in Brussels. When the provincial center bought goods from the National Committee, its Brussels agent paid the *National Committee* out of the funds the Province held in Francqui's bank. Quite ingenious. The food was invoiced to the *Provincial Committee* at a profit and the *Provincial Committee* had to invoice to the smaller districts also at a profit and, out of this profit, remit part to the Francqui *National Committee* for its expenses, so that the *National Committee* was not only making a profit on direct sales but a share in the profits of indirect sales.

And what did they sell? Everything. Not only the food bought with the funds provided for the Belgian Government, but also the food purchased with the millions contributed by private charity throughout the world and even the gifts of clothing, even the dolls that women in this and other countries sat up at night to dress for Belgian babies. This was a cash "relief" business. As the war dragged on the demands for food grew, and the amounts put up in Francqui's bank became inadequate. So he organized co-operatives in the various centers, taking the joint promissory notes of the members, which the Belgian Government in Havre agreed to redeem after the war, if defaulted on. The Germans, too, allowed him to issue paper currency against these promissory notes. Monsieur Francqui was taking no chances. Everything was sold, sold for cash and at a profit, with payment guaranteed.

Hoover's C. R. B. organization was quite simple as compared with Francqui's. It consisted of three main offices: one in New York, to collect all money and gifts from America, purchase supplies there and attend to shipments; one in London, to collect all money and gifts from other countries, order supplies from America and attend to the banking arrangements; and one in Rotterdam, to receive all shipments, and reship to Belgium, *or elsewhere,* and at a profit, a thumping big profit. He had also a representative in Brussels, with a large number of young assistants throughout occupied Belgium, young well meaning boys, but ignorant of the Flemish language or Walloon dialect, who were to act as "buffers" between the German authorities and the Belgians and check up on the distribution of supplies. The Germans showed the greatest consideration for these young Americans, treating them as officers and giving them free quarters and transportation when required. But the Germans thoughtfully did not allow them to run around unaccompanied or travel on such a lowly conveyance as a freight train. No, they must not know what became of the merchandise in those freight trains or where they were going to. The Germans, otherwise, gave every assistance to the food relief business. It meant all the more food for Germany. They charged no custom dues on the imported food and transported it by water and rail at half the ordinary rates.

Now, let us see how food expert Hoover swung into action. He had a lot of pots on the fire just then. He had just been round to the Britsh Board of Trade for a subvention for his Zinc Corporation. His Burma goose was cooking nicely. The Russian bear in the Kyshtim pot was fit for carving. There was still plenty of "gravy" in the Australian *Lake View* and *Oroya.* But the *Camp Bird* was leaner than expected. And then there was that Nicaraguan stew and that Klondike Granville mess! That California oil, too, was rancid, oh, so rancid! On October 27th, 1914, he put his Siberian Irtysh pot on the fire and was waiting for investors to come in and fill it.

Then he turned to relief.

On November 1st, 1914, Hoover published an appeal to the world in which he stated that his *Belgian Relief Commission* had to feed seven million people—the entire Belgian population—that there was no money in the country, that eighty per cent of the Belgian people were unemployed. Then he went on to tell how Belgian imports in normal times averaged two hundred and thirty thousand tons of cereals monthly and that this, together with accumulations, was now exhausted and that Belgium required a monthly supply of sixty thousand tons of wheat, fifteen thousand tons of corn and fifteen thousand tons of peas and beans, besides bacon and lard, to save her from starvation.

This report was inaccurate as it applied to conditions in Belgium. It did coincide, though, with the German program for the rationing of supplies to the total population. On the next day, November 2nd, Hoover sent the following cable to the American press:

"I have received reports from members of our Commission, from the American Minister in Brussels and from local officials that within three weeks the last vestiges of foodstuffs in Belgium will have been exhausted and the entire population of over seven million people will be faced with starvation."

This was what the Germans wanted America to believe!

The American newspapers of March 2, 1915, contained a further statement issued by Hoover in London on March 1st to the effect that Belgium imports five-sixths of her foodstuffs. The statement continued:

"Every Belgian is today on a ration from the Commission. Food and money are not interchangeable. A Belgian man with a million dollars in cash can obtain no more bread than the man who is destitute."

Pure German propaganda to have foodstuffs sent to Belgium.

The facts are that Belgium for its size was the most productive agricultural country in the world. Over sixty per cent of its area was cultivated intensively. It produced normally (and in 1914 the crop was much larger) 410,000 tons of wheat and 620,000 tons of rye, also available for flour, a total equipment to 38,000,000 bushels, or 2,280,000,000 lbs. of grain which, at 75 per cent milling, gives flour for 2,280,000,000 lbs. of clear bread, besides over 250,000 tons of feed and bran. Take the Belgian population of 7,350,000, of which 350,000 were under arms and 500,000 refugees in Holland and England, and we find that Belgium produced enough wheat and rye to give every man, woman and child of the 6,500,-000 left 351 lbs. of clear bread a year, which, for the average large Belgian family of six, is equivalent to almost 6 lbs. of clear bread per day per family without any importation whatever. Of course, Belgium did import large quantities of wheat in normal times. But this mostly went in transit to Germany and France (see British Consular reports for 1910-1911).

Then Belgium also produced 3,250,000 tons of potatoes a year, equal to a ration of 17 lbs. per family of 6 per day. The yearly production of beets was 1,750,000 tons, yielding 250,000 tons of sugar, and enormous quantities of vegetables were raised. Indeed, a month or so after Hoover issued the above statement, the Spanish and American Ministers in Belguim authorized the export of huge quantities of vegetables to Germany, because the Belgian population could not possibly consume them all!

At the commencement of the war, Belgium had also 1,500,000 cattle, 320,000 horses, 600,000 sheep and goats, 1,500,000 pigs, over 12,000,000 fowl, and countless millions of pigeons and rabbits, besides having one of the richest fishing grounds in the world on the North Sea coast. Outside the strictly industrial centers, it was a farmer's paradise. Do not imagine, either, that production decreased under German occupation. Quite the contrary. The Germans were buying up everything at high prices, and, to encourage production, they authorized the unemployed to cultivate any unoccupied or waste land, so that there was not a patch the size of a table-cloth left untilled. Almost everybody took up the breeding of small animals, such as pigeons, chickens, rabbits, sheep and goats. To give an idea of how the Germans fostered production, Francqui's *National Committee* itself tells us in its report that from January 15, 1915, to January 15, 1916, the stocks of animals increased in spite of the War and of the enormous quantities requisitioned by Germany—cattle by 34 per cent, pigs by 42 per cent, sheep and goats by 57 per cent—so that, on January 15th, 1916, despite the hundreds of thousands of cattle slaughtered for the German armies, there still remained in Belgium 606,281 milk cows, an average of more than one to every two families!

Francqui's *National Committee* itself quite completely contradicts Hoover. This National Committee, by the way, issued no fewer than eleven volumes of reports, which have subsequently been bought up at great expense and taken off the market for reasons that are very evident. They simply "gave the game away," and could not make their accounts gibe with Hoover's. The General Report of the National Committee, 4th part, page 267, states:

"When the war started, Belgium was, from the food standpoint, in a very favorable situation. The cataclysm that struck the country was so unforeseen that commercial transactions continued up to the very day of the outbreak of war. Important stocks of the most various kinds of merchandise were accumulated on spot and the new crop of cereals had been exceptionally favorable. Thanks to these circumstances, in spite of the destruction due to acts of war, there was no shortage of foodstuffs at first and they hardly advanced in price."

The report of the National Committee's Provisioning Department, volume 1, chapter 1, pages 5 and 6, reads:

"At the start of operations, the Provisioning Department met with very extensive competition from private business firms which were still supplied with all kinds of provisions. Domestic foodstuffs were plentiful and many households, moreover, had laid in reserve supplies. An important part of the population therefore did not *buy* its provisions in the stores of the *National Committee* * * * There were times even when it was difficult to place some of the cargoes shipped and the provincial committees had to be forced to take their share of all the foodstuffs imported."

Compare these officials' reports of the National Committee with Hoover's appeals and statements broadcasted throughout the world for the purpose of tapping the fountain of human charity allegedly for the Belgians, but, in reality, to keep Germany supplied with food. Here in America thousands of committees were formed to collect funds throughout the length and breadth of this great land. There were men's committees, women's committees, and even the Belgian Kiddies committees. Institutions collected, newspapers and magazines collected (the *Literary Digest* alone over $300,000). People gave till it hurt, both rich and poor, for years. And what do Hoover's accounts show? Total cash contributions from the United States—$4,949,098.93. Not even five million dollars!

In November, 1914, the Belgian "Relief" was already under way. The food purchased in England by Shaler was shipped. Further supplies in accordance with the German programme were ordered in America with the $5,000,000 monthly advanced by England and France for account of the Belgian Government. Everything was done to grease the wheels and make operations easy. Twenty-three Belgian steamers were commandeered for the service by the Belgian Government. All kinds of facilities were given. Gay's *Statistical Review of Relief Operations*, published on behalf of Hoover's Commission, tells us:

"Most of the firms engaged in commercial operations on behalf of the Commission either returned their fees or made no charge. Inland purchases and conveyance from America, Canada and the Argentine necessitated extensive rail transportation arrangements in which connection the Comsion enjoyed many generous concessions in rates and a large amount of entirely free transport, to say nothing of continuous and general favors in the way of extra facilities as to handling and delivery.

The chartering and management of an entire fleet of vessels, together with agency control practically throughout the world, was carried out for the Commission quite free of the usual charges by large transportation firms who offered these con-

THE STRANGE CAREER OF MR. HOOVER

cessions in the cause of humanity. Banks generally gave their exchange services, and paid the full rate of interest on deposits; insurance was facilitated by the British Government Insurance Commissioners, and the firms who fixed the insurance subscribed the equivalent of their fees. Harbor dues and port charges were remitted at many ports, and stevedoring firms made important concessions in rates and afforded other generous services. In Holland exemption from harbor dues and telegraph tolls was granted, and rail transport into Belgium provided free of charge. The German military authorities in Belgium itself abolished Customs and canal dues on all Commission imports, and reduced railway rates one half."

How can Hoover's Relief Commission then justify the outrageously extravagant prices at which the provisions were charged to the Belgian National Committee?

As we have already seen, Belgium was in no need of this organized relief when the war broke out, and, consequently, the first shipments were hard to place. The Germans began requisitioning food right and left, in contravention of the Law of Nations, and also bought up large quantities of these relief supplies, which the Belgians did not want. But the British Government was receiving reliable information from Belgium of these enormous shipments of food to Germany, and called Hoover on the carpet. Which brings us to one of the most villainous murders in human history!

CHAPTER THE TWENTIETH

Edith Cavell Was Betrayed

A FEW years prior to the War an English nurse named Edith Cavell had opened a private hospital and training school for nurses in the residential section of Uccle in Brussels, and had been quite successful. After hostilities began, wounded soldiers and officers of British, Belgian and even German nationality were taken care of in her institute. The German authorities did not interfere with her. Indeed, the Germans were always considerate of enemy civilians during the War. A few months after entering Brussels they organized a train for English doctors and nurses who wished to leave Belgium, and return to England. Miss Cavell, who was forty-nine years old and had her old mother and her sister in England, did not leave with them. Dr. Tacquin, a Belgian, asked her why she did not want to leave with them for her own country, where she would be of such service and probably obtain a very responsible position. She gave him no reply. She had her own reasons for staying behind.

When the first so-called relief supplies arrived from England, they were offered for sale. But there was no demand for them, as Belgium had enormous food supplies of its own at cheaper prices. The Germans, taking advantage of the low prices, bought up a considerable quantity of the relief food, notably large quantities of rice, which was purchased in Brussels and reshipped to Germany. This was reported from some reliable source in Brussels to the British Government. The result was that Sir Edward Grey, the British Foreign Minister, wrote to Hoover on February 22nd, 1915, withdrawing the offer he had made of a subvention to the "relief," and practically threatening to put a stop to the whole "relief" business unless steps were taken to see that the supplies did not fall into the hands of the Germans. Hoover immediately countered with a statement which appeared in the press on February 24th, 1915, and which read:

> "The destitute in Belgium are the wards of the world. There is no solution to their misery save Charity, and as we have so far failed to secure the help of Governments in this department we can but continue to appeal to the mercy of the people in every land."

This, of course, was untrue; for the Belgian Government had already granted monthly a subvention of $5,000,000 (soon after increased to $7,500,000) for relief purposes. But Hoover wanted to exploit the world's charity in addition, and build up the fiction that Belgium was solely dependent on it.

The distribution of the relief supplies, which were mostly purchased in America, was made by Francqui's *National Committee* in stores opened for the sale of them. The enormous quantities of Belgian domestic produce, however, such as meat, potatoes, fruit, vegetables, milk, sugar, butter, etc., were distributed by the Germans themselves, who established Centrals for that purpose, and which provided a minimum ration for the Belgians, reserving all the rest for the German troops or for shipment to Germany. This was in contravention of the Law of Nations but, as the Germans paid well for the food requisitioned, the Belgian farmers earned enormous profits, and did not worry much about their brethren in the industrial centers who had to suffer in consequence. Indeed, all during the War, one half of the Belgian population was living in luxury—feasting, drinking, dancing, dog racing, and all the rest of it. The peasants did not know what to do with their money, which they carried around by the pailful. The farm girls who milked the cows were dressed in silk, and kept the diamond merchants of Antwerp busy. "Impoverished" Belgium profited by the war so much that, despite the destruction of industrial establishments, its wealth was estimated after the war as being more than twice as much as when the war began. All the above mentioned German Food Centrals came under the control of a rather mysterious personage named Count von der Lancken, who was head of the so-called Political Department, which represented the German Foreign Office. Prior to the war, Lancken had been for six years Counsel to the German Embassy in Paris, with the rank of Ambassador Extraordinary, and is even supposed to have been in direct communication with the Kaiser over the head of the Ambassador. It is certain that he was a man of great prestige and great power.

As the war progressed, the shortage of food in Germany began to cause suffering to certain classes of the German population, and still greater quantities of food were requisitioned and shipped from Belgium into Germany. Hoover, of course, denied this. In a statement issued by him to the press on March 1st, 1915, he stated:

"The German authorities agreed with us in December, that there should be no further requisition or purchase of foodstuffs by the German army in the occupied zone of Belgium. * * * The German authorities have carried out this undertaking with scrupulous care."

To show how much truth there was in this statement

— 327 —

of Hoover's, here is just one quotation from the Belgian side. The *Independance Belge* of December 31st, 1914, tells us:

> "The Germans are making disconcerting requisitions. * * * At Ghent they demand per soldier per day 2 1/5 lbs. of bread and over 1 3/4 lbs. of meat. This quantity of food is evidently too much for one man. It is consequently nothing exceptional to see the rascals get rid of their excess meat by throwing it into the toilets."

Now what do the Germans themselves tell us about requisitions at this period. The *Cologne Gazette* of October 24th, 1914, had already advertised a public auction in Cologne of horses plundered in Belgium. In its issue of January 15th, 1915, the same great newspaper reports the speech of General von Wandel, Deputy Minister for War, from which we give the following extract:

> "We owe it in great part to the skillful and untiring activity of the economic committees that our soldiers in the field are fed as well as they are, and that large stocks, which have made it easier to feed our people, have been brought from the occupied territories into Germany. The officers who co-operated in this work have rendered a great service to the Fatherland."

The same paper, in its issue of February 14th, 1915, reports the following from a speech of a member of the German House of Representatives:

> "In the matter of food we can look forward calmly to a long duration of the war, and also to the maintaining of our industrial activity. This will be considerably helped if the vast quantities of materials bought up in the occupied ter-

ritories are shipped to Germany as speedily as possible."

The *Norddeutsche Allgemeine Zeitung* of March 13th, 1915, tells us that railroad arrangements had been made to expedite shipments from Belgium to Germany and, in its issue of March 30th, 1915, under the caption *Early Vegetables from Belgium,* it reports that great quantities would be available for about three weeks at five to six cents per pound.

From Schmoller's internationally known *Yearbook for Legislation, Administration and Political Economy* for 1916, we learn on page 84, that the amounts of food requisitioned by the German troops in the first four months of the war were estimated at 963,600,000 lbs. of meat, 1,445,400,000 lbs. of potatoes, 1,445,400,000 lbs. of bread and 121,000,000 lbs. of butter and fats, equivalent to 12 to 14% of the meat consumption and 6% of the bread and potato consumption of all Germany. This was saved to Germany. The same article goes on to state:

> "Also in grain for flour the requirements of the soldiers were mostly covered in the occupied territory, for, as we know, American grain (about 600,000 tons) was imported for the necessitous Belgians."

The above report does not include the 400,000 tons of flour and 1,000,000 tons of other provisions removed to Germany after the fall of Antwerp and which would have been saved to Belgium but for the treachery of Louis Frank of the Belgian Relief Committee in surrendering Antwerp and its supplies when the forts could have held out at least two weeks longer.

These quotations are given solely to show that the whole aim and object of the Belgian Relief was to provide Germany with food, and at the same time divert a vast amount of food and immobilize an enormous tonnage which would otherwise have been available for the service of the allied countries, thus cruelly and unnecessarily prolonging the terrible war which, without the slightest shadow of a doubt, would otherwise have come to an end in 1916 through the breakdown of Germany from hunger.

The British Government was mysteriously learning of these requisitions, and of the diversion of relief supplies from Belgium to Germany as well. But, though faced with the awful dilemma of losing the sympathy of America or suffering the breakdown and surrender of the Belgians who were ever and always led to believe that the "relief" was a gigantic work of charity, they had to occasionally protest, and frequently warned Hoover that they would have to put a stop to this relief "business" altogether.

There was someone in Belgium "spilling the beans." Something would have to be done about it. Hoover left his London home for Belgium in June, 1915, and interviewed von der Lancken. What the conversation was, we do not know, but it can well be imagined. It was up to the Germans to find out who was informing the British Government of the leakage in the relief supplies.

Now, was Nurse Cavell a spy? The British Government, of course, does not recognize its spies. But all the facts point to it. In the first place, the enquiries about her arrest, to Minister Wheelock in Brussels, through Ambassador Page in London, show that she was considered a person of importance. Then the *Nursing Mirror* in London received a communication from her on April 15th, 1915, which had been reforwarded through the Post Office without passing the Censor, which is evidence that it must have gone through some Government Department. And lastly, Nurse Cavell was receiving mail in Brussels through the American Consulate, which would not take charge of it unless it had come through a Department of the British Government, which America officially represented in Belgium. The German authorities themselves have always referred to her as "that spy" Cavell.

Edith Cavell was arrested at her private hospital on August 5th, 1915, and lodged in the prison of St. Gilles. Her rooms were searched by the German detective O. Meyer, who found only one letter which she had received from England through the American Consulate and which, being considered of importance, was at once sent to von der Lancken. Here is an extract from O. Mayer's report:

> "I made a search in the course of which a letter from England was found, which had been sent through the American Consul. * * * This letter was handed by the Central Police Office to the Political Department of this city in order that the necessary steps may be taken."

What were the contents of that letter? It was never produced at the trial. Therein lay the secret of the fate of Edith Cavell.

It was the duty of the American Minister Brand Whitlock and his Secretary of Legation, Hugh Gibson, as representing the British Government, to look after the interests of the British, especially those who got into trouble. But their conduct in this case is enough to bring a blush of shame to every genuine American.

Brand Whitlock, in his book *Belgium*, admits that all Brussels knew of the arrest of Miss Cavell. Yet he did absolutely nothing in the matter, until he received a telegram on August 27th, from Ambassador Page in London, making enquiries. Even then, he did not write to von der Lancken until August 31st, and, not obtaining a reply, wrote again on September 10th. To this letter von der Lancken replied on September 12th informing Whitlock that Miss Cavell was under arrest in the prison of St. Gilles and that her case was in the hands of lawyer Thomas Braun.

Ambassador Page wrote again to Whitlock on September 23rd enquiring about Miss Cavell, but Whitlock did not reply until October 9th. And what did he write? "The case will come on for trial next week." When Whitlock wrote that letter Miss Cavell had already been sentenced to death!

On October 5th, De Leval, the Belgian Counselor to the American Legation, had received a letter from Miss Cavell's defender that the case was coming on for trial on the 7th. This conclusively shows all the interest that Brand Whitlock took in it. On October 11th, Whitlock again wrote to Ambassador Page informing him that the Cavell trial was completed but that she had not yet been sentenced. He added:

"I have thus far done everything possible to secure a fair trial for Miss Cavell."

What had he done? Nothing. When he wrote that letter, the death sentence had already been read to Nurse Cavell. She was shot the next morning.

There were a large number of Belgians, thirty-seven of them, including the Princess De Croy and the Countess De Belleville, arrested at this period, and they were all put on trial together before a German Military Court on October 7th and 8th, 1915, on charges of having aided Belgian, French and English soldiers to escape from Belgium, the technical charge reading: "conducting troops to the enemy."

Who undertook the defense of Edith Cavell? Francqui's *National Relief Committee*. It appointed Emm.
Hanssens, one of its members to defend her. Hanssens,
however, was not authorized to plead before a German
military tribunal, and he named as substitute Thomas
Braun. But Braun happened to be under suspension at
the time, and he, with the approval of Hanssens, selected
lawyer Sadi Kirschen, a naturalized Belgian of Ruman-
ian birth, as Miss Cavell's defender. G. De Leval, the
Belgian Counsel at the American Legation, took an interest in the case and arranged with Kirschen to let him
know when it would come for trial. This Kirschen did,
advising De Leval that the case would be heard on Thurs-
day, October 7th. De Leval then arranged with Kirschen
an appointment for Saturday morning, the 9th, to let
him know how things turned out, but on the Saturday
Kirschen was not to be found, nor on the Sunday nor on
the Monday. He had gone to the country! Meanwhile
Edith Cavell had been sentenced to be shot!

A rather strange occurrence, one must admit. The
sequel is even more disgusting. A month later, Whitlock
fired De Leval at the instigation of the Germans for
mixing up in the affair. It is in the hands of men like
this that American prestige abroad is placed.

What had happened at the trial? Miss Cavell's
lawyer, Sadi Kirschen, pleaded guilty to the charge
of "conveying troops to the enemy" which, on conviction, according to the German military Code, carried
with it the possibility of a death sentence. This, however, was a rather common offense, and the sentences imposed were generally light, ranging from a few months'
imprisonment for aiding a private to a few years in the
case of an officer or an aviator. Here are a few of the
sentences passed at this period by German Military

— 333 —

Courts, and they are typical:

Sentenced in Antwerp from October 8th to 15th, 1915 (the very same week as Edith Cavell) (*L'Independance Belge,* November 15, 1915) K. Vermesoen of Welsele —2 months imprisonment for not having delivered up his arms and ammunition.

Alphonse Gehard of Berchen—3 months for trying to cross the frontier.

W. van Winshen of Druten—3 months prison for having helped Belgians who wanted to cross the frontier and only a month later the Rector De Vroeg was sentenced in Brussels to 14 months for sending young Belgians to the Front, but sentence was suspended!

The Germans were even more lenient with women. Why, then, did they pick on Edith Cavell, who had nursed German soldiers back to health? Nothing was proved against Edith Cavell. There was only her own admission that she had aided some soldiers to escape to Holland and had received a letter from one who managed to get back to England. The Germans took advantage of the technicality that this offense carried with it a death penalty to apply it to Miss Cavell, although the offense of "conducting troops to the enemy" was never proved against her, and her sentence on this charge was nothing but a judicial murder. But what did the charge matter? The one she was tried on was merely a "blind." They did not want to try her on a charge of spying and let the facts come to light. That is why they cunningly prosecuted her on the subterfuge charge of "conveying troops to the enemy," which carried with it a death penalty. The result would be the same. She would be suppressed. This frail little middle-aged woman was more dangerous than a dozen army corps. She knew what the "relief" meant to Germany.

All the difference between victory and disaster. So she was suppressed.

To conceal their real object, the German Military Court sentenced to death five of the thirty-eight on trial. But only two were executed, Edith Cavell and a poor architect named Philippe Baucq, whose only offense was that of distributing a patriotic Belgian news sheet, and who was evidently doomed so that the world might not think that the Germans had picked on a frail woman as their only victim.

On Saturday, October 9th, 1915, Edith Cavell was sentenced to death by shooting. It did not take the Military Governor, General von Sauberzweig, long to confirm the sentence. The very next day, Sunday, after church service, he sent this message to the Military Court. It was brief enough:

"Brussels, 10. 10. 15

I confirm the sentence

(signed) Von Sauberzweig,

Brigadier General."

On the next day, Monday, he issued the following order:

"Court of the German Imperial Government
Brussels, October 11, 1915

Brussels, 11b 3301/15

1. I consider that the interests of the State require that the death sentence against Philippe Baucq and Edith Cavell should be carried out *immediately* (underscored in red pencil), and hereby order this to be done.

2. I adjourn the execution of the death sentence against the other persons until such time as a decision has been come to concerning the appeals for mercy now pending.

3. Immediate. The original to be returned to the Kommandantur here for it to be examined and the necessary steps taken.

4. In two days.

The Governor

(signed) Von Sauberzweig,

Brigadier General."

The order reached 1st Lieutenant Behrens. He noticed the significant word "immediately" and reported as follows:

Brussels 11.10.15

Sentence to be returned after examination thereof.

The death penalty against Baucq and Cavell will be carried out 12.10.15 at seven o'clock A. M.

(signed) Behrens, Lieutenant.

The above original documents, which can be found in Ambroise Got's book "Le Cas Cavell," are pretty clear evidence that there was some very definite and urgent reason for the murder of Edith Cavell.

De Leval, the Belgian counsel to the American Legation, was astounded at not being able to locate Sadi Kirschen, Miss Cavell's lawyer, on either the Saturday, Sunday or Monday after the trial. On Monday, the 11th, he telephoned to von der Lancken's office, where von der Lancken's assistant, Conrad, assured him positively that she had not yet been sentenced. For some extremely grave reason, the most extraordinary precautions were being taken to keep the sentence secret so that she should be executed before there could be any intervention to save her. It was only when the office of the American Legation was closing for the day on Monday, October 11th, that De Leval and two nurses arrived with the news they had received through some underground channel that Miss Cavell had been sentenced to death and would be shot early the next morning.

Brand Whitlock professed to be ill, but wrote an appeal for clemency, and sent Hugh Gibson, Secretary of Legation, with De Leval to get hold of the Marquis de Villalobar, the Spanish Minister, and make a last minute effort for Miss Cavell with von der Lancken. They found Villalobar at the house of Baron Lambert, where he was having supper with Lambert and Francqui. Villalobar at once accompanied Gibson and De Leval to Lancken's house. Singularly enough, however, Francqui did not accompany them, Francqui who controlled the food situation and one word from whom, or from Hoover to von der Lancken, might have saved her.

On arrival at Lancken's house, they found he was at the theatre. They sent for him and he replied he would come when the show was over. When Lancken arrived home, it was already after ten o'clock and, on being told the object of the mission, he, according to Brand Whitlock's account, gave vent to an outburst of feeling against "that spy," as he called Miss Cavell. On recovering his temper, he expressed the greatest surprise, saying that it was quite impossible that sentence could have been passed. At the same time, however, he was very insistent to know where the information originated from. Simulating ignorance, he went through the farce of telephoning to the presiding judge of the Court Martial when he apparently learned for the first time of the sentence.

The appeal for clemency was then presented to him by Hugh Gibson, but it was the Spaniard Villalobar who did all the pleading, for, according to Lancken himself, Gibson did not say a word. Lancken said it was too late to do anything, for the decision rested with General von Sauberzweig, and he could not disturb him at that late hour. However, at the insistence of Villalobar, he either went, or pretended to go and see von Sauberzweig, and returned in about half an hour with the report that von Sauberzweig was insistent on the death of Miss Cavell, *because the circumstances in her case were of such a character that he considered the infliction of a death sentence imperative.*

Lancken then told them he was very sorry, but that there was no further remedy as, under the circumstances, the Kaiser himself could not interfere. This was, of course, a falsehood. These men wanted their prey. Only a few months ago, von der Lancken published a book in Germany, in which he takes great pains to show his innocence of the death of Miss Cavell. He throws all the blame on Von Sauberzweig, who is dead and cannot defend himself. The fact remains, however, that von der Lancken must have known of the death sentence on October 9th, and was directly implicated in the murder (for it was a murder, Miss Cavell not having been proved guilty of the offense charged), if for no other reason than that the execution of the death sentence was carried out by 1st Lieutenant Behrens of the Kommandantur, attached to von der Lancken's staff in the Food Administration!

The shot that snuffed out the life of Edith Cavell was heard around the world, a challenge to humanity. It was not that the Germans killed a woman (the French had shot two women spies only a few months previously), but that she was a woman working at the noble profession of nursing for the benefit of mankind, British, Belgian and German without distinction, and was not proved guilty of the charge brought against her, which was only a fictitious one. Her real offense was never disclosed. It was an affair of calories, of bread and fat and

beans, the fuel of the great German army machine, which
she must not be allowed to clog. The London *Times* in a
leading article on October 22nd, 1915, wrote:

"We do not know whether the hidebound bru-
tality of the military authorities or the lying
trickery of the civilians is the more repulsive.
Both were determined that Miss Cavell should die,
and they conspired together to shoot her before
an appeal could be lodged."

The London *Daily News,* writing on the same date,
said:

"It is perfectly clear from these papers that
the German military authorities were determined
to destroy Miss Cavell. Why, is a mystery, and
will perhaps remain so; but the intention cannot
be doubted any more than the extraordinary means
taken to realize it. * * *   But it is a mistake to
lay this crime to the door of the German judicial
machinery, cruel and stupid as that is; for the
machinery was deliberately tampered with to
murder a woman."

The correspondence between the American Legation
and Ambassador Page in London was issued to the London press on October 22nd, 1915. It was the first anniversary of the foundation of the Commission for Relief
in Belgium, and a dinner was to be held to commemo-
rate the event. A busy day for Hoover. We can well
picture him swinging out of the porch gate of his London
home, the Red House, down Hornton Street to the corner
of Kensington High Street to catch the Underground to
the City. At the street corner he snatches a paper from
a newsboy. Across the page is splashed in huge letters:
THE MURDER OF MISS CAVELL. Horrors, the whole ter-

rible stink was out! He grows faint. Is it any wonder that the anniversary celebration of the founding of the Belgium Relief, which was to have been held that day, never came off?

A few days after the body of Miss Cavell was riddled with bullets, a meeting of the Relief Committee was held in Brussels. It was they who had appointed the lawyer for her defense, whose substitute the ex-Roumanian Kirschen had pleaded guilty and disappeared during the two and a half days between her sentence and her execution. Her death had been made a text of warning against spies in posters pasted up throughout Brussels by the German Governor General. It was the sensation of the day. It was echoing around the world. But at this meeting in Brussels held just after her execution by the *National Committee,* her name was not even mentioned. Hush, hush! The dark secret must be buried with her. Was it that she loved England more and Germany less? Oh, dear, no. She knew too much about wheat and lard, rice, beans and peas. She was "put on the spot." She stood in the way of ruthless men.

CHAPTER THE TWENTY-FIRST

How America Was Brought into the War

Aᶠᵀᴱᴿ the death of Edith Cavell, the Belgian Relief continued as before. The Belgian Government increased its subvention to $7,500,000 monthly. England, however, insisted on closer control. A service of inspection and control was set up to prevent requisitioning of relief supplies by the Germans. It was only in May, 1916, that this service started operating, and one can imagine what a farce it was from the fact that the inspectors were young American boys ignorant of the dialects spoken in Belgium, and that they were not allowed to accompany freight trains. The Germans continued, of course, to take relief supplies. There is one authenticated instance where they took 3,500 tons at one time. They did spare the grain and flour, but they certainly did not spare the bread. The German crop of 1915 was a poor one, owing to the shortage of fertilizers, and prices rose considerably, the German food rations costing in October, 1915, butter and bacon 60 cents per lb., beans 15 cents, and rice 17 cents per lb. Germany thereupon began a systematic plundering of Belgium. The Centrals allotted to the inhabitants the minimum rations of sugar, butter, meat and potatoes, and left the poorer classes dependent on Francqui's *National Committee* for bread, lard, peas and beans, etc. Of course the well-to-do Belgians could have everything they wanted, for everything was for sale at a price. There were the Belgian co-operatives, which purchased enormous quantities of foodstuffs, especially white bread, in Holland. There were also hundreds of charitable organizations, each helping out in its own way. Even the poorer classes of Belgians managed to get along very nicely until the middle of 1916, when the Germans, at the instigation of Francqui's *National Committee,* which wanted to control the sale of all food, prohibited the further purchase of provisions, including bread, from Holland on the pretext that it meant the sending of German money out of Belgium to Holland, whereas all the German money that came into Francqui's bank and against which it issued Belgian notes, was being sent to Germany!

A great part of the Belgian population was thus condemned to eat the vile bread supplied by the *National Committee.* All accounts agree that this bread was not fit for pigs. It was like a ball of putty when fresh and fell into dust when toasted. It had always a bad taste, was the cause of all kinds of gastric troubles and kept the grave diggers busy. The lard, too, was often rancid, and the bacon diseased. Indeed, it would seem that Hoover's organization was supplying to Belgium whatever rubbishy food it could get away with. In 1916, however, Germany was even in a worse situation. The crop of 1916 was again disastrous for want of fertilizers and hundreds of thousands of Germans were dying of starvation. If it had not been for the tremendous supplies of food—meat, potatoes, eggs, bread, vegetables, fodder, millions of tons that Germany was enabled to draw from Belgium through the operation of the Relief plan—the great war would undoubtedly have ended in August, 1916, at the battle of the Somme.

It was in the first week in August of that anguishing summer of 1916 that the Germans had Hoover come to Berlin with von der Lancken to see their Quarter Master General von Sauberzweig (the one who as Military Governor of Brussels had put Edith Cavell on the spot nine

months before) to see what could be done regarding
getting more food into Germany by organizing a Relief
for Poland on the same lines as had been done for
Belgium. Maybe Hoover was ready to take this next
step, but the British Government was certainly not.
They had had enough of the Belgian Relief, which was
costing them the war. (See British document "Miscel-
laneous No. 32 (1916)"—Correspondence respecting the
relief of allied territory in the occupation of the enemy.)
They would have abolished it if they could. The Belgian
Relief, had, however, been so widely advertised throughout the world as a great American work of charity that
England was powerless to stop it, for fear of losing
American sympathy when the necessity of the intervention of the United States was becoming daily more apparent. England had a knife in her throat, and dared
not pull it out for fear that she would bleed to death.

One has only to read the "Report on Food Conditions
in Germany" (the result of a thorough investigation on
the spot after the war) published by the British Government in 1919, to see that Germany was actually on her
last legs from starvation in 1916. The average man requires to take a daily supply of food equal to about 3,400
calories in value, and the average woman 2,700 calories,
to maintain health and efficiency. Children over thirteen
require as much as the average man or woman, and children from one to five, half as much. Heavy workers need
4,000 to 5,000 calories per day in the form of food. Now
let us see what this report tells us of conditions in Germany in 1916:

"In the first two years of the war, these effects
had not begun to make themselves felt. Some food
was still to be obtained through neutral countries,
and up to Easter of 1916 the food supply of the

population as a whole was not much inferior to that obtaining before the war. At Easter 1916, it was found necessary to reduce the meat ration. No very serious effects were, however, anticipated by the Food Ministry. The ration per head per day, which was guaranteed, had a value of 1,985 calories, i. e., nearly 2,500 per "average man," and it was anticipated to be possible to obtain, besides this, a considerable amount of unrationed food, such as fruit, vegetables, fish and polished barley. When the autumn of 1916 came, this ration was found to be impossible from lack of supplies, and the ration actually distributed had a calorie value of only 1,344 with a protein content of only 31 grams per day. Bread and potatoes constituted the bulk of this inadequate diet, and very small quantities of unrationed foods were available. Then the potatoes failed and their place had to be taken by swede turnips.

The winter of 1916-1917 is acknowledged by all to have been the time of the severest food shortage that has occurred throughout the war. The weight of the population rapidly diminished on the starvation diet. They were only maintained alive by the using up of the fat in their own tissues, and a reduction of 60, 70 and 80 pounds in weight was not infrequent. On an average it may be asserted that during this time that part of the population who were not producers and who were not given specially favorable treatment, such as workers in munition factories, etc., lost from 15 to 25 per cent of their previous weight."

Page 7 of the same report tells us:

"In consequence, however, of the large propor-

tion of vegetable food in the diet, and the large proportion of bran in the bread, the food is much less
digestible than normally, and there must be a loss
of at least 15 to 20 per cent in digestion. It is thus
certain that the ordinary individual, if living in a
family, obtained less than two-thirds of the amount
regarded by all authorities as adequate for health
and efficiency, and if a bachelor living alone, he
was receiving only one-half of his necessary allowance. The food, moreover, was seriously deficient
as regards quality. For the normal repair of the
wear and tear of the tissues, especially the muscles,
a certain amount of protein must be taken. The
minimum figure to which this can be safely reduced, according to the Royal Society, is 70 grammes per man per day. In the German rations, the
amount varied from 30 to 40 grammes, and even
with other possible purchases, did not exceed 45
grammes. This amount might have been sufficient
if it had been animal protein, and had formed part
of a diet sufficient in all other respects. It was,
however, for the most part, vegetable protein of
little more than one-half the value of animal protein, and was therefore absolutely insufficient for
the maintenance of health. As regards fat, 70
grammes per man per day (56 per head) has been
accepted by the Allied countries as the necessary
minimum for the average man. The rations contained only 15 to 20 grammes of fat per day, and
the food obtainable outside the ration was almost
entirely deficient in fat. A diet thus restricted in
quantity and defective in quality signifies slow
starvation. When food is suddenly and entirely
withdrawn from an animal or a man, death occurs

when the body has lost, on the average, 40 per cent of its weight. In Germany a number of deaths have actually occurred as a direct result of this slow starvation. These deaths were numerous in the winter 1916-1917."

The London *Economist* has estimated that 800,000 Germans died from starvation. What would have happened if Germany had not obtained those millions of tons of food from Belgium, made possible by the rationing plan of the Belgian Relief? It would never have been able to go through that dread year of 1916. The war would have ended, millions of lives and maimed and crippled spared, and the brave American boys would have never had to sink into that horrible inferno of slaughter.

The prolongation of the war with all its terrors and atrocities in the bitter cold of that dreadful winter campaign of 1916-1917, with all the monumental human sacrifice to Moloch, and especially America's entering the war, are directly due to the provisioning of Belgium by the Relief Commission, enabling Germany to plunder Belgium of countless millions of tons of food, and hold out till the conquest of Roumania again brought it bread.

DEPARTAMENTO DE MATAGAEPA

Jurisdiccion	Nombre de la propiedad	Nombre del propietario	Clase de metal
San Ramón	Yankee Boy..........	William A. Wheeler............	Oro
«	Yankee Girl	Herbert Clark Emery	«
«	La Constancia	William A. Wheeler............	«
«	La Blanquita.........	id. id. id	«
«	Santa Rosa...........	id. id. id..............	«
«	Perú	José Vita...............	«
«	Lima	Anibal Paracca...	«
«	San Basilio...........	id. id	«
«	Delicias	id. id...............	«
«	California	id. id	«
«	Prinzapolka..........	José Vita...............	«
«	Montserrat..........	William A. Wheeler	«
«	La Leonesa	La Leonesa Mining Cía	«
«	San Basilio	id. id. id. id	«
«	Leonecita	id. id. id. id	«
«	Alaska....	id. id. id. id.......	«
«	Providencia	id. id. id. id.......	«
«	Tacoma	id. id. id. id	«
«	Boston	id. id, id. id.......	«
«	La Tranquilidad.. ...	id. id. id. id......	«
«	La Reina	Adler & Eister	«
«	La Española	id. id. id	«
«	Zola...............	José Vita....	«
Muymuy	Santa Rita	Benicio Guerrero	«

POBLACION—CENSO PROVISIONAL DE 1906

NUEVA SEGOVIA

MUNICIPIOS	Población de la cabecera		Población rural		Total por sexos		Total general	% de la población de la cabecera		% de la población rural		% por sexos	
	V	M	V	M	V	M		V	M	V	M	V	M
Somoto.........	624	729	3,432	3,491	4,056	4,220	8,276	7,54	8,81	41,47	42,18	49,01	50,99
Telpaneca........	185	193	2,431	2,499	2,616	2,692	5,308	3,48	3,65	45,79	47,08	49,27	50,73
Palacaguina....	97	111	961	996	1,058	1,107	2,165	4,48	5,12	44,39	46,00	48,87	51,13
Yalaguina.......	70	90	426	427	496	517	1,013	6,91	8,89	42,05	42,15	48,96	51,04
Totogalpa	123	161	1,292	1,388	1,415	1,550	2,965	4,15	5,43	43,57	46,85	47,72	52,28
El Jícaro........	195	266	1,416	1,373	1,611	1,639	3,250	6,00	8,18	43,57	42,25	49,57	50,43
Jalapa......	235	264	609	559	844	823	1,667	14,10	15,84	36,53	33,53	50,63	49,37
San Fernando...	85	98	172	165	257	263	520	16,34	18,85	33,08	31,73	49,42	50,58
Ciudad Antigua..	88	116	194	205	282	321	603	14,60	19,23	32,17	34,00	46,77	53,23
Santa María.....	35	44	695	747	730	791	1,521	2,30	2,90	45,69	49,11	47,99	52,01
Macuelizo........	101	112	262	265	363	377	740	13,65	15,13	35,41	35,81	49,05	50,95
Ocotal..........	546	752	107	110	653	862	1,515	36,04	49,64	7,06	7,26	43,10	56,90
Dipilto.........	89	111	195	203	284	314	598	14,88	18,56	32,61	33,95	47,49	52,51
Murra	119	100	157	159	276	259	535	22,24	18,69	29,35	29,72	51,58	48,41
Quilalí.........	47	53	486	474	533	527	1,060	4,43	5,00	45,85	44,72	50,28	49,42
Mosonte........	60	78	512	513	572	591	1,163	5,16	6,71	44,02	44,11	49,18	50,82
Total......	2,699	3,278	13,347	13,575	16,046	16,853	32,899						
%........	8,20	9,96	40,57	41,27	48,77	51,23	....						

2

From the official record of the Republic of Nicaragua.
Note the name underlined.

CHAPTER THE TWENTY-SECOND

BENEVOLENCE

So the war did not end in the Fall of 1916. Germany, hunger-desperate, late in that year overran Rumania and captured sixty million bushels of grain, enabling her to carry on until the new crop and the receipt of fresh Belgian plunder in 1917. In desperation, the Germans, in January, 1917, proclaimed unrestricted submarine warfare, and began sinking English cargoes Then England, too, began to feel the pinch of hunger. The English did not yelp, but they punished their stomachs voluntarily—two ounces of bread (one slice) and one ounce of flour daily. At that juncture, fifteen cargoes of food supplies, purchased for Belgium by Hoover's Commission, arrived in England. Hoover refused to allow them to proceed to Rotterdam, where the relief cargoes were unloaded, unless the Germans gave them a safe conduct. Germany, on March 2nd, 1917, asked the British for the names of the fifteen steamers for the purpose of giving the safe conduct. Instead of doing so, however, Sir Maurice De Bunsen, the British Under Secretary of State, issued a communication to the Associated Press in New York (see *N. Y. Times* of March 6, 1917), stating that it had been agreed with Hoover's *Belgian Relief Commission* to unload the cargoes, and store them until such time as they might be conveyed to Rotterdam with safety. This was pure hokum, for the cargoes had already been sold to England. England needed those cargoes. Not only that. But, at the same time, England also took over the stocks of food accumulated on her wharves for Belgian account, so that ninety-five thousand tons of food were lost to Belgium. By this time the Germans had so thoroughly cleaned up the available food supplies in Belgium that a great part of the Belgian population was left dependent on the relief rations in accordance with the original German plan. Thus, all of a sudden, supplies were cut off from Belgium. The sale of this food at this terrible juncture put Hoover right with the British Board of Trade. The food situation was desperate in England, and prices were rising in America. Something would have to be done to control them. Hoover got Ambassador Page, who was a great Anglophile, to recommend him for the job. After the sale of the cargoes, Hoover left for the United States to interview President Wilson. The plan was being prepared.

When he arrived here at the end of January, 1917, Hoover thought it was time to jack up the American public for some more contributions to his commission. Receipts from other countries had fallen off. Indeed, at this very time, New South Wales in Australia, which had been the most generous of all subscribers, having given $2,250,000 from a population of 2,000,000, had had so many reports from Australian soldiers of the Relief supplies going to Germany, that it cabled Hoover's Commission not to spend any more of their money, and to return $220,000 of it that had not yet been spent!. Did this disturb Hoover? No. On February 1st, 1917, he issued an appeal to the Chamber of Commerce in New York for contributions of $5,000,000 to $8,000,000 per month with an additional $10,000,000 a month on loan. On February 9th, 1916, after the sale of the ninety-five thousand tons of Belgian relief food to England, Mr. Hoover told the City Club in Philadelphia that there was then no starvation in Belgium. Just see what daily rations these poor

unfortunates were on when Hoover made that statement:
Rations for January, February, March, 1917:

Black bread—300 grams (a little over one pound)—690 calories	
Rice, peas or beans 16 grams (a little over ½ ounce)— 60 "	
Bacon or lard 13 grams (a little under ½ ounce)— 90 "	
Herrings, coffee (a very small quantity)	50 "
Soup 1 Liter (about one quart)	150 "
Sugar 20 grams (less than ¾ ounces)	70 "
Butter 3 grams (less than 1/10th ounces)	20 "

Total 1,130 calories

(*La Metropole,* 3 October, 1917, page 2).

When it requires 3,400 calories for a normal active man to support life!. The Dutch newspaper *Nieuwe Rotterdamsche Courant* of May 1, 1917, tells us that the Belgian workers were half starved since January, and that the mortality was enormous! The grave diggers were busy that winter in the biting cruel cold. What did Hoover care? Men had died for him in Australia, in China, in Africa, in Burma. What were a few thousand Belgians more or less? On with the racket!

The relief supplies in Belgium, as we have seen, were sold by Francqui's National Committee in stores established for the purpose. It came to a point where the poorer classes of people had pawned all their belongings for money to buy the food, which, with the exception of bread (the price of which was kept down by the Germans), was sold at the highest prices they could get away with. Here are the prices of "relief" foodstuffs in June, 1918:

Bacon and lard, 45c; rice, peas and beans, 14c; coffee, 73c per lb. There was only the bread, which the Germans knew to be essential and would not allow them to racketeer on. They got around this by importing the grain, milling it in Belgium and making such an admixture that the bread made out of it was not fit for pigs. They had to get their profit somehow. Francqui, however, was under obligation to the Belgian Government, which was advancing $7,500,000 a month (increased in April, 1917, to $15,000,000 monthly on loans from the American Government), to provide relief for the destitute. He had, from the beginning, established soup kitchens, the expenses of which were defrayed by the parishes. In the summer of 1916, however, as the resources of the poorer classes had been spent in buying food, there was a good deal of unrest and rioting broke out in several places. Francqui thereupon decided to give the unemployed an out-of-work allowance of fifty cents a week. However, the Germans were shortly thereafter provided with the names of the unemployed, so that they could be deported to Germany to the horrors of forced labor, coupled with starvation. Then there were the lacemakers, of whom there were hundreds of thousands in Belgium. He allowed them a wage of forty-seven cents a week and took their produce to sell at extravagant "relief" prices. This high rate of wages resulted in the loss of a few million dollars, that is, in Francqui's books. Then there were the unfortunate wives of soldiers in the battlefield. They got no relief from Francqui until the starvation days of January, 1917, when they were allowed a few cents a week, and that in food tickets. Francqui's relief was all given in food tickets. The money had to be spent in the relief stores.

Francqui's arrangement with the Belgian Government had provided that he was to keep a separate account of money expended for the benefit of Government employees, soldiers' wives and other disbursements that would normally be for account of the Government. This he did until the Americans entered the war, and a subvention of $15,000,000 monthly was arranged, when he jumbled the two accounts together. Indeed, in his eleven volumes of reports, Francqui time and again reminds both the Government and the Public that what became of the money is none of their business, that his was a private organization responsible to nobody. It was just the same with Hoover's Commission for Relief in Belgium. It was responsible to nobody.

Francqui's *National Committee* report Part 1, page 39 (published in 1919), tells us that up to December 31st, 1918, the Committee had spent 1,300,000,000 francs (roughly $260,000,000) in relief. This corresponds with their accounts published in 1919. In 1921 when trying to make their accounts gibe, they stretched this amount to 2,214,836,054.72 francs (roughly $442,400,000). What became of the difference of $182,000,000? It was nobody's damned business, and Francqui had the gall to say so. His statement of relief expenses included such items as

Co-operative loan society (approx.)	$59,654,000
Building society	702,000
Advances to savings banks	3,400,000
Advances to provinces and towns	2,675,000

and many others, all of which were investments and not permanent expenditures. To stuff his accounts, he even shows an expenditure for relief in December, 1918 (after the war was over), of over $40,000,000, four times as much as reported for any previous month.

If the accounts of Francqui were erratic, those of Hoover were fantastic. His relief commission issued volumes and volumes of reports, taking care to give the quantities in metric tons and foreign measurements, with a maze of figures. These reports have been condensed and embodied in a work published from Stanford University in 1925, entitled:

Commission for Relief in Belgium
Statistical Review of Operations

by one George I. Gay of Stanford, who was connected with this relief business. Hoover has written a foreword to this volume under date of June 20, 1925, in which he writes of the work of the bookkeepers:

> "But the work of these men was of the utmost importance to those in official direction, not only that the relief undertaking might be effectively performed and presented to the World, but that our honor and the honor of our country in this trusteeship should never be challenged."

This *Statistical Review of Operations* gives over four hundred large pages of statistics, accounting practically for every pound of food supposed to have gone to Belgium and Northern France, when we know that practically half the population of Belgium was trafficking in these supplies, and, apart from the enormous sales to Germany, there were important robberies time and again, one authenticated instance being the plunder of three thousand five hundred tons of relief supplies by the Germans at Roubaix. And yet practically every pound is accounted for!

In February, 1917, General Hurt, the German Governor of Brussels, had to post up the following notice:

> "The underground dealing in these foodstuffs has attained such proportions that a fair distribution of them and uniform rationing of all classes of the population has become almost impossible."

These statistics are so much "boloney" just as the reading matter of this *Statistical Review* bristles with contradictions.

Page 4 of this *Statistical Review* tells us:

> "Herbert Hoover, an American engineer, who happened to be in London, whither he had gone from California on behalf of the Panama Pacific

Exposition in the summer of 1914."

Hoover had resided in London since 1901 continuously. He had no official connection whatever with the Panama Pacific Exposition. Instead of being on a visit to London, he had just returned from a visit to California, where he had been making his desperate efforts to secure an oil reserve for England.

In connection with these accounts, there are two things to bear in mind. The first is that no money whatever passed between Francqui's *National Committee* and Hoover's *Commission for Relief,* and the other is that Northern France was rationed by Francqui's Committee, to which all these supplies were invoiced.

The report of Francqui's Provisioning Department, 2nd part, vol. 1, chapter 1, page 5, tells us:

"Although the Provisioning Department might be compared to a commercial organization, still it differed in many respects. First of all, it did not itself buy the goods it imported. They were shipped to it from abroad by the Commission for Relief in Belgium (C. R. B.) which bought them in foreign markets with funds placed at its disposal chiefly by the Belgian Government. These goods were shipped to Rotterdam and from there to Belgium by the C. R. B. office in that city. The latter invoiced them to the National Committee which, in turn, invoiced them to the Provincial Committees. The proceeds of the sale of goods by the National Committee to the provincial committees supplied the funds which the Provisioning Department turned over to the Relief Department. As a matter of fact, if the National Committee was charged in the books of the C. R. B. with the value of all the goods shipped to it, it did

not pay for them and transferred no funds abroad."
No funds were received by Hoover's Commission from
Francqui's Committee. All the money Hoover had to
spend was what he received from charity and from the
subventions put up on behalf of the Belgian Government.
These accounts show that Hoover's Commission received in cash:

Subsidies from Governments		$700,540,443.38
Charitable cash donations		19,435,076.83
		719,975,520.21
Refunded to U. S. Treasury		23,033,683.43
		696,941,836.78
On hand at close of a/cs (approx.)	$4,000,000	
Administration expense	4,000,000	8,000,000.00
		$688,941,836.78

so that all the money they had to spend did not amount
to 689 million dollars. And yet his accounts show that he
purchased for this sum provisions costing $646,829,568.07
on which he paid freight and insurance amounting to
$165,239,023.32, a total of over eight hundred and twelve
million dollars. In other words, he bought goods costing
a hundred and twenty-two million dollars more than he
had to spend and still had many millions left over. He
accounts for the difference by saying that this represented
marginal charges. But these marginal charges do not
represent money spent.

The *General Summary of Operations* shows, under B.
World Charity: from United States $6,051,859.82.

The same item is shown in the *Statement of Financial
Operations* under 2. World Charity: from the United
States $4,906,614.85.

This, however, is only one detail. Look at the *Statement of Financial Operations* where the *Comite d'Ali-
mentation du Nord de la France* (Northern France Provisioning Committee) is charged as having received $216,-

033,665.27 worth of supplies. Now Hoover's Commission *did not supply this Northern France Committee at all!* The C. R. B. shipped everything to Francqui's Committee, which resold at a profit to the Northern France Committee. Then what does that entry of $180,922,696.56 charged against the Northern France Committee represent?

At the outbreak of war, Lord Kitchener had estimated that it would last at least three years. It is reasonable to suppose that Hoover with the guarantee of Governments behind him, and not risking his own money, would make purchases for at least twelve months in advance. He knew all about "options" and "futures," this wizard of the London Stock Market. Well, when he began to buy in December, 1914, he could have covered his wheat to the new crop at $1.15 a bushel, for New York or Buenos Aires, his maize at 60 cents and his bacon and lard at 11 cents. In August, 1915, he could have covered to June, 1916, at $1.00 for wheat, 60 cents or less for corn and 10 cents for bacon and lard, and in June, 1916, could have covered again at the same prices until the summer of 1917. Did he do it? We suppose he did. That is where the money was to be made, juggling in options and futures. Did the Belgians get the benefit of it? They did not. Look at the prices. All along the line they are the highest of the day. Just imagine billing a starving people, for they were starving in 1917, with fat backs and lard at 35½ cents per lb. in cargo lots, corn at over $4.37 per bushel, Rio coffee at 21¾ cents per lb. And then Francqui had to get his profits on top of these prices!

Here are the prices over four years at which Hoover billed "relief" supplies to Francqui:

	Dec. 1914	Oct. 1915	Oct. 1916	Oct. 1917	Oct. 1918
Wheat rye, per bushel	$1.51	$1.80	$2.32	$3.86	$4.80

Corn, per bushel	1.10	1.50	2.06	3.86	4.38
Barley, per bushel					4.10
Flour, per 100 lbs.					9.53
Rice, per 100 lbs.	4.33	3.90	4.33	7.36	12.58
Peas, beans, per 100 lbs.		5.20	6.93	10.82	13.85
Bacon fat backs, 100 lbs.	14.72	15.59	19.48	28.14	35.50
Lard, per 100 lbs.	14.72	12.99	17.32	28.14	35.50
Pickled meat, per 100 lbs.		14.72	12.57	21.22	25.98
Coffee, Rio, per 100 lbs.	4.50	12.99	14.72	17.32	15.16
Cocoa, per 100 lbs.			25.98	25.98	18.18
Condensed milk, 100 lbs.	7.36	10.10	12.56	10.86	12.56
Sugar, per 100 lbs.		4.33	8.66	8.66	9.53

And of course, they obtained a rebate of the amount of duty on sugar and on sugar content of condensed milk.

Hoover's Commission never paid these prices, or anything near them. They were invoicing the food to Francqui at a tremendous profit, so that Francqui could make a huge profit on the resale of the goods. They even profited on the freight rates. Just to give a few examples: The S/S "St. Helena" was chartered by Hoover's Commission for Atlantic Coast to Rotterdam April, 1915, sailing at 7/— per quarter—$7 per ton. The freight was charged up at $15 per ton. The S/S "Cambrian King" from Newport News to Rotterdam, April/May 1915, at $9/—per quarter—$9 per ton. The freight was charged up at $14 per ton. The S/S "Elfland" chartered for Baltimore/Rotterdam, April, 1915, at 9/9 per quarter—29¼ cents per bushel. The freight was billed at forty cents per bushel. And remember that every cent per bushel on a vessel of 200,000 bushels means $2,000! They juggled with the steamers, too, swapping and rechartering at higher rates. Some that were chartered never made the voyages. The Belgian steamers requisitioned by the Belgian Government were not used to any great extent. The rates for them were fixed and there was no way of juggling them.

When on April, 1917, President Wilson made Hoover Food Administrator, he had even richer fields opened up for him. He had control of all American food production and the spending of over a hundred and fifty million dollars of American money. But he was not satisfied. He still clung to the relief business.

He took over with him to America one of his relief aides, Prentiss Gray, who had been a shipping clerk on the Pacific Coast before the war. Gray was launched in the grain and flour business. Enormous profits were made. Gray is now president of a bank and a trust company and director of about a dozen large corporations. He got his start working for nothing in the relief racket.

Another that Hoover took with him to the States was Edgar Rickard, who before the war business had been agent of a small mining publication in London and was lucky if he could pay his laundry bill every Saturday night. Hoover actually had this Englishman appointed Food Administrator of the United States in his absence! Rickard is now president and director of many corporations, including some controlling patents issued while Hoover had control of the Patent Office.

We all know the later history of Mr. Hoover since he rediscovered the United States, in 1917. How, as soon as the war was over, he rushed to Europe to organize the "European" relief, and control the spending of another billion of dollars worth of food. Edgar Rickard had sole charge of the Polish and Russian relief, and Prentiss N. Gray, Inc., were in the grain and flour shipping business.

It was at that time, also, that Hoover tried to put a quantity of American shipping under the control of the Inter-Allied War Council, in other words, England. He was only prevented from doing so by the prompt action of Chairman Hurley of the Shipping Board.

After the relief business was exhausted, we find him taking his place in Harding's cabinet as Secretary of

Commerce, and earning great applause by finding jobs for inexperienced young men, and promoting American commerce by having the naked Patagonians circularized for the purchase of washing machines.

CHAPTER THE TWENTY-THIRD

THEY BECAME RICH BY WORKING FOR NOTHING

OF Hoover's associates in early days, there were Jack Means and George Wilson of Stanford, with the latter of whom he seems to have broken later, for Wilson went back to the law. Then there were Newberry, the Australian, and Agnew, the New Zealander, both mining engineers, and S. C. Magennis, the accountant of the National Bank in Coolgardie, whom he wangled into Tilden Smith's office and who evidently remained loyal to his new employer. Of these the one closest to Hoover was long headed John Agnew, who left Moreing in 1912 to join Hoover, and "substituted" for Hoover in many mining enterprises when Hoover took up the relief business. Agnew is now one of the greatest figures in the mining world. But how much of his holdings are his own, or are still Hoover's, it is impossible to say.

After the "taking" of the Kaiping coal mines his associates were mostly mining racketeers and stocketeers like Forger Rowe, Musketeers Davis and Turner, Carbine Govett, Tailor Doolette, Boulder Deep Robinson, Silent Tilden Smith, Gambler Grenfell, Granville Beatty, Bolshevik-eating Urquhart, and the like.

His connection with Edmund Davis of the Nigerian tin and other rackets appears to continue. Davis is now the dominant factor in the great Rhodesian copper properties, which have been promising dividends for the last thirty years and in which considerable American capital has been invested within the last few years. It would be interesting to know at whose suggestion these investments were made, just as it would be interesting to learn who is back of the movement to curtail production of American copper for the benefit of this Rhodesian gang. With Urquhart Hoover probably is still friendly, if for no other reason than that little claim of two hundred and eighty million dollars against the Soviet Government.

In the years of the California oil business, Hoover's closest American connection, apart from Beatty, seems to have been with Mark Requa, whom he made his assistant in the Food Administration in 1917, as soon as he had settled down in this country, and afterwards placed in charge of the Oil Division, that same Requa who was so eager to lease the naval oil reserves and afterwards became a vice president in the Sinclair oil organization.

All Hoover's recent associations in America, apart from political ones, date from this relief and food business. His main relations in that business were with the Belgians, Francqui and De Wouters, his old pals in the Chinese robbery, both of whom are now financial magnates, especially Francqui, who must be one of the world's richest men. He controlled the distribution of the "benevolence" in Belgium. There were, however, a number of men connected with this relief and food business who seem to have had important claims on benevolence and have benefited accordingly. Take that mysterious individual, Lawrence Richey, the former obscure secret service man who was assistant office manager of the Food Administration from 1917 to 1919. He managed to put so much gum on his "gum shoes" that there was no prying his heels loose from the job. He is the high priest of the tabernacle. Then there is Walter Lyman Brown. No, not a shipping man, but a mining engineer, brought all the way from the Gold Coast of Africa to attend to the shipping of relief supplies from the port of Rotterdam to Belgium and elsewhere.

"And he did his work with such pep and vim
That America's no longer good enough for him."

Oh, no! My word, no! He lives in Belgravia in London, right among all the snobs and "haristocrats." He is now Vice President of a large investment security firm. And all accomplished by working five years for nothing at the relief game. Our old friend, Robert Grant, the Canuck, who resigned from one of Hoover's mines in 1905 rather than risk the lives of his men for want of timber (good luck to him!) was put in charge of the *U. S. Food Administration* in Colorado from 1917 to 1919, and is now director of the Mint in Washington, D. C.!

It would take a volume to tell of all these good boys who made their way in life by working for nothing. Let us limit ourselves to a few—Prentiss Gray, Julius Barnes and Edgar Rickard. Nobody can accuse these gentlemen of having been capitalists before the outbreak of war. Prentiss Gray, at the start of hostilities, was in charge of shipping for a lumber concern on the Pacific coast. It was not much of a job and he left it to join Hoover's Commission for Relief in Belgium, where he would get his food and expenses, anyway. In 1916, he was Hoover's director of relief in Brussels. When Hoover returned to the U. S. in April, 1917, to take over the control of all American food supplies for the benefit of England and the other allied countries, Gray was brought along. He was made chief of the Marine Transportation Division of the U. S. Food Administration and, on the termination of the war, director of the American Relief Administration. There were still many hundreds of millions of dollars worth of grain and flour to go to Europe under the control of Hoover. Gray

blossomed forth in the grain and flour export trade.
Prentiss N. Gray Inc. did an enormous business. Was
it because it was such an old established firm? In
1922, Gray was already president of the J. Henry
Schroder Banking Corporation! He is a great capitalist.
You remember the lines from Gilbert and Sullivan's
comic opera *H. M. S. Pinafore*:

> *"I cleaned the windows and I swept the floor*
> *And I polished up the handle of the big front door,*
> *And I polished up that handle so carefully*
> *That now I am the ruler of the Queen's Navy."*

Gray appears to have been equally efficient. Here is a
list of some of his directorships, as taken from the *New
York Directory for Directors*, 1930/1931 edition:

American, British & Continental Corporation	Vice President
Electric Shareholdings Corporation	Director
European Mortgage & Investment Corporation	President
Hydro Electric Securities Corporation	Director
International Holding & Investment Company, Ltd.	Director
International Railways of Central America	Director
J. Henry Schroder Banking Corporation	President
J. Henry Schroder Trust Company	President
Manati Sugar Company	Director
Minor C. Keith, Inc.	Director
Petroleum Heat & Power Company	Director
Prudential Investors, Inc.	Director
St. Regis Paper Company	Director
Swiss American Electric Company	Director

It will be noted that one of these companies is a
Cuban sugar company. Another holds mortgages on land
in Central Europe. Another, the *Hydro Electric Securities Corporation,* has very large stockholdings in U. S.
hydro-electric and public utility companies, in which
Hoover takes such interest. This is the company that
was formed by Alfred Loewenstein, the Belgian flying
financier, who was also connected with the Belgian Relief and who so mysteriously disappeared from one of
his planes a few years ago, that no one can yet say
whether he fell, or was pushed. Then there is the *Inter-*

national Holding and Investment Company, Limited,
with tremendous holdings in shares of artificial silk
companies (Tubize, Enka, Snia Viscosa and Glanzstoff).
Mr. Hoover would probably deny that he knows anything
about artificial silk. But do you remember when he
went to the tiny little town of Elizabethton, Tenn., to
read his campaign speech on October 6, 1928, how people
wondered why he had selected such a hole in the woods?
A huge artificial silk factory had just been erected there
for the American Glanzstoff Co., and the little town
needed advertising very badly in order to secure the
influx of an adequate supply of labor. Of course, there
may have been no connection, but it was certainly a
remarkably strange coincidence. Another very peculiar
coincidence is that both the *Hydro Electric Securities
Corporation* and the *International Holding & Investment
Company, Ltd.,* are controlled by the *Societe Generale,*
Francqui's bank in Brussels. Gray, too, is a director
of the huge *St. Regis Paper Co.,* of which H. E. Machold
is chairman of the executive committee, which owns
twenty-one mills and controls the *North Eastern Power
Company.* Prentiss Gray has certainly vast interests,
if they are his own.

Julius Barnes, at the outbreak of war, was a grain
commission man in Duluth, connected with the Ames
firm. In August, 1917, Hoover appointed him president of
the *Grain Corporation,* one of those dollar a year jobs.
He also flourished. Here is a list of some of his directorships:

J. Henry Schroder Banking Corporation	Chairman
Northwest Bancorporation	Director
Barnes-Ames Corporation	President
Klearflax Linen Looms, Inc.	Chairman
Chamber of Commerce of U. S.	Chairman
General Bronze Corporation	President
Intercontinental Development Company	President
Pejepscot Paper Company	Chairman

American Industries, Inc.	President
Highway Lighthouse Company	Director
Pitney-Bowes Postage Meter Company	Chairman
Erie & St. Lawrence Corporation	President

Edgar Rickard is an English mining engineer who, at the start of hostilities, was business manager of a mining publication in London just earning a living and no more. He had been associated since 1909 with Hoover, who, for reasons of his own, had helped to launch Rickard's mining magazine. Hoover at once appointed Rickard honorary secretary and publicity man on his *Relief Commission*. When Hoover came to America in 1917, to take charge of the U. S. Food Administration, he brought along Rickard as his assistant, and actually had him placed in charge of the entire U. S. Food Administration when he, Hoover, went to Europe in 1918. Rickard also at the same time took Hoover's place as Chairman of the *Commission for Relief in Belgium*, is one of the two liquidators of that commission, and Director General of the *American Relief Administration*. He gave his services gratis for all those years and has, like the others, prospered exceedingly. According to the *New York Directory of Directors* and *Poor's Register of Directors*, he is on the boards of the following companies:

American Industries, Inc.	Vice President
Androscoggin Water Power Company	President
Belgo American Trading Company	President
Erie & St. Lawrence Corporation	Vice President
Hazard Wire Rope Company	President
Hazeltine Corporation	President
Intercontinental Development Corporation	Vice President
Latour Corporation	President
Fred T. Ley Co., Inc.	Director
Pejepscot Paper Company	President
Pitney-Bowes Postage Meter Company	Vice President
Wood Fibre Board Corporation	Chairman

Not only that, but he occupies the somewhat mysterious position of Chairman of the Executive Committee of Secretary Mellon's *Port Improvement Committee*, which gives him much to do with Custom House matters.

Both Julius Barnes and Edgar Rickard occupy the same suite of offices at 42 Broadway, New York. Another who has offices on the same floor of the same building right across from Rickard, is Edwin Shattuck, Hoover's attorney, the man who represented the Cuban sugar interests before the Tariff Commission, on the recommendation of Mr. Hoover, it was said at the time. Those are the same Cuban sugar interests in which Prentiss Gray is interested. Well, Edwin Shattuck, Mr. Hoover's attorney, is also a director of the following companies:

A. R. A. Child Health Association	Director
Belgo American Trading Company	Vice President
C. R. B. Educational Foundation, Inc.	Director
Intercontinental Development Corporation	Director
Pejepscot Paper Company, Inc.	Director
Pitney-Bowes Postage Meter Company	Director
Poso Land & Products Company	Director
Welsbach Street Lighting Co. of America	Director

There is a strange interlocking and intertwining of the directorship held by these gentlemen in the above companies:

J. Henry Schroder Banking Corporation	Gray, Barnes
C. R. B. Educational Foundation	Rickard, Shattuck
Intercontinental Development Corp.	Barnes, Rickard, Shattuck
American Industries, Inc.	Barnes, Rickard
Belgo-American Trading Company	Rickard, Shattuck
Pejepscot Paper Company	Barnes, Rickard, Shattuck
Pitney-Bowes Postage Meter Company	Barnes, Rickard, Shattuck
Erie & St. Lawrence Corporation	Barnes, Rickard

Three at least of the companies mentioned—the *Hazard Wire Rope Co.*, the *Pitney-Bowes Postage Meter Co.* (which owns the Mailometer) and the *Hazeltine Corporation* (which controls the Neutrodyne radio patent) are dependent for their income to a great extent on royalties on their patents. Indeed, this is the only source of income of the *Hazeltine Corporation*, which collects over a million dollars yearly in royalties. Some of our readers may be aware of the rather peculiar circumstances under which this patent was issued in 1925, while the Department of Commerce was in charge of the Patent Office, and it appears to be a remarkable coincidence that the board of directors of this corporation are almost exclusively mining engineer associates of Herbert Hoover.

The President of the Company is Edgar Rickard. The Office of the Company is at 42 Broadway, Suite 2000.

Note the address. It is the headquarters of various other corporations whose seamy history we have been tracing. It is the office of Edgar Rickard. It is the office of Julius Barnes.

It is also listed as the New York address of Herbert Hoover, President of the United States of America.

INDEX

INDEX

Maikop Combine, The, 243
Maikop & General Petrolum Trust, The 241
Maikop New Producers, The 242
Maikop Oil Fields, The 219, 222, 240, 241, 242, 243, 298
Maikop Oil & Petroleum Producers, The 242
Maikop Shirvansky, The 241
Mammoth Oil Co., The, 257
Mandalay Canal Works, The, 262
Manet, 102
Manual of Extinct or Obsolete Companies, The, 291
Martin, A. C. 262, 263
Maryanski, Prof. Modest, 33
May, P. L., 296
Mayflower, The, 23
McCalla, Captain, 62
McCullagh, Dean, 116
McElmore, 8, 9, 10
McGee, Van Norman, 61
McLeish, Captain, 66
McPhail, John, 226
Meade, Colonel, 68
Means, Jack, 57, 61, 232, 359
Meekatharra, The, 218, 219
Mein, The, 41
Mellon, 136
Menzies' Consolidated Gold Mines, 33
Menzies' Gold Development, 33
Menzies' Gold Estates, 33
Mercer, W. A., 30
Merchants Association, The, 9
Merode, Baron de, 312
Merton's Reward, The, 119
Mertzy's Reward, The, 33
Messina Copper Mine, The, 294, 295, 296
Mestress, Father Ramon, 52
Midway Field, The, 250
Milner, Lord, 153, 154
Mine Managers' Institute, The, 45, 49

Minerals Separation, Ltd., The, 200, 207
Mines, School of, 137
Mining Journal, The, 35, 48, 148, 260, 278, 290
Mining Magazine, The, 238, 283, 293
Mining News, The, 34
Mining Trust, The, 304
Mining World, The, 42, 136
Minthorn, John, 13, 14, 15, 16, 17, 37
Mitchell, D. P., 57, 61
Moffit Mines, The, 137
Money Market Review, The, 174
Monypenny, Mr., 154
Moolort Goldfields, The, 169, 170, 175, 176
Moonta, The, 210
Moreing, Charles Algernon, 25, 26, 27, 29, 30, 31, 32, 40, 44, 45, 46, 49, 50, 51, 53, 54, 55, 58, 59, 69, 70, 71, 72, 73, 74, 75, 77, 83, 84, 85, 86, 88, 90, 91, 93, 100, 101, 103, 104, 105, 106, 110, 111, 126, 127, 133, 136, 139, 147, 148, 157, 168, 169, 178, 179, 180, 187, 188, 189, 191, 193, 208, 209, 210, 211, 212, 213, 243, 280, 281, 359
Morgan, Pritchard, 44, 53, 55, 131
Morning Leader, The, 241
Morning Star, The, 97, 98, 114
Morrison, Dr., 56
Moss, Frank, 214
Mountain Queen, The, 217, 218
Mount Isa Lead, Zinc, Silver Mines, The, 302, 303, 304
Mount Lyell, The, 210
Mount Morgans, The, 210
Mueller, A. H., & Sons, 291
Mutual Oil Co., The, 257
Myer, O., 331
My War Experiences in China, 60
Nathan, Sir Matthew, 136
National Bank, The, 122, 359

INDEX

Prichard, W. A., 95, 133, 139, 143, 144, 147

Principles of Mining, The, 223, 224

Provincial Committee, The, 317

Purcell, Sir John, 122, 133, 134

Quenneau, A. L., 198, 200

Railways, Bureau of Control of, 55

Ravensthorpe Syndicate, The, 221, 232

Rees, Crole, 173

Remington, Charles, 254

Requa, Mark, 250, 255, 256, 257, 360

Rhodesia, Ltd., The, 197

Rialto, The, 201, 231

Richey, Lawrence, 360

Rickard, Edgar, 293, 294, 357, 361, 364, 365, 366

Rickard, T. A., 293

Ridder & Kirgiz Concession, The, 300

Ridgeway, George, 214

Riuz, Jose del Carmen, 225

Roberts, Lord, 30, 140

Roberts & Lubbock, 140

Robinson, Lionel, 106, 142, 195, 204

Robinson, Sir J. B., 150

Roosevelt, 82

Roosevelt, Theodore, Jr., 257

Ropp, Alfred von der, 289

Rowbotham, E., 209

Rowe, Anthony Stanley, 84, 88, 89, 104, 105, 106, 107, 108, 109, 110, 111, 142, 171, 359

Royal Commission of Enquiry, The, 140, 147, 148, 149

Royal Commission on Immigration, The, 113, 114, 115

Rumbold, W. R., 237, 238

Russo-Asiatic Consolidated, The, 301, 302, 303, 304, 305

Russo-Asiatic Corporation, The, 299, 300, 301

Russo-Canadian Development Co., The, 301

Russper Syndicate, The, 244, 245

Sabla, Eugene de, 251

Saint Gertrudis Silver Mine, The, 294, 295

Salisbury, Lord, 73

Saltykoff, Prince, 298

Samuel, Sir Edward, 209

San Francisco Chronicle, The, 254

Santa Maria Fields, The, 250

Sarkies, A., 263

Saton, Sir Ernest, 102

Saturday Evening Post, The, 10

Scaddan, Mr., 117

Schaar, Johann, 230

Schmoller, 329

Schroder, J. Henry, Banking Corporation, The, 362

Scudder, Marvyn, 291

Seely, General, 158

Senate, The, 8, 9, 12

Seymour, Sir Edward, 59, 60, 62, 66

Shaler, Millard K., 309, 312

Share Guarantee Trust, The, 197, 252, 263

Shattuck, Edwin, 365

Sikh, The, 161

Silver Falls City, 16, 17, 169

Sinclair Consolidated Oil Co., The, 256

Sinclair, Harry, 256, 257

Sinclair Oil & Refining Co., The, 257

Sin Wan Pao, 103

Swain, Dr., 18

Skinner, 155

Smithfield Market, The, 232, 233

Smith Mines, The, 137

Smith, Professor J. P., 20

Smith, Richard Tilden, 196, 197, 251, 252, 263, 264, 266, 267, 271, 273, 275, 276, 277, 278, 279, 359

Societe Generale, The, 310, 317, 363

Somerset House, The, 197

Sons of Gwalia Gold Mine, The, 44, 45, 46, 48, 49, 51, 53, 56, 96, 97, 98, 110, 114, 115, 208, 213, 236